Torrey
Les philosophes

Les Philosophes

THE PHILOSOPHERS OF THE ENLIGHTENMENT AND MODERN DEMOCRACY

EDITED, WITH AN INTRODUCTION, BY

Norman L. Torrey

PROFESSOR EMERITUS OF FRENCH,
COLUMBIA UNIVERSITY

CAPRICORN BOOKS

New York, N.Y.

Library of Congress Catalog
Card Number: 60-11991

MANUFACTURED IN THE UNITED STATES OF AMERICA

CONTENTS

Suggested Reading

George R. Havens: *The Age of Ideas*, Henry Holt & Co., 1955

Kingsley Martin: *French Liberal Thought in the Eighteenth Century*, Little, Brown, 1929

R. R. Palmer: *The Age of the Democratic Revolution*, Princeton Univ. Press, 1959

Alfred N. Whitehead: *Science and the Modern World* (various editions)

Ernst Cassirer: *The Philosophy of the Enlightenment*, Princeton Univ. Press, 1951

Irwin Edman: *Fountainheads of Freedom*, Reynal & Hitchcock, 1941

Howard Robinson: *Bayle the Sceptic*, Columbia Univ. Press, 1931

S. G. Tallentyre: *The Life of Voltaire*, G. P. Putnam's Sons

H. N. Brailsford: *Voltaire*, Henry Holt & Co., 1935

Norman L. Torrey: *The Spirit of Voltaire*, Columbia Univ. Press, 1938

Lester G. Crocker: *Diderot, the Embattled Philosopher*, Michigan State Univ. Press, 1954

Montesquieu: *The Spirit of Laws* (various editions)

Jean Stewart and Jonathan Kemp (eds.), *Diderot, Interpreter of Nature*, London: Lawrence and Wishart 1937. (Excellent translations)

J.-J. Rousseau: *The Confessions* (various editions)

Diderot: *Jacques the Fatalist* (tr. J. Robert Loy), New York Univ. Press, 1959

Voltaire: *Candide, Zadig, and Selected Stories* (tr. Donald M. Frame), Indiana University Press, 1961 (and other various editions)

Voltaire: *Candide and Other Writings* (ed. Haskell M. Block), The Modern Library

The Portable Voltaire (Ben Ray Redman, ed.), The Viking Press

Author's Foreword

TRANSLATIONS

WITH THE following exceptions, the translations here presented are my own:

For Voltaire's *Letters Concerning the English Nation* (except the letter on Locke) the text is taken from the first English edition of 1733.

Montesquieu's *Spirit of Laws:* Thomas Nugent.

Rousseau's *Discourse on Inequality* and *Social Contract*: G. D. H. Cole.

Helvetius, *On the Mind:* a contemporary translation, revised.

D'Holbach, *On Supernaturalism*: H. D. Robinson.

The selections from Fontenelle are from an English translation of the period.

A number of the Voltaire translations appeared previously in *Voltaire and the Age of Enlightenment*, F. S. Crofts & Co., Inc.

ACKNOWLEDGMENTS

It is a great pleasure to express here my debt to Otis E. Fellows of Columbia University, who collaborated with me in editing *The Age of Enlightenment* (copyright, 1942, F. S. Crofts & Co., Inc.) which has been a model for the present undertaking; also to Appleton-Century-Crofts, Inc., for permission to reuse almost verbatim an introductory paragraph on Voltaire's religion and other incidental introductory phrases.

General Introduction

In an age of wilful irrationalism and dehumanization of the arts, when interests are captivated by myths, symbols and abstractions, it is refreshing to renew our acquaintance with the writers of an age of common sense, reason and humanity. Fashions, customs, habits of thought, are ceaselessly changing, philosophical systems succeed one another in an endless chain, but human nature remains essentially the same, and reason and common sense still wage an uneven battle against the powers of darkness. The writings of the French *philosophes* of the eighteenth century continue to remind us of fundamental human truths.

They have, in addition, the advantage of being of great historical significance. As James Harvey Robinson once wrote, we cannot fully comprehend what we are until we know how we got that way. The ideas of liberalism and democracy that flourished in France at this time have shaped the social and philosophical thinking and the political institutions of the western world and constitute a chapter of American history that is too often neglected. The American and French revolutions, with their constitutions and declarations of civil liberties, are only the most important of many similar developments.

A number of terms have been used to characterize the spirit of the times. Among the most common has been the Age of Reason. Its only disadvantage is its connotation of pure rationalism, or deductive reasoning, more descriptive of the century following Descartes. By 1750, the rapid development of the biological sciences, the publication of the first volumes of Buffon's monumental *Natural History*, and the adoption of the scientific method gave priority again to natural phenomena and the observed facts of the material universe. The Age of Ideas and the Age of Humanism are descriptive, but not distinctive, while the Age of the Democratic Revolution is not broad enough to be entirely satisfying. D'Alembert, spokesman for his fellow *philosophes*, considered his era the Age of Enlightenment, "l'age des lumières," the splendid illumination that was kindled by the rebirth of the thought of the ancients during the Renaissance, smouldered during the Age of Classicism, and burst into flame in the eighteenth century. It was this concept that gave the name of "Aufklärung" to the derivative German liberal movement.

The Age of Enlightenment, then, is a term applied to a definite Revolution in the history of thought which took place in France in the eighteenth century. The leaders of the movement were called *philosophes*, although they established no definite systems of philosophy. Among the *philosophes*, Voltaire was by far the most powerful figure. The main tenets of the group were a firm belief in the idea of progress, the application of the experimental method in science, the free and unfettered use of the God-given faculty of reason in all affairs, human and divine, and the ardent faith that reason, with all its limitations, was the final judge and the best guide available for the conduct of life.

Historical Setting

In seeking the place of the Enlightenment in the history of thought it is useful to note that many of the anomalies of modern civilization arise from the incomplete amalgamation of our two great cultural heritages, the Judeo-Christian and the Greco-Roman. During the Middle Ages the former played the dominant role, epitomized by its greatest literary production, Dante's *Divine Comedy*. The fourteenth century witnessed the beginnings of the revival of learning as long lost manuscripts of the ancients were being recovered: the texts of Homer and Cicero and

Lucretius and many other Greek and Latin authors, and the works of Aristotle, which had been known only through his commentators. As the Renaissance, or rebirth of pagan culture, spread into France, the excitement of these discoveries inspired a bevy of scholars to produce grammars, lexicons, glossaries, translations and commentaries. As D'Alembert observed, the patient labors of these often pedantic and arrogant scholars were necessary for the full understanding of the riches of the wisdom of the ancients. The rapid development of printing facilitated communication between scholars and contributed greatly to the revival by making possible the wide dissemination of discovered treasures.

The most notable authors in sixteenth-century France were Rabelais and Montaigne. It was no accident that Rabelais earned his medical degree by a translation from the Greek physician Galen, and that linguistic concerns loom so large in his histories of Gargantua and Pantagruel. He showed Protestant leanings before the line was sharply drawn by Calvin, but was wise enough not to follow Calvin in his exodus to Geneva. The Pantagruelian philosophy is a robust and whole-hearted acceptance of the joys of life, both physical and intellectual, a revolt against the asceticism of the Middle Ages; for Rabelais pictured God as the beneficent creator of carp, sausages and wine, rather than the stern author of Lent.

Later in the century Montaigne's *Essays*, which are still considered one of the world's great masterpieces, were nourished by the learning of the ancients. Although Montaigne was no rebel and remained faithful to the Church as a matter of civic duty, in his retirement during the bloody religious wars of the period his essays were an attempt to find the salvation of individual men in the fulfillment of their human possibilities. Because of his Stoicism and genial skepticism, Montaigne's work became the bible of later generations of "libertines," or freethinkers, who kept alive the traditions of pagan culture even during the most repressive years of the reign of Louis XIV. At the end of the seventeenth century, at the very threshold of the Enlightenment, Pierre Bayle adopted Montaigne's skeptical philosophy in his *Historical and Critical Dictionary*, from which the *philosophes* derived so much of their information and inspiration.

The philosophical thought of seventeenth-century France was dominated, however, by Descartes, whose discourse on methodical reasoning (1636) denied the validity of the axiomatic truths and syllogisms of the Scholastics and established a system of rationalism deduced from clear and innate intuitions. His belief in the fixed and immutable laws of nature, of inertia and the conservation of energy, gave a firm foundation to modern philosophies of science and a guarantee of the validity of scientific research. The material universe, ordered by the laws of motion, which were determined once and for all by the Divine Intelligence and never abrogated, is, in his system, submitted to a rigorous scientific determinism, from which man alone is exempt; for man's nature is dualistic, partaking through the union of soul and body of the realms of mind and matter. In so far as he is body, he is, like the lower animals, an automaton, a beast-machine. In the realm of the mind, his thought, which Descartes equated with soul, and his will, even when it yields to the evidence of intuitive, clear, innate ideas, set him free. A century later, as we shall see, La Mettrie, one of the most radical and original of the *philosophes*, will deny the distinction and attempt to prove that man, too, is a machine.

Descartes' philosophy met considerable opposition, even in his own century. Chief among the opponents was Pierre Gassendi, priest and doctor of theology. He upheld against Descartes' innate ideas and intuitions the scholastic doctrine that there is nothing in the intellect which does not originate in sense perceptions. This theory of sensationalism, stripped of its scholastic overtones, was passed on to the *philosophes* through John Locke and Condillac and became one of the burning issues of the struggle for freedom of thought. Voltaire's defense of John Locke in his *Letters on the English Nation* was the chief cause of the condemnation of that work and subsequent persecution of its author. Diderot's *Encyclopedia*, too, was condemned and publication suspended because of the adoption of the sensationalist philosophy. His original and scientifically valid *Letter on the Blind*, a study of persons who are deprived of one of the gateways by which sense perceptions enter the mind, was likewise condemned. This generally accepted theory was that sense perceptions recalled by memory gave rise to comparisons, reflection, judgment, and finally to self-awareness. The story of Helen Keller and the slow and patient opening of her mind through the sense of touch confirms the theory, as does also the observation of the gradual development of intelligence and self-awareness in the child.

Gassendi was noted also for his rehabilitation of Epicurus, so mistreated by Christian apologists, and of the atomic theory of his forerunners, Leucippus and Democritus. Epicurean philosophy is known to us chiefly through the treatise of the Latin poet Lucretius, *On the Nature of Things*, on a translation of which it is reported that Cyrano de Bergerac and Molière worked under Gassendi's tutelage. The influence of Lucretius injected a large element of epicureanism into the philosophy of Voltaire and his co-workers. As friend and correspondent of Galileo, Gassendi gave strength and support to the Copernican theory of the universe, which was the most revolutionary and violently opposed idea of the age, and accepted by the Church only in the nineteenth century. Descartes had prudently withheld his own views from publication and based his own theories on a carefully elaborated system of vortices, in which the earth was still left as the center of the universe; around it revolved the sun and the moon and the starry firmament, according to the Ptolemaic system so beautifully popularized by Dante. Gassendi's disciple, Cyrano de Bergerac, in his posthumously published *Voyage to the Moon* (1655), gave an imaginative account of Copernican astronomy and the theory of gravitation, of which Newton was soon to discover the mathematical laws.

The great popularizer of Copernican theory, however,

was Fontenelle (1657-1757). His widely published and often translated *Conversations on the Plurality of Worlds* first brought the new system to the attention of the general educated public. As a primer of astronomy, it was not surpassed for over a century. Because of its clarity and discussions of other possibly inhabited universes, it still holds its fascination for the modern reader. Fontenelle's *Origin of Fables* gave to the *philosophes* their conviction that myths arose in times of ignorance and were maintained through the connivance of priests and princes. His *History of Oracles* is a concrete example of the ease and pleasure with which man can be fooled and become a prey to superstition. Fontenelle prudently excepted Christian priests and miracles from his attack, which was, none the less, a worthy forerunner of *The Golden Bough*. Many *philosophes*, and especially Voltaire, were not so prudent.

Towards the end of the seventeenth century, as a result of the persecutions and forced conversions of French protestants and the revocation of the Edict of Nantes, promulgated in 1598 by Henri IV to give them the rights of public worship, Bayle's attack on the dissolute morals of all-Catholic France and his plea for religious toleration added greatly to the fuel of the Enlightenment. Most of the ideas developed by the *philosophes* were already at hand. What was lacking was a dynamic program of social and political action, based on the faith that man's condition could be meliorated. This program Voltaire and his associates provided. Montaigne had sought his ideal in retirement from the bloody world of civil war and in the dream of individual perfection. Pascal, in general submissive to the authority of pope and king, considered man's condition hopeless and this world a vale of tears, at best a painful preparation of the Elect for the glorious life to come. The eighteenth-century ideal was a society which would limit the authority of State and Church, protect the citizen from arbitrary powers, submit man only to established law, and thereby increase his chances of finding happiness on this earth. In the development of this program most of the cherished traditions and institutions of the Old Régime were doomed to perish.

General Themes

For readers today, the most significant of the general themes treated by the *philosophes* is the rapid growth and development of the democratic spirit. Since their contributions to the rise of modern democracies are still very much alive and not yet fully realized, illustrations of this theme have received special attention in the following pages. History had contributed comparatively little for them to draw upon since the democracies of the Athenian and other Greek city-states. The new ideas developed only gradually in the struggle to liberate mankind from the authoritarian repressions of the Old Régime.

Rather than a model, the Greek city-state presented a political ideal, most nobly expressed in the Funeral Oration of Pericles: an administration by the many regardless of wealth or station, in the duties and privileges of which all free citizens (the great body of slaves of course was excluded) could share equally according to their virtues. The Greeks also deified Justice, the mark of all superior civilizations, as Montesquieu said all nations must do if justice were not the main attribute of their God. The famous trilogy, the *Oresteia* of Aeschylus, ends with the glorification of the Athenian court of justice, in which all citizens had the right to appeal and be judged by their peers.

Montesquieu admitted, too, that if he had not been born a Christian, he would be a Stoic: for it was chiefly from the Stoics and from their disciple, Cicero, that the modern world inherited the principles of natural law and rational justice. We find in Cicero the idea of the essential equality of men as men and of the natural rights of man based on his submission to reason; also an exaltation of law as an expression of reasonableness. Long after the decline and fall of Rome, Roman law was recognized throughout great regions of western Europe as superior to local customs and exerted its stabilizing influence. The Stoics emphasized, too, the sense of the dignity and self-sufficiency of the individual, an idea which was strengthened by the Judeo-Christian insistence that all men are brothers in the sight of God, their common father. It appears paradoxical that the chief proponent among the *philosophes* of the brotherhood of man was Voltaire who, because of the persecuting power of the Church, did his utmost to sap the foundations of Christianity. His prayer for universal tolerance, the noblest expression of this ideal, was widely disseminated in Europe and often republished in the newspapers and magazines of eighteenth-century America from colonial times. It was Voltaire, too, who bade all men forget their petty differences and remember their essential dignity as men ("Souviens-toi de ta dignité d'homme").

In modern times John Locke exerted the greatest influence on the political thought of the *philosophes*, and both directly and through them, on Franklin, Jefferson and Madison. Considered superficial by systematic philosophers, Locke's political principles, like his philosophical theory of sensationalism, were developed more fully in France and given more solid foundations. Chief among them were a plea for religious toleration, a somewhat intuitively conceived defense of inalienable rights and free enterprise, and the proposal that the only legitimate form of government was by consent of the people and in the interests of the people, with emphasis on the happiness of the individual.

Locke's *Letters on Toleration* supported, but did not surpass the somewhat earlier *Philosophical Commentary* of Pierre Bayle, whose defense of the rights of the "erring conscience" was more broadly conceived and more solidly grounded. Locke's constitution for the Carolinas, like William Penn's laws for the colony of Pennsylvania, granted freedom of worship, but excluded atheists, whom Bayle defended. Bayle's proposal that a multiplicity of religions would be beneficial to the state was accepted by Montesquieu in his *Persian Letters* and by the *philosophes* in general. Voltaire was the most powerful propagandist in favor of religious toleration. Largely through his successful propaganda the principle of freedom of worship was firmly established in the *Declaration of the Rights of Man and of the Citizen*, which became the preamble to the French Constitution of 1791, and in the American Bill of Rights of the same year. The development of the theme of religious toleration led to the subordination of the Church to the State in France (Article III of the *Declaration*) and the principle of the separation of Church and State in America.

Locke's theories of inalienable property rights and free enterprise were developed by early English economists and exaggerated by Bernard Mandeville in his *Fable of the Bees* (1714). Voltaire drew upon these sources and from Pierre Bayle to expound, in his famous poem, *The Worldling*, the economic doctrine of *laissez-faire*. Apart from its epicurean aspects, this poem is a forceful apology for luxury. Voltaire's periods of exile in the commercial nations of Holland and England convinced him that the wealth of these nations, shared in varying measure by their people, was the result of free and unfettered trade, and the encouragement of commerce. One generation's luxuries became the next generation's necessities and the general standard of living was thereby raised. Voltaire believed, too, that free enterprise and freedom of trade were essential to the other freedoms which he so ardently championed. The democratic principles emerging from the thought of the *philosophes* were thus capitalistic rather than socialistic. The *Declaration* at the end of the century explicitly confirmed the "inviolable and sacred" right to property (article XVII).

The idea of progress and the defense of capitalism were not achieved without a struggle. Rousseau attacked them in his first published discourse, in which he attempted to prove that progress in the arts and sciences was always attended by corruption of morals and consequent unhappiness. A second discourse on the origins of inequality among men was a thoroughgoing denunciation of private property and capitalism. Rousseau's attempt to revive primitivistic and equalitarian principles drew satirical replies from Voltaire and were doomed to failure in an age that stood at the threshold of the Industrial Revolution. The *Declaration* (article I) granted that men were born and remain free, but equal only before the law. Diderot's insistence on hereditary traits and his interest in the phenomena of genius suggested a refutation of Helvetius' theory of the equal natural endowments of all men of sound constitution. Voltaire, who through wise speculation and business acumen became one of the wealthiest men of his century, adopted the Christian precept that the poor we have with us always, otherwise no one would till our fields or cobble our shoes. But even they would greatly benefit from the decline of superstition and fanaticism and the general rise in standards of living.

Rousseau's great contribution to the advance of democratic thought was his stirring proclamation of the sovereignty of the people, to be safeguarded by periodic free elections. In the first chapters of the *Social Contract*, the primordial right of the people to govern themselves through public servants and administrations of their own choosing is emphatically and eloquently maintained. The sovereignty of the people is alone legitimate and inalienable in the sense that if it has been usurped in the past the people have the right and obligation to reclaim it. Rousseau himself was soon to abandon the struggle, but this principle, echoed in the American Declaration of Independence, remained as the great inspiration of democratic revolutions throughout western Europe.

Our ideas of what constitutes the basic principles of democracy thus emerge from the writings of the *philosophes*. Democratic administration was another matter, in respect to which it can be readily argued that not one of the *philosophes* was truly a democrat. In their writings are found the intellectual origins of the French Revolution, but they were not revolutionaries. Montesquieu included in his *Spirit of Laws* a history of the origins and a defense of the feudal privileges which he shared as a member of the nobility. One aspect of his theory of the balance of powers was a House of Lords to serve as a stabilizing force between the king and the lower House. Voltaire, as a benevolent landlord, mistrusted the people who were ever a prey to superstition and fanaticism, and believed that a constitutional monarchy was the best solution for France. Rousseau shared Plato's mistrust of democracies and the almost universal belief that democratic administrative procedures were impossible in large nations. Government by representation, they felt, could only lead to usurpation and corruption. Faced with this dilemma, Montesquieu suggested a federated republic, or society of societies, through which democratic institutions might be saved and the defensive strength of its members maintained. Jefferson was later to institute the ward system, in an effort to obtain true representation of the people's desires and opinions.

It is often argued that the theory of the natural rights of man rests on very shaky foundations. The natural law to which the *philosophes* appealed has fallen into disrepute. There must, however, have been a sense of equity, the feeling that there ought to be a law, antecedent to every positive and written law. This sense of equity, believed by the Cartesians to be innate, was explained by D'Alembert as being acquired through experience with injustice, a theory of which Voltaire's overriding passion for justice was a notable example. Also, with the advance of scientific thought, natural law came to be thought of as the laws of nature, including the laws of human nature. Its source was sought in the psychosomatic organism that is man. Abandoning innate ideas, Voltaire, in his *Poem on Natural Law,* had recourse to the more scientifically acceptable instincts, and Diderot habitually sought physical causes for all mental phenomena. Men living in society cannot long tolerate universal license and anarchy at one extreme or the restraints of authoritarianism at the other. Democracy is the attempt to find the point of balance between the requirements of law and order and the desire for civil liberties which reduces psychological frictions and tensions to a minimum. Herein lies the assurance that as long as human nature remains essentially the same, democracy will, in the long run, not perish from the earth.

Fontenelle
1657-1757

GENIAL philosopher, playwright, popularizer of the sciences, and socially minded epicurean, Fontenelle enjoyed life into his hundredth year. Only the protection of influential friends saved him from censorship and prison for the boldness of his early works. His later years were more discreetly devoted to eulogies of the great scientists of the age and a history of the French Academy of Sciences.

In his *Crisis of the European Conscience*, covering especially the years from the revocation of the Edict of Nantes (1685) to the death of Louis XIV (1715), Paul Hazard gives a prominent place to the methodical doubt and critical spirit of Pierre Bayle and Fontenelle. The major cause of the crisis was the popularization of the Copernican system in the latter's *Conversations on the Plurality of Worlds* (1686). Up to that time only a handful of scientists understood and accepted the theories of Copernicus. Because of its extraordinary clarity and simplicity, Fontenelle's work remained the best initiation to astronomy for well over a century. It enjoyed immense popularity and numerous editions both in France and England.

The geocentric system of Ptolemy, poeticized in Dante's *Divine Comedy*, in which the sun, the moon, the planets and the fixed stars revolved about the earth, center of the universe, gave way among all educated people to the heliocentric system propounded by Copernicus. Fontenelle, however, retained the vortices, spheres and celestial matter of Cartesian physics. A few years later, Newton divulged the gravitational laws that governed the movement of the heavenly bodies through the void.

Fontenelle's *History of Oracles* (1687) was an adaptation of a book by a learned Hollander, whose theory was that the oracular demons of the pagans were silenced by the coming of Christ. In discussing the cheats of priests, Fontenelle explicitly excepts those of Christianity, the true religion. However, irony and sly innuendo can be read between the lines.

These works of Fontenelle were almost immediately

"made English." The language of over two and a half centuries ago has been retained in the passages below. It does not want—today we would say *lack*—a certain charm.

Conversations on the Plurality of Worlds (1686)

[The Copernican System]

. . . Imagine then a German called Copernicus confounding every thing, tearing in pieces the beloved circles of antiquity, and shattering their crystal heavens like so many glass windows. Seized with the noble rage of astronomy he snatcheth up the earth from the center of the universe, sends her packing, and placeth the sun in the center to which it did more justly belong. The planets no longer turn round the earth, and do not enclose it in the circles they describe; if they give us light, it is but by chance, and as they meet us in their way. All now turns round the sun, the earth herself goes round the sun, and Copernicus, to punish the earth for her former laziness, makes her contribute all he can to the motion of the planets and heavens. And now stripped of all the heavenly equipage with which she was so gloriously attended, she hath nothing left her but the moon, which still turns round about her. Fair and softly, saith the Countess, I fancy you yourself are seized with the noble fury of astronomy; a little less rapture, and I shall understand you the better. The sun you say is in the center of the universe, and is immovable; what follows next it is Mercury, said I; he turns round the sun so that the sun is the center of the circle wherein Mercury moves; above Mercury is Venus, who turns also round the sun; after comes the earth, which being placed higher than Mercury and Venus, makes a greater circle round the sun than either of them; at last come Mars, Jupiter, Saturn, in the same order I name them, so that Saturn hath the greatest circle round the sun, which is the reason he is a

BERNARD DE FONTENELLE.

longer time in making his revolution than any of the other planets. And the moon, you have forgot her, said she. We shall quickly find her again, said I; the moon turns round the earth, and doth not leave her, but as the earth advanceth in the circle, which she describes about the sun, and if the moon turns round the sun, it is because she will not quit the earth. I understand you, said she, and I love the moon for staying with us when all the other planets do abandon us; nay I fear your German would have willingly taken her away too if he could, for in all his proceedings, I find he had a great spite to the earth. 'Twas well done of him, said I, to abate the vanity of mankind, who had taken up the best place in the universe, and it pleaseth me to see the earth in the crowds of the planets. Sure, said she, you do not think their vanity extends itself as far as astronomy! Do you believe you have humbled me, in telling me the earth goes round the sun? For my part I do not think myself at all the worse for it. I confess, said I, Madam, I believe a fair lady would be much more concerned for her place at a ball, than for her rank in the universe; and the precedence of two planets will not make half such a noise in the world, as that of two ambassadors. However the same inclination which reigns at a ceremony, governs in a system, and if you love the uppermost place in the one, the philosopher desires the center in the other; he flatters himself that all things were made for him, and insensibly believes a matter of pure speculation to be a point of interest. This is a calumny, said she, you have invented against mankind. Why did they receive this system if it was so abasing? I know not, said I, but I am sure Copernicus himself distrusted the success of his opinion. He was a long time before he would venture to publish it, nor had he done it then without the importunity of his friends. But do you know what became of him? The very day they brought him the first proof of his book, he died; he foresaw he should never be able to clear all the contradictions, and very wisely slipped out of the way.

I would be just to all the world, said the Countess. But 'tis hard to fancy we move and yet see we do not change our place; we find ourselves in the morning where we lay down at night. Perhaps you will tell me the whole earth moves. Yes certainly, said I, it is the same case as if you fell asleep in a boat upon the river; when you awake you find yourself in the same place, and the same situation in respect to all the parts of the boat. 'Tis true, she replied, but here's a great difference; when I awake I find another shore and that shows me my boat hath changed place. But 'tis not the same with the earth, I find all things as I left them. No, no, said I, there is another shore too; you know that beyond the circles of the planets are fixed stars; there is our shore. I am upon the earth, and the earth makes a great circle round the sun. I look for the center of the circle and see the sun there. I then direct my sight beyond the sun in a straight line, and should certainly discover the fixed stars which answer to the sun, but that the lights of the sun effaceth them. But at night I easily perceive the stars which corresponded with him in the day, which is exactly the same thing. If the earth did not change its place in the circle where it is, I should see the sun always against the same fixed stars, but when the earth doth change its place, the sun must answer to other stars and there again is your shore which is always changing. And seeing the earth makes her circle in a year, I see the sun likewise in the space of a year answer successively to the whole circle of the fixed stars, which circle is called the zodiac. I will draw you the figure of it, if you please, on the sand? 'Tis no matter, said she, I can do well enough without it; beside, it will give an air of learning to my park which I would not have in it.[1] For I have heard of a certain philosopher, who being shipwrecked and cast upon an unknown island, seeing several mathematical figures traced on the seashore, cried out to those that followed him: Courage, courage, my compan-

[1] Molière had recently ridiculed women astronomers in *The Learned Ladies*.

ions, the isle is inhabited, behold the footsteps of men. But you may spare your figures, such footsteps are not decent here.

I confess, said I, Madam, the footsteps of lovers would better become this place; that is, your name and cypher graved on the trees by your adorers. Tell not me, said she, of lovers and adorers. I am for my beloved sun and planets. But how comes it to pass that the sun as to the fixed stars completes his course but in a year, and yet goes over our heads every day? Did you never, I replied, observe a bowl on a bowling green? It runs towards the block, and at the same time turns very often round itself so that the parts which were above are below, and those which were below are above. Just so it is with the earth. At the same time that she advanceth on the circle which in a year's space she makes round the sun, in twenty four hours she turns round her self; so that in twenty four hours every part of the earth loseth the sun, and recovers him again, and as it turns towards the sun, it seems to rise, and as it turns from him, it seems to fall. It is very pleasant, said she, that the earth must take all upon herself, and the sun do nothing. And when the moon, the other planets, and the fixed stars seem to go over our heads every twenty four hours, you'll say that too is only fancy? Pure fancy, said I, which proceeds from the same cause. For the planets complete their courses round the sun at unequal times, according to their unequal distances, and that which we see today answer to a certain point in the zodiac or circle of the fixed stars, tomorrow we see answer to another point, because it is advanced on its own circle as well as we are advanced upon ours. We move, and the planets move too, which must make a great alteration; so that what seems irregular in the planets, proceeds only from our motion, when in truth they are all very regular. I will suppose them so, said the Countess, but I would not have their regularity put the earth to so great trouble; methinks you exact too much activity from so ponderous a mass. But, said I, had you rather that the sun and all the stars, which are vast great bodies, should in twenty four hours travel such an infinity of miles, and make so prodigious a tour as they needs must, if the earth did not turn round itself every twenty four hours?

Oh, said she, the sun and the stars are all fire, their motion is not very difficult; but the earth, I fancy, is a little unwieldy. That signifies nothing, I replied, for what do you think of a first rate ship, which carries near an hundred guns, and a thousand men, besides her provisions and other furniture? You see one puff of wind makes it sail on the water, because the water is liquid, and being easily separated doth very little resist the motion of the ship. So the earth though never so massive is as easily borne up by the celestial matter, which is a thousand times more fluid than the water, and fills all that great space where the planets float; for where would you the earth should be fastened to resist the motion of the celestial matter, and not be driven by it? You may as well fancy a little block of wood can withstand the current of a river.

But pray, said she, how can the earth with all its weight be borne up by your celestial matter, which must be very light, because it is so fluid? It doth not argue, said I, that what is most fluid is most light; for what think you of the great vessel I mentioned but now, which with all its burden is yet lighter than the water it floats on? I will have nothing to do with that great vessel, said she, and I begin to apprehend myself in some danger on such a whirligig as you have made of the earth. There is no danger, I replied; but Madam, if you are afraid, we will have the earth supported by four elephants, as the Indians believe it. Hey day, cried she, here's another system; however I love those people for taking care of themselves; they have a good foundation to trust to, while you Copernicans are a little too venturous with the celestial matter; and yet I fancy if the Indians thought the earth in the least danger of sinking, they will double their number of elephants. They do well, said I, laughing at her fancy. Who would sleep in fear? And if you have occasion for them tonight, we will put as many as you please in our system, we can take them away again by degrees as you grow better confirmed. I do not think them very necessary, said she, I have courage enough to turn. You shall turn with pleasure, Madam, said I, and shall find delightful ideas in this system. For example, sometimes I fancy myself suspended in the air, without any motion, while the earth turns round under me in twenty four hours.[1] I see I know not how many different faces pass below, some white, some black, and some tawny. Sometimes I see hats, and sometimes turbans, now heads with hair, and then shaved heads; here I see cities with steeples, others with spires and crescents, others with towers of porcelain, and anon great countries with nothing but cottages; here I see vast oceans, and there most horrible deserts; in short I discover the infinite variety which is upon the surface of the earth. I confess, said she, twenty four hours would thus be very well bestowed, so that in the same place where we are now, I do not mean in the park, but we will suppose ourselves in the air, other people continually pass by who take up our place, and at the end of twenty four hours we return to it again.

Copernicus himself, said I, could not have comprehended it better. First then we see some of our neighbors passing by us, up to the ears in politics, yet settling their nation no better than we do the world in the moon; then follows a great sea, perhaps a fleet of ships, perhaps a mackerel boat, no matter whether; then come some of the Iroquois going to eat a prisoner for their breakfast, who seems as little concerned as his devourers. After appear the women of the land of Jesso,[2] who spend all their time in dressing their husbands' dinners and suppers, and painting their lips and eyebrows blue, only to please the greatest villains in the world. Then the fair Circassians, who

[1] On a fanciful trial voyage to the moon (1655), Cyrano de Bergerac was lifted up by the attraction of the sun for the vials of dew that he had attached to his belt. As the dew evaporated, he came down after some hours in French Canada, the earth having turned under him during his ascent and descent.

[2] Northern Japanese island.

are very free of their favors, and grant all to the first comer, except a little they reserve for their husbands; then the Tartars going to steal concubines for the Turks and Persians; and at last our own dear countrymen, it may be in some points as ridiculous as the best of them.

It is very pleasant, said the Countess, just to imagine what you tell me, though if I was above and saw all this, I would have the liberty to hasten or retard the motion of the earth according as the objects pleased me more or less, and I assure you I should quickly send packing the politicians and maneaters, but should have a great curiosity for the fair Circassians, for methinks they have a custom very particular. They are so extremely beautiful, said I, that their husbands have enough and to spare to a stranger. I fear then, said she, the women of our country are very ugly, in respect to those fair ladies, for the husbands part with nothing here, but keep all to themselves. 'Tis because they make more use, I replied, of —— Hold your peace, said she, and no more of your fooleries. I have a difficulty to clear, and you must be serious. As the earth moves, the air changeth every moment, so we breathe the air of another country. Not at all, I replied, for the air which encompasseth the earth doth not extend above a certain height, perhaps 20 leagues. It follows us and turns with us. Have you not seen the work of a silkworm, the shells which those little animals imprison themselves in, and weave with so much art? They are made of a silk very close, but are covered with a down very slack and soft; so the earth which is solid is covered from the surface 20 leagues upwards with a kind of down, which is the air, and all the shell of the silkworm turns at the same time. Beyond the air is the celestial matter, incomparably more pure and subtle, and much more agitated than the air. Your comparison, said she, is somewhat mean and yet what wonders are wrought, what wars, what changes in this little shell? 'Tis true, I replied, but Nature takes no notice of such little particular motions, but drives us along with the general motion, as if she were at bowls. Methinks, said she, 'tis very ridiculous to be upon a thing that turns, and not be well assured that it doth turn; and to tell you the truth, I begin to distrust the reasons you give, why we should not be sensible of the motion of the earth; for is it possible there should not some little mark be left, by which we might perceive it?

All motions, said I, the more common and natural they are, are the less perceptible, and this holds true even in morality; the motion of self-love is so natural to us, that for the most part we are not sensible of it, and we believe we act by other principles. You are moralizing, said she, when it is a question of natural philosophy. But 'tis enough for the first time, let us now go home and meet here again tomorrow; you with your systems and I with my ignorance. [The First Evening]

The History of Oracles and the Cheats of the Pagan Priests (1687)

[The Golden Tooth]

It is very difficult to give an account of those stories and oracles which we have mentioned without having recourse to demons. But the question is, whether they be true. Let us be assured of the matter of fact, before we trouble ourselves with enquiring into the cause. It is true that this method is too slow and dull for the greatest part of mankind, who run naturally to the cause and pass over the truth of the matter of fact; but for my part, I will not be so ridiculous as to find out a cause for what is not.

This kind of misfortune happened so pleasantly at the end of the last age to some learned Germans, that I cannot forbear speaking of it. In the year 1593 there was a report that the teeth of a child of Silesia of seven years old dropped out and that one of gold came in the place of one of his great teeth. Hortius, a physicist in the University of Helmstad, wrote in the year 1595 the history of this tooth and pretended that it was partly natural, and partly miraculous, and that it was sent from God to this infant to comfort the Christians, who were then afflicted by the Turks. Now fancy to yourself what a consolation this was and what this tooth could signify, either to the Christians or the Turks. In the same year (that this tooth might not want for historians) a certain Rolandus wrote a book of it. Two years after, Ingolsteterus, another learned man, wrote against the opinion of Rolandus concerning this golden tooth, and Rolandus presently made a learned reply. Another great man, named Libavius, collected all that had been said of this tooth, to which he added his own opinion. In fine, there wanted nothing to so many famous works, but only the truth of its being a golden tooth. For when a goldsmith had examined it, he found that it was only a thin plate of gold fixed to the tooth with a great deal of art. Thus they first went about to compile books and afterwards they consulted the goldsmith.

Nothing is more natural than to do the same thing in all other cases. And I am not so convinced of our ignorance by the things that are, and of which the reasons are unknown, as by those which are not, and for which we yet find out reasons.[1] That is to say, as we want those principles that lead us to truth, so we have those which agree exceedingly well with error and falsehood.

Some learned physicists have found out the reason why places under ground are hot in winter and cool in summer, and greater physicists have since discovered that they are not so.

Historical enquiries are much more liable to this error. For when we argue from what is said in history, what assurance have we that these historians have never been biassed, nor credulous, nor misinformed, nor negligent? It is necessary therefore that we should look out for one that has been an eye-witness, unconcerned by interest,

[1] A saying attributed later to many others, among them "the Iowa farmer": "It ain't so much what people don't know as what they know that ain't so."

and diligent. But especially when men write of such matters of fact as have a relation with religion, it is very hard not to favor (according to the party of which they are) a false religion with those advantages which are not due it; or not to give a true one those false assistances of which it has no need. And yet we may be assured that we can never add more truth to what is true already, nor make that true which is false. . . . [I, iv]

[Location of Oracles]

We shall now enter upon the history of those artifices and cheats practised by the priests, which contains many things of antiquity very agreeable and particular.

Countries that were mountainous (and by consequence full of holes and caverns) were always fullest of oracles; such was Bœotia, which anciently, as Plutarch says, had a number of them. Where, by the way, you may observe that the Bœotians were reputed to be the foolishest nation of the world; and therefore it was a fit country for oracles, being full of blockheads and caverns.

I cannot believe that the first establishment of oracles was a designed cheat; but that the people fell into some superstition which gave them a beginning, and that afterwards men of wit made their advantages of them. For the weakness of the people is often greater than could have been foreseen; and many times those that deceive them think of nothing less, until they themselves give some opportunity for the fraud.[1] And my opinion is that the oracles were not therefore placed in Bœotia because it is mountainous; but because the oracle of Delphos had by chance its beginning there, after the manner which we have related, therefore others, that were made in imitation of that in the same country, were situated also in the caverns, the conveniences of which for that purpose were very well known to the priests.

This custom afterwards spread itself everywhere, for

[1] This is Fontenelle' theory of the beginning and perpetuation of myth (see, *The Origin of Fables*, 1724).

the pretense of divine exhalations rendered these caverns necessary; and besides, caverns of themselves affect one with a certain horror, which does not a little advance superstition, and in things that are only to make impressions on the imaginations of men, nothing is to be neglected. It may be also that the situation of Delphos contributed to the making it be esteemed as a holy town. It was built on a small level which was half way up the mountain of Parnassus, and encompassed with precipices which fortified it without the help of art. That part of the mountain which was above it had the resemblance of a theater; and the voice of men and the sound of trumpets was multiplied by the echoes of the rocks. Do you not believe then that they knew how to make even these echoes of great use to them?

The advantages of the priests and the majority of the oracles do equally require caverns; for which reason there was no great number of these prophetic temples situated on plains; but yet there were some whose defects the priests knew how to remedy, and instead of natural caverns, to accommodate them with artificial ones, that is to say, what they call sanctuaries, which were a sort of caves where divinity perpetually resided and where none but the priests ever entered. . . . [I, xii]

Pierre Bayle
1647-1706

Bayle was the great inspirer of the *philosophes*. The accumulation of facts and the skeptical spirit of his *Historical and Critical Dictionary* (first edition, 1697, fifth edition, 1730) supplied both the weapons and methods with which the authoritarian principles of the Old Régime were destroyed.

The son of a Protestant pastor in southern France, his intellectual ability won him the chair of philosophy in the Protestant University of Sedan. The unfortunate attempt to wipe out all non-conformity in France shut down the university in 1681 and forced Bayle to take refuge in the newly-established Free School of Rotterdam. During the following years, he lost his entire family from the direct or indirect effects of persecution.

The Miscellaneous Thoughts on the Comet of 1680 not only attacked the prevalent notion that comets were omens of disaster, but attempted to undermine superstition of all varieties, and especially religious superstition. In claiming that morality depended in no way upon religious principles, reasoning led him to assert that even a society of atheists could be more moral than a society founded on religious fanaticism. In his *Philosophical Commentary on the Words of Jesus Christ, "Compel them to come in"*—the excuse of the Church for persecution since St. Augustine—he defended the legitimacy of "heretical" opinions and surpassed even John Locke in the cogency and liberalism of his plea for religious toleration.

After early years of vacillation, Bayle lost his faith and adopted a philosophy of skepticism. The fanatical and sectarian zeal of his colleague, Jurieu, brought about his condemnation by Dutch Protestant authorities. He gave up his professorship and devoted the rest of his life to his *Dictionary*, which became the bible of liberalism, not only in France, but in England and America. Boswell reports that Dr. Johnson, when he was told that Leibniz had published a confutation of Bayle, exclaimed: "A confutation of Bayle, sir! What part of Bayle do you mean? The greatest part of his writings is not confutable: it is historical and critical." And Voltaire, with typical irony, wrote: "Would to God that Bayle had been drowned, along with the rest of his Dutch heretics! Did you ever see such an abominable man! He gives facts with such odious fidelity, he exposes the arguments for and against with such dastardly impartiality, he is so intolerably intelligible, that he leads people of only ordinary common sense to judge and even to doubt. It's more than a man can bear, and I for one confess that I enter into a state of righteous indignation whenever that man and his kind are mentioned."

Miscellaneous Thoughts on the Comet (1682)

The Antiquity and General Acceptance of an Opinion Is No Assurance of Its Truth

Now let us undertake the task of considering whether or not the general agreement among ancients and moderns that comets are evil omens should bear much weight. Again I say, it is pure illusion to claim that a notion that has passed from one century to the next, from generation to generation, cannot be entirely false. If only we examine the causes of the establishment of certain opinions in the world about us, we readily see that nothing is less reasonable than such a claim. You will certainly grant me that it is easy to persuade the people of certain false opinions which are in accordance with the prejudices of childhood or the desires of the heart, as are all the so-called rules in regard to omens. That is all I ask, for that admission is enough to perpetuate such opinions forever; for except for a few philosophical minds, no one thinks of submitting to examination what is universally held to be true. We assume that the ancients once examined it and were sufficiently on their guard against error; and therefore we teach it in our turn to our children as infallible fact. If you remember, too, what I have said else-

BAYLE

where about man's intellectual indolence and the pains that must be taken for thorough reconsideration, you will see that we will not say, with Minucius Felix, "Everything is uncertain in human affairs, but the more uncertain it is, the more reason to be astonished that some, disgusted with the exacting search for the truth, prefer rashly to embrace the first opinion that lies at hand, rather than take the time and the care that deep thought requires"; we should rather say, "The more uncertain everything is, the less reason we have to be astonished at such a solution." The author of the *Art of Thinking* observes very judiciously that most men decide to accept one notion rather than another because of certain superficial and extraneous traits which they consider to be more in conformity with truth than with falsehood and which are easily discernible; whereas solid and essential reasons which reveal truth are difficult to come by. Hence, since men are prone to follow the easier course, they almost always take the side on which these superficial traits are apparent.

It is a common occurrence to see people avoid marriage in the month of May, because it has been believed from time immemorial that May weddings bring bad luck; and I have no doubt that this superstition, which came down to us from ancient Rome and was founded on the fact that the festival of evil spirits, or Lemuralia, was celebrated in May, will subsist among Christians until the end of time. For it will be kept alive in a family, if only it is remembered that some grandfather or uncle took such precautions. And the reasoning becomes invincible and all the more impressive when we see intelligent people observe the same practice. In fact many persons, not superstitious themselves, delay or speed up their marriage to avoid the month of May, because it is important that the belief should not be spread around that they have courted misfortune. In this society of ours, all precautions should be taken. A merchant can become truly unlucky just because people entertain the ridiculous idea that he is threatened with bad luck; for no one will be willing to extend him credit or associate in business with him. If anyone wanted to seek out all the reasons for popular misconceptions, it would be an unending task. (C)

Men Do Not Act According to Their Principles

That man is a reasoning animal, we are all agreed; it is no less true that he almost never acts in accordance with his principles. He is well able, in speculative matters, to avoid drawing false conclusions, for in this field he sins much less through the ease with which he entertains false principles than through the false suppositions that he derives from them. But in questions of moral conduct, it is an entirely different matter. Almost never yielding to false principles and almost always retaining in his conscience ideas of natural equity, he nevertheless almost always concludes to the advantage of his unbridled desires. Tell me, please, how it happens that although there exists among men a prodigious diversity of opinion concerning the manner of serving God and living according to the laws of propriety, we see nonetheless that certain passions constantly hold sway in all countries and have done so through all ages; that ambition, avarice, envy, the desire for vengeance, indecency, all the crimes that satisfy these passions are everywhere apparent; that the Jew, the Mohammedan, the Turk, and the Moor, Christian and infidel, Indian and Tartar, continentals and islanders, noblemen and commoners, all these kinds of people who, in other respects, we might say have only their humanity in common, are so alike in respect to these passions that we would think they copy one another? How can all that be true unless we admit that the true principle of all our actions (I except those in whom the grace of the Holy Spirit is fully operative) is our temperament, our natural inclination to seek pleasure, the taste that we acquire for certain objects, the desire to please someone, a habit contracted in dealing with our friends, or some other disposition which arises from the depths of our natures, in whatever country we may be born, and with whatsoever knowledge our minds may be imbued?

That must be so, since the ancient heathen, overwhelmed with an unbelievable multitude of superstitions, perpetually busy appeasing the anger of their gods, terrified by an infinity of prodigies, imagining that the gods were dispensers of adversity and prosperity according to the lives that they had led, did not fail to commit all crimes imaginable. And if that were not so, how would it be possible that Christians, who know so clearly through a revelation upheld by so many miracles that they must renounce vice in order to be eternally happy and not to be eternally damned; who have such excellent preachers to present to them in these matters the most vivid and pressing exhortations possible; who have all around them so many zealous and learned directors of conscience and so many books of devotion; how would it be possible, I say, that in the midst of all that, Christians could lead, as they do, the most sinful of lives? (CXXXVI)

Reflections on the Charge Made by Certain Infidels Against Christians That Their Religion Is Fit Only to Form Cowards

. . . The charge has sometimes been made against Christians that the principles of the Gospel are not suited to safeguarding the commonwealth, because they undermine courage and inspire horror for blood and all the violence of war. . . .

Evangelical courage only makes us despise the insults of poverty, the persecution of tyrants, prisons, torture, and all the throes of martyrdom. It quite properly makes us brave with heroic patience the most inhuman rage of persecutors of the faith. It resigns us to the will of God in the most painful of maladies. In that consists the courage of the true Christian. That is enough, I confess, to convince infidels that our religion does not undermine courage and inspire cowardice. But that does not prevent them from being able to say with reason that if we take the word courage in its commonly accepted sense, the Gospel is not apt to foster it. It is understood that by a courageous man we mean a man who makes it a point of honor not to suffer the least insult, who avenges himself gloriously and at the peril of his life for the slightest offense given him; who loves war, seeks the most perilous occasions to dip his hands in the blood of enemies, who is ambitious and wants to shine above all other men. It would be completely nonsensical to say that the counsels and precepts of Jesus Christ inspire us with that spirit; for it is a notorious conviction among all who know the first elements of the Christian religion that it recommends above all else that we suffer insults, walk humbly, love our neighbor, seek peace, and render good for evil, and abstain from every semblance of violence. I defy all living men, no matter how expert they may be in the military arts, ever to make good soldiers of an army in which are found only men resolved to follow punctually all these maxims. The best that could be expected would be that they would not be afraid to die for their country and their God. But I leave it to those who know what war is to decide if that is sufficient to qualify as a good soldier and if men who want to succeed in that calling must not inflict all possible harm on the enemy, outguess him, take him by surprise, put him to the sword, burn his supplies, reduce him to starvation and destitution. . . .

It may be said that if the principles of Christianity were truly followed, we would see no conqueror among Christians nor offensive war, and we would restrict ourselves to a defense against the invasions of infidels. That being so, how many nations in Europe would we see enjoying a profound peace for very long who because of that would be the least fit of all peoples in the world to wage war? It is therefore true that the spirit of our holy religion does not make us warlike: and yet there are no more warlike nations on the face of the earth than those which make a profession of Christianity. . . .

We Christians daily improve upon the art of war by inventing an infinite number of machines to make sieges more deadly and horrible; and from us Christians infidels learn to use better weapons. I know very well that we do not do that because we are Christians, but because we are more skilful than infidels: for if they were clever and valorous enough to wage war better than Christians they would do so without fail. Nevertheless I find here a very convincing argument to prove that in daily life we do not follow the principles of our religion, since I show that Christians employ all their knowledge and passions in improving upon the art of war, without the slightest hindrance from a knowledge of the Gospel in pursuing this cruel design. (CXLI)

Philosophical Commentary on the Words of Jesus Christ: Compel Them to Come In (1686-1687)

Political Evils Caused by Intolerance

If a multiplicity of religions is harmful to the State, that is only because one religion will not tolerate the other but wants rather to swallow it up by dint of persecution. *Hinc prima mali labes,* that is where trouble begins. If each religion adopted the spirit of tolerance that I recommend, there would be the same concord in a state with ten religions as in a city in which different artisans and craftsmen mutually support one another. The most that could happen would be honest rivalry in outdoing one another in piety, good conduct and knowledge; each religion would take pride in proving its favored share of God's love by exhibiting a firmer attachment to moral conduct; all would boast of greater love for their country, if the sovereign protected them all and through his justice held them in balance. Such handsome emulation would give rise to innumerable blessings; consequently toleration is of all things the most conducive to the return of the golden age and the formation of a concert and harmony of a number of voices and instruments of different tones and notes as agreeable at the very least as the uniformity of a single voice. What then prevents this beautiful concert composed of such different voices and tones? It is only because one of two religions wants to exercise cruel tyranny over men's minds and force others to act against their conscience; because kings foment this unjust partiality and lend secular force to the furious and tumultuous desires of a populace of monks and clerics; in short the whole disorder springs not from toleration but from non-toleration. (Pt. II, ch. vi)

The Impossibility of Discovering Absolute Truth —Respect for the Rights of the Erring Conscience

. . . It is impossible in our present condition to know with certainty whether or not what appears to us to be the truth (I am speaking of the particular truths of religion and not of the properties of numbers or the first principles of metaphysics or the demonstrations of geometry) is absolute truth; the best we can do is to be fully convinced that we hold to absolute truth, that we are right and other people are wrong, all very dubious indications of truth, since they can be found among pagans and the most damnable of heretics. It is therefore certain that there is no trustworthy indication which will enable us among our beliefs to distinguish the true from the false. This distinction cannot be deduced from evidence; for on the contrary everyone says that the truths of God's revealed word are profound mysteries which require us to surrender our intelligence in obedience to the Faith. This is not because of incomprehensibility, for what is more false and altogether incomprehensible than a squared circle, than an essentially vicious first principle, than God a father through carnal generation, as Jupiter was among the pagans? Nor is it to satisfy our conscience, for a Papist is as satisfied with his religion, and a Turk and a Jew with theirs, as we are with ours. Nor is it because of the courage and zeal that belief inspires, for the falsest of religions have their martyrs, their incredible austerities, their spirit of proselytism which very often overcomes the charity of true believers, and their unshakable attachment to superstitious ceremonies. Nothing in short can assure a man of the distinction between truth and falsehood. Thus it is asking too much of him to hope that he can make this distinction. The best he can do is to judge certain questions under examination by their appearances, whether or not they seem true or false to him. He can then be asked to see to it that those that are true appear to him to be true; but whether he succeeds in this or whether the false seem to him to be true, he must follow his own persuasion.

. . . This consideration, if it were carefully weighed and thoroughly meditated upon, would surely reveal the truth of what I am here claiming: which is that, in man's present condition, God is content to demand that he seek the truth as diligently as possible and when he thinks he has found it that he cherish it and make it the rule of his life. As everyone can see, this proves that we are obliged to have the same respect for presumptive as for real truth. Whence it follows that all the objections that can be brought to bear on the difficulty of examination disappear like idle phantoms, since each individual is surely capable of finding a meaning in what he reads or hears, and of feeling that that meaning is true; and thus his particular brand of truth is established. It is enough that every man consult sincerely and in good faith the light that God gives him and seize accordingly upon the idea that seems to him the most reasonable and the most conformable to God's will. In this way he is a true believer in respect to God, although through a flaw for which he cannot be blamed his thoughts may not be a faithful image of reality, just as a child is a true believer in taking for his father his mother's husband, of whom he is not the son. The important consideration is then to act virtuously; thus everyone should try as hard as he can to honor God through prompt obedience to moral precepts. In this respect, that is, in respect to the knowledge of our moral obligations, the light of revelation is so clear that few can mistake it if only they seek it in good faith.

. . . Whence I conclude that ignorance founded on good faith is excusable in the most criminal of cases, such as robbery or adultery, and that thus ignorance in every domain is excusable, to the extent that a heretic of good faith or even an infidel will be punished by God only for evil acts that he has committed knowing well that they were evil. As for acts committed in all good conscience, a conscience, I say, that he has not himself maliciously stultified, I cannot be convinced that they constitute a crime.

. . . Judging by our ideal of a man most accomplished in wisdom and justice, we believe that if, after leaving an order with his servants as he departed on a long journey he found upon his return that they understood it differently and that while they were all agreed that their master's will was their sole guide, they disagreed only on what that was, he would declare that they were all equally respectful of his orders; but that some were more intelligent than others in their understanding of the real meaning of his instructions. Certainly, we would clearly and distinctly expect that to be his pronouncement; therefore Reason requires that God should declare likewise in regard to both true believers and conscientious heretics. . . . (Pt. II, ch. x)

Fénelon
1651-1715

FÉNELON, Archbishop of Cambrai, and member of an aristocratic family, was not a *philosophe*. The *philosophes*, however, thought of him as a fellow-martyr in the cause of enlightenment. His eminent position as Archbishop and tutor of the Duke of Burgundy, heir to the throne, allowed him to be much more daring than they in his criticisms of Louis XIV's despotic reign. A quarrel with Bossuet, upholder of the divine prerogatives of kingship in ecclesiastical matters, led to his banishment from Paris to Cambrai.

The Adventures of Telemachus (1699), his greatest literary accomplishment, was designed to teach the young Duke the duties of a benevolent king towards his flock. From this work Voltaire borrowed many criticisms of royal power and also the spirit and wording of cosmic mysticism. Rousseau and Chateaubriand were more influenced by Fénelon's theories of the natural goodness of man and the uncorrupted felicity of "the noble savage" as described by Jesuit missionaries. The death of the young prince in 1712 was a tragic blow to Fénelon, who did not live to see the succession to the throne.

The *Lettre à Louis XIV* given below is a forceful denunciation of the abuses of the Old Régime, all the more convincing in that it comes from an eminent Churchman who lived long in the intimacy of the court.

Letter to Louis XIV
(1694)

The person, Sir, who takes the liberty of writing you this letter has no worldly interest in view. He writes it not from chagrin, nor ambition, nor a desire to occupy himself with affairs of state. He loves you without being known to you; he sees God in your person. With all your power you can give him no boon that he desires, and there is no ill that he would not gladly suffer to make you recognize truths that are necessary to your salvation. If he speaks to you forcefully, do not be surprised, for the truth is strong and free. You are not often accustomed to hear it. People who are accustomed to flattery readily mistake for chagrin, asperity and immoderation what is nothing but plain truth. It would be a betrayal of truth not to reveal it to you to the fullest extent. God is witness that the person who speaks to you does it with a heart full of zeal, respect, fidelity, and affection, in all matters that concern your true interests.

You were born, Sir, with a just and equitable heart; but those who brought you up have given you, instead of the science of government, only a spirit of defiance, jealousy, estrangement from virtue, fear of all outstanding merit, a liking for compliant, groveling men, haughtiness, and narrow self-interest.

For about thirty years your principal ministers have undermined and overturned all the ancient maxims of the State, to make full show of your authority, which had become theirs because it was left in their hands. The State and the rules of State were no longer spoken of, only the King and his good pleasure. They have increased your revenues and expenses to the utmost limit. They have extolled you to the skies for having effaced, so they said, the grandeur of all your predecessors together, that is, for having impoverished all France in order to introduce monstrous and incurable luxury into your court. They have tried to raise you upon the ruins of all orders of the State: as if you could be great through the ruination of all your subjects, upon whom your grandeur is founded. It is true that you have been jealous of authority, perhaps even too much so in foreign affairs; but at bottom each minister has been master of his administrative domain. You thought you were governing because you have set the limits of the departments of those who govern. They have shown the public their power, which has been only too keenly felt. They have been heartless, haughty, unjust, violent, treacherous. They have recognized no other rule, either for the administration of the internal affairs of State or for foreign negotiations, but the crushing and annihilation of all resistance. They have spoken to you only for the purpose of keeping away from you all men of merit who might give them umbrage. They have accustomed you to accept a steady stream of extravagant adulation, which reaches the point of idolatry and which, for your own honor, you should have indignantly rejected. Your name has been rendered odious, and the whole French nation unbearable in the eyes of our neighbors. All former allies have been lost, because only slaves were wanted. Bloody wars have been instigated for more than twenty years. For example, Sir, your Majesty was made to undertake, in 1672, the war against Holland for your glory and the punishment of the Hollanders, who had scoffed in annoyance over the upsetting of the commercial regulations established by Cardinal Richelieu. I cite this war in particular because it was the source of all the others. Its only grounds were the desire for glory and vengeance, which can never make a war just; whence it follows that all the frontiers that you have extended through this war were from the beginning unjustly acquired. . . .

This war is still the true source of all the ills that France is suffering. Ever since, you have sought to make peace as a master and impose conditions instead of measuring them equitably and moderately. That is why there has been no enduring peace. Your enemies, shamefully overwhelmed, have had no thought but to rise up and unite against you. Is it any wonder? You have not even confined yourself within the terms of that peace that you so haughtily granted. In wholly peaceful times, you have waged war and made prodigious conquests. You have established an assembly in order to be both judge and party thus adding insult and derision to usurpation and violence. You have sought, in the Treaty of Westphalia, dubious arms for a surprise assault on Strasbourg. Never over such a long period of years had a single one of your ministers dared to allege these terms in any negotiation to show that you had the slightest claim upon that city. Such conduct has united and animated all Europe against you. . . .

Meanwhile your people, whom you should cherish as your children and who have been until now so devoted to you, are dying of hunger. The cultivation of the fields is nearly abandoned; cities and countryside are becoming depopulated; all trades are languishing and no longer provide a living for workmen. Commerce is at a standstill. As a consequence you have destroyed half of the real strength within your nation in order to make and defend vain conquests without the realm. Instead of extracting money from this impoverished populace, you should rather give it alms and food. All France is nothing but a great poor-house, desolate and unfed. Magistrates are debased and enervated. The nobility, whose total wealth is under decree, live only on state subsidies. . . . Popular uprisings, which had been so long unknown, are becoming frequent. Even Paris, so near you, is not exempt. Magistrates are forced to tolerate insolence from the rebellious and to pay them off secretly to appease them; thus those are paid who should be punished. You are reduced to the shameful and deplorable extremity of leaving sedition unpunished and fostering it through this impunity or inhumanly massacring people that you have reduced to despair by snatching from them through your war-taxes the bread that they try to gain by the sweat of their brows. But while they lack bread, you yourself lack money and are unwilling to face the extremity to which you are reduced. . . . [1]

[1] La Bruyère forcefully describes the same period of famine and popular uprisings in his *Caractères* (ed. of 1694): "Wild creatures, male and female, can be seen throughout the countryside, dark, ghastly, all burned beneath the sun, attached to the soil which they work with invincible obstinacy: they have something that resembles an articulate voice, and when they stand on their feet, they disclose a human face; and they are indeed men. They withdraw at night to their lairs, where they live on black bread, water and roots: they spare other men the trouble of sowing, cultivating, and reaping in order to live, and thus do not deserve to be deprived of the fruit of their labors."

Everyone sees the dilemma and no one dares bring it to your attention—you will perhaps see it too late. True courage consists in not flattering yourself and in taking a firm stand in the face of necessity. You willingly lend an ear, Sir, only to those who deceive you with vain hopes. The people that you consider the most worthy are those whom you fear and avoid the most. You should be prepared for the truth, since you are king, urge people to tell it to you bluntly, and encourage those who are too timid to do so. Quite to the contrary, your sole desire is to keep it dark; but God can finally lift the veil that covers your eyes and show you what you turn your face from. He has long held his arm lifted against you: but he is slow to strike, because he has pity for a prince who has all his life been besieged by flatterers and because, moreover, your enemies are also his. But he will be able to separate the justice of his cause from yours, which is not just, and humiliate you in order to convert you. For you will be a Christian only in humiliation. You do not love God: you fear him even only as a slave fears; for you fear Hell, and not God. Your religion consists only in superstitious and superficial observances. You are like the Jews of whom God said: "While they honor me with their lips, their hearts are far from me." You are very scrupulous in observing trivialities and hardened in the face of terrible wrongs. You love only your glory and your ease. You relate everything to yourself as if you were Lord of the earth and all the rest were created only as a sacrifice to you. But on the contrary, God gave you to the world only for the sake of your people. But alas! you do not understand these truths: how could you take pleasure in them? You do not know God, you do not love Him, you do not pray to Him in your heart, and you make no effort to know Him.

You have an archbishop [Harlay] who is corrupt, scandalous, incorrigible, deceitful, malicious, sly, hostile to every virtue, the despair of all honorable people. You put up with him because his sole preoccupation is to please you with flattery. For more than twenty years, by prostituting his integrity, he has enjoyed your confidence. You deliver honorable people into his hands, you allow him to tyrannize the Church, and no virtuous prelate is treated as well as he.

As for your confessor [Father Le Tellier], he is not vicious; but he fears sound virtue and likes only worldly people of loose morals; he is jealous of his authority, which you have increased beyond all bounds. Never before have the King's confessors alone appointed bishops and decided all cases of conscience. You are the only person in France, Sir, who does not know that he is ignorant, that his spirit is deficient and vulgar, and that with all his coarseness he does not lack cunning. Even the Jesuits despise him and are indignant to see him so compliant with the ridiculous ambition of his family. You have made of a monk a minister of State. He is no better judge of men than of anything else. . . .

It had been hoped, Sir, that your Council would turn you back from your erroneous ways; but your Council has neither the strength nor moral courage for righteousness. At least Madame de M*** and M. le Duc de B***[1] should take advantage of your confidence in them to open your eyes; but their weakness and timidity do them no honor and are a public scandal. . . . You will perhaps ask, Sir, what they should tell you; just this: they should show you that you must humble yourself beneath the powerful hand of God, if you do not want Him to humiliate you; you must ask for peace and expiate in shame all the glory which has become your idol; you must reject the unjust counsels of political flatterers; and finally you must surrender immediately to your enemies, for the safety of the State, the conquests that you could not in any case retain without injustice. Are you not all too lucky in your misfortunes that God will put an end to the prosperity which has blinded you and constrained

[1] It is believed that Mme de Maintenon and the Duc de Beauvilliers brought this letter to the king's attention. It was of course suppressed and was therefore unknown to the *philosophes* and to the eighteenth century.

you to make a restitution which is essential to your salvation and which you never could have resolved to make in a peaceful and triumphant state of mind? The person who tells you these truths, Sir, far from being opposed to your interests, would give his life to see you such as God wants you to be, and will not cease praying for you.

Voltaire

1694-1778

Born a commoner in Paris in 1694, François-Marie Arouet was sent to the Jesuit school of Louis-le-Grand. There he received an excellent education in rhetoric, philosophy and the Latin humanities, and made many lifelong friends among his Jesuit masters and noble schoolmates. His free-roving wit and the facility of his light verse led him into the libertine society of the Temple and gave him an early acquaintance with the dreaded "lettres de cachet," some instigated by the father against his wayward son, others by the strict censorship exercised by Church and State. Banishment from Paris for brief periods was the commonest punishment, but once, on order of exile, he was lucky enough to be sent only to Holland rather than to the French West Indies, and in 1717 was shut up in the Bastille for eleven months for satirical poems which he might have written, but apparently did not. On his release in 1718, the production of his first successful tragedy gave him the reputation of the greatest playwright of the century, a position which he successfully maintained for sixty years. His *Henriade*, an epic poem celebrating the virtues of Henri IV, France's tolerant king, served greatly to increase his fame.

In 1726, an insignificant altercation with a member of the powerful Rohan family led to a second imprisonment in the Bastille, from which he was released to go into exile in England. While there, he thoroughly mastered the English language, saw many productions of Shakespeare's plays, met Pope and Swift, and studied English manners and customs. His *Letters Concerning the English Nation*, in its surreptitious French publication in 1734, led to an order of arrest. He left France again and returned secretly to Lorraine, where he was welcomed by Mme du Châtelet, his mistress and intellectual companion, with whom he lived until her death in 1749. During this period he popularized the physics and optics of Newton, began his history of *The Age of Louis XIV*, and wrote two of his best philosophical tales, *Zadig* and *Micromégas*. (For Voltaire's later activities, see page 233.)

Letters Concerning the English Nation (1733)

Voltaire reveals himself in these sprightly Letters *as the undisputed master of French prose. Presented as if written in England in 1728, they were composed for the most part in 1732, after Voltaire had had time to study more thoroughly the scientific findings of Isaac Newton, the psychology of John Locke, and various aspects of the English religious and political scene. They first appeared in England in translation, in 1733. Voltaire then added a twenty-fifth letter of* Remarks on Pascal's Thoughts *and sought permission to publish the book in France under the title of* Philosophical Letters. *When permission was denied, surreptitious editions appeared in 1734. Voltaire's arrest was ordered and the book was officially burned.*

Harmless as the Letters *seem to us today, they have been described as the first bomb hurled against the Old Régime. Voltaire's object was to describe the English customs, institutions, and philosophy which contrasted most notably with French failings and abuses. He had been particularly struck by the religious freedom that had been won through the Toleration Act of 1689, although, being Voltaire, he is not blind to certain of the ridiculous aspects of the Quakers and Dissenters. He was also greatly impressed by the liberal and democratic aspects of England's political and judicial systems, the respect paid to her great scientists and philosophers and the thriving commerce that was enriching the nation. Most serious of all was his letter on John Locke, from whom he derived many of his life-long political and philosophical opinions.*

On the Quakers

I was of the opinion that the doctrine and history of so extraordinary a people were worthy the attention of the curious. To acquaint myself with them, I made a visit to one of the most eminent Quakers in England, who after having traded thirty years, had the wisdom to prescribe limits to his fortune and to his desires, and was settled in a little solitude not far from London. Being come into it, I perceived a small, but regularly built house, vastly neat, but without the least pomp of furniture. The Quaker who owned it was a hale ruddy-complexioned old man, who had never been afflicted with sickness, because he had always been insensible to passions and a perfect stranger to intemperance. I never in my life saw a more noble or a more engaging aspect than his. He was dressed like those of his persuasion, in a plain coat, without pleats in the sides, or buttons on the pockets and sleeves; and had on a beaver, the brims of which were horizontal, like those of our clergy. He did not uncover himself when I appeared, and advanced towards me without once stooping his body; but there appeared more politeness in the open, humane air of his countenance than in the custom of drawing one leg behind the other, and taking that from the head which is made to cover it. "Friend," says he to me, "I perceive thou art a stranger, but if I can do anything for thee, only tell me." "Sir," says I to him, bending forwards, and advancing as is usual with us, one leg towards him, "I flatter myself that my just curiosity will not give you the least offence, and that you'll do me the honor to inform me of the particulars of your religion." "The people of thy country," replied the Quaker, "are too full of their vows and compliments, but I never yet met with one of them who had so much curiosity as thyself. Come in, and let us first dine together." I still continued to make some very unseasonable ceremonies, it not being easy to disengage one's self at once from habits we have been long used to; and after taking part of a frugal meal, which began and ended with a prayer to God, I began to question my courteous host. I opened with that which good Catholics have more than once made to Huguenots. "My dear sir," says I, "were you ever baptized?" "I never was," replied the Quaker, "nor any of my brethren." "Zounds," says I to him, "you are not Christians then." "Friend," replies the old man in a soft tone of voice, "swear not; we are Christians, and endeavour to be good Christians, but are not of the opinion that the sprinkling water on a child's head makes him a Christian." "Heavens!" says I, shocked at his impiety, "you have then forgot that Christ was baptized by St. John." "Friend," replies the mild Quaker once again, "swear not. Christ indeed was baptized by John, but he himself never baptized anyone. We are disciples of Christ, not of John." I pitied very much the sincerity of my worthy Quaker, and was absolutely for forcing him to get himself christened. "Were that all," replied he very gravely, "we would submit cheerfully to baptism, purely in compliance with thy weakness, for we don't condemn any person who uses it; but then we think that those who profess a religion of so holy, so spiritual a nature as that of Christ, ought to abstain to the utmost of their power from the Jewish ceremonies." "O unaccountable!" says I, "what! baptism a Jewish ceremony?" "Yes, my friend," says he, "so truly Jewish that a great many Jews use the baptism of John to this day. Look into ancient authors, and thou wilt find that John only revived this practice; and that it had been used by the Hebrews long before his time, in like manner as the Mahometans imitated the Ishmaelites in their pilgrimage to Mecca. Jesus indeed submitted to the baptism of John, as he had suffered himself to be circumcised; but circumcision and the washing with water ought to be abolished by the baptism of Christ, that baptism of the spirit, that ablution of the soul, which is the salvation of mankind. Thus the forerunner said, 'I indeed baptize you with water unto repentance; but he that cometh after me, is mightier than I, whose shoes I am not worthy to bear: he shall baptize you with the Holy Ghost and with fire.' Likewise Paul the greatest apostle of the Gentiles, writes as follows to the Corinthians: 'Christ sent me not to baptize, but to preach the Gospel'; and indeed Paul never baptized but two persons with water, and that very much against his inclinations. He circumcised his disciple Timothy, and the other dis-

ciples likewise circumcised all who were willing to submit to that carnal ordinance. But art thou circumcised," added he? "I have not the honor to be so," says I. "Well, friend," continues the Quaker, "thou art a Christian without being circumcised, and I am one without being baptized." Thus did this pious man make a wrong, but very specious application of four or five texts of scripture which seemed to favour the tenets of his sect; but at the same time forgot very sincerely a hundred texts which made directly against them. I had more sense than to contest with him, since there is no possibility of convincing an enthusiast. A man should never pretend to inform a lover of his mistress's faults, no more than one who is at law, of the badness of his cause; nor attempt to win over a fanatic by strength of reasoning. Accordingly I waived the subject.

"Well," says I to him, "what sort of a communion have you?" "We have none like that thou hintest at amongst us," replied he. "How! no communion," says I? "Only that spiritual one," replied he, "of hearts." He then began again to throw out his texts of scripture; and preached a most eloquent sermon against that ordinance. He harangued in a tone as though he had been inspired, to prove that the sacraments were merely of human invention, and that the word *sacrament* was not once mentioned in the gospel. "Excuse," says he, "my ignorance, for I have not employed a hundredth part of the arguments which might be brought to prove the truth of our religion, but these thou mayest thyself peruse in the Exposition of our Faith written by Robert Barclay. 'Tis one of the best pieces that ever was penned by man; and as our adversaries confess it to be of a dangerous tendency, the arguments in it must necessarily be very convincing." I promised to peruse this piece, and my Quaker imagined he had already made a convert of me. He afterwards gave me an account in few words of some singularities which made this sect the contempt of others. "Confess," says he, "that 'twas very difficult for thee to refrain from laughter when I answered all thy civilities without uncovering my head, and at the same time said *Thee* and *Thou* to thee. However, thou appearest to me too well read not to know that in Christ's time no nation was so ridiculous as to put the plural number for the singular. Augustus Cæsar himself was spoke to in such phrases as these, *I love thee, I beseech thee, I thank thee;* but he did not allow any person to call him *Domine*, Sir. 'Twas not till many ages after that men would have the word *You*, as though they were double, instead of *Thou* employed in speaking to them; and usurped the flattering titles of lordship, of eminence, and of holiness, which mere worms bestow on other worms, by assuring them that they are with a most profound respect, and an infamous falsehood, their most obedient, humble servants. 'Tis to secure ourselves more strongly from such a shameless traffic of lies and flattery that we *thee* and *thou* a king with the same freedom as we do a beggar, and salute no person; we owing nothing to mankind but charity, and to the laws respect and obedience.

"Our apparel is also somewhat different from that of others, and this purely that it may be a perpetual warning to us not to imitate them. Others wear the badges and marks of their several dignities, and we those of Christian humility. We fly from all assemblies of pleasure, from diversions of every kind, and from places where gaming is practised; and indeed our case would be deplorable should we fill with such levities as those I have mentioned the heart which ought to be the habitation of God. We never swear, not even in a court of justice, being of opinion that the most holy name of God ought not to be prostituted in the miserable contests between man and man. When we are obliged to appear before a magistrate upon other people's account (for law-suits are unknown among the Friends), we give evidence to the truth by sealing it with our *yea* and *nay;* and the judges believe us on our bare affirmation, whilst so many other Christians forswear themselves on the holy Gospels. We never war or fight in any case; but 'tis not that we are afraid, for so far from shuddering at the thoughts of death, we on the contrary bless the moment which unites us with the Being of

Beings; but the reason of our not using the outward sword is that we are neither wolves, tigers nor mastiffs, but men and Christians. Our God, who has commanded us to love our enemies, and to suffer without repining, would certainly not permit us to cross the seas, merely because murderers clothed in scarlet and wearing caps two foot high enlist citizens by a noise made with two little sticks on an ass's skin extended. And when, after a victory is gained, the whole city of London is illuminated; when the sky is in a blaze with fireworks, and a noise is heard in the air of thanksgivings, of bells, of organs, and of the cannon, we groan in silence, and are deeply affected with sadness of spirit and brokenness of heart, for the sad havoc which is the occasion of those public rejoicings." (Letter I)

Such was the substance of the conversation I had with this very singular person; but I was greatly surprised to see him come the Sunday following and take me with him to the Quakers' meeting. There are several of these in London, but that which he carried me to stands near the famous pillar called The Monument. The brethren were already assembled at my entering it with my guide. There might be about four hundred men and three hundred women in the meeting. The women hid their faces behind their fans, and the men were covered with their broad-brimmed hats. All were seated, and the silence was universal. I passed through them, but did not perceive so much as one lift up his eyes to look at me. This silence lasted a quarter of an hour, when at last one of them rose up, took off his hat, and, after making a variety of wry faces and groaning in a most lamentable manner, he, partly from his nose and partly from his mouth, threw out a strange, confused jumble of words (borrowed, as he imagined, from the Gospel) which neither himself nor any of his hearers understood. When this distorter had ended his beautiful soliloquy, and the stupid, but greatly edified, congregation were separated, I asked my friend how it was possible for the judicious part of their assembly to suffer such a babbling? "We are obliged," said he, "to suffer it, because no one knows when a man rises up to hold forth whether he will be moved by the Spirit or by folly. In this doubt and uncertainty we listen patiently to everyone; we even allow our women to hold forth. Two or three of these are often inspired at one and the same time, and it is then that a most charming noise is heard in the Lord's house." "You have, then, no priests?" said I to him. "No, no, friend," replies the Quaker, "to our great happiness." Then opening one of the Friends' books, as he called it, he read the following words in an emphatic tone:—" 'God forbid we should presume to ordain anyone to receive the Holy Spirit on the Lord's Day to the prejudice of the rest of the brethren.' Thanks to the Almighty, we are the only people upon earth that have no priests. Wouldst thou deprive us of so happy a distinction? Why should we abandon our babe to mercenary nurses, when we ourselves have milk enough for it? These mercenary creatures would soon domineer in our houses and destroy both the mother and the babe. God has said, 'Freely you have received, freely give.' Shall we, after these words, cheapen, as it were, the Gospel, sell the Holy Ghost, and make of an assembly of Christians a mere shop of traders? We don't pay a set of men clothed in black to assist our poor, to bury our dead, or to preach to the brethren. These offices are all of too tender a nature for us ever to entrust them to others." "But how is it possible for you," said I, with some warmth, "to know whether your discourse is really inspired by the Almighty?" "Whosoever," says he, "shall implore Christ to enlighten him, and shall publish the Gospel truths he may feel inwardly, such a one may be assured that he is inspired by the Lord." He then poured forth a numberless multitude of Scripture texts which proved, as he imagined, that there is no such thing as Christianity without an immediate revelation, and added these remarkable words: "When thou movest one of thy limbs, is it moved by thy own power? Certainly not; for this limb is often sensible to involuntary motions. Consequently He who created thy body gives motion to this earthly tabernacle. And are the several ideas of which thy soul receives the impression formed by thyself? Much less are they, since these pour in upon thy mind whether thou wilt or no; consequently thou receivest thy ideas from Him who created thy soul. But as He leaves thy affections at full liberty, He gives thy mind such ideas as thy affections may deserve; if thou livest in God, thou actest, thou thinkest in God. After this thou needest only but open thine eyes to that light which enlightens all mankind, and it is then thou wilt perceive the truth, and make others perceive it." "Why, this," said I, "is Malebranche's doctrine to a tittle." "I am acquainted with thy Malebranche," said he; "he had something of the Friend in him, but was not enough so." These are the most considerable particulars I learned concerning the doctrine of the Quakers. In my next letter I shall acquaint you with their history, which you will find more singular than their opinions. (Letter II)

You have already heard that the Quakers date from Christ who, according to them, was the first Quaker. Religion, say these, was corrupted a little after His death, and remained in that state of corruption about sixteen hundred years. But there were always a few Quakers concealed in the world, who carefully preserved the sacred fire, which was extinguished in all but themselves, until at last this light spread itself in England in 1642.

It was at the time when Great Britain was torn to pieces by the intestine wars which three or four sects had raised in the name of God, that one George Fox, born in Leicestershire, and son to a silk weaver, took it into his head to preach, and, as he pretended, with all the requisites of a true apostle—that is, without being able either to read or write. He was about twenty-five years of age, irreproachable in his life and conduct, and a holy madman. He was equipped in leather from head to foot, and travelled from one village to another, exclaiming against war and the clergy. Had his invectives been levelled against the soldiery only he would have been safe enough, but he inveighed against ecclesiastics. Fox was seized at Derby, and being carried before a justice of peace, he did not once offer to pull off his leathern hat, upon which an officer gave him a great box of the ear, and cried to him, "Don't you know you are to appear uncovered before his worship?" Fox presented his other cheek to the officer, and begged him to give him another box for God's sake. The justice would have had him sworn before he asked him any questions. "Know, friend," says Fox to him, "that I never swear." The justice, observing he "thee'd" and "thou'd" him, sent him to the House of Correction, in Derby, with orders that he should be whipped there. Fox praised the Lord all the way he went to the House of Correction, where the justice's order was executed with the utmost severity. The men who whipped this enthusiast were greatly surprised to hear him beseech them to give him a few more lashes for the good of his soul. There was no need of entreating these people; the lashes were repeated, for which Fox thanked them very cordially, and began to preach. At first the spectators fell a-laughing, but they afterwards listened to him; and as enthusiasm is an epidemical distemper, many were persuaded, and those who scourged him became his first disciples. Being set at liberty, he ran up and down the country with a dozen proselytes at his heels, still declaiming against the clergy, and was whipped from time to time. Being one day set in the pillory, he harangued the crowd in so strong and moving a manner, that fifty of the auditors became his converts, and he won the rest so much in his favour that, his head being freed tumultuously from the hole where it was fastened, the populace went and searched for the Church of England clergyman who had been chiefly instrumental in bringing him to this punishment, and set him on the same pillory where Fox had stood. . . .

The Quakers were several times persecuted under Charles II; not upon a religious account, but for refusing to pay the tithes, for "theeing" and "thouing" the magistrates, and for refusing to take the oaths enacted by the laws.

At last Robert Barclay, a native of Scotland, presented to the King, in 1675, his "Apology for the Quakers," a work as well drawn up as the subject could possibly admit. The dedication to Charles II is not filled with mean, flattering encomiums, but abounds with bold touches in favor of truth and with the wisest counsels. "Thou hast tasted," said he to the King at the close of his epistle dedicatory, "of prosperity and adversity; thou knowest what it is to be banished from thy native country; to be overruled as well as to rule and sit upon the throne; and, being oppressed, thou hast reason to know how hateful the oppressor is both to God and man. If, after all these warnings and advertisements, thou dost not turn unto the Lord with all thy heart, but forget Him who remembered thee in thy distress, and give up thyself to follow lust and vanity, surely great will be thy condemnation.

"Against which snare, as well as the temptation of those that may or do feed thee and prompt thee to evil, the most excellent and prevalent remedy will be, to apply thyself to that light of Christ which shineth in thy conscience, which neither can nor will flatter thee nor suffer thee to be at ease in thy sins, but doth and will deal plainly and faithfully with thee, as those that are followers thereof have plainly done.—Thy faithful friend and subject, Robert Barclay."

A more surprising circumstance is, that this epistle, written by a private man of no figure, was so happy in its effects as to put a stop to the persecution. (Letter III)

[*Voltaire's interest in the Friends and especially in the colony that William Penn had founded in America continued throughout his lifetime. Their religion, a primitive form of Christianity founded on the dictates of conscience, having no rigid dogmas, priests, or theological litigations, resembled his own deistic beliefs and represented for him the road towards a better, more highly civilized humanity, which he described in golden terms as the utopia, or "El Dorado," of* Candide.

In his Questions on the Encyclopedia *(1771-2) he wrote: "I will say, to avoid repetition, that I like the Quakers. Yes, if the sea did not make me unbearably sick, it is in thy bosom, oh Pennsylvania, that I would pass the rest of my life, if indeed there is any life left for me." And in the same work, in a further article on the subject, he described the laws promulgated by Penn in 1681, which granted full civil liberty, forbade lawyers and attorneys to accept remuneration for legal services, and permitted all citizens to worship according to the dictates of their own hearts. This last law he took pains to translate: "Liberty of conscience being a right which all men have received from nature as a birthright and which should be maintained by all peaceful peoples, it is firmly established that no person shall be forced to attend any public religious worship. But full power is expressly given everyone to worship freely either in public or in private, without let or hindrance under any pretext whatsoever, provided that he profess to believe in one God, eternal, all-powerful, creator and preserver and ruler of the universe, and that he fulfill all civic duties and social obligations in respect to his fellow citizens." This law Voltaire describes as "more indulgent and humane than that given to Carolina by John Locke, the Plato of England, who was so superior to the Plato of Greece."]*

On the Church of England

England is properly the country of sectarists. *Multæ sunt mansiones in domo patris mei* [in my Father's house are many mansions]. An Englishman, as one to whom liberty is natural, may go to heaven his own way.

Nevertheless, though every one is permitted to serve God in whatever mode or fashion he thinks proper, yet their true religion, that in which a man makes his fortune, is the sect of Episcopalians or Churchmen, called the Church of England, or simply the Church, by way of eminence. No person can possess an employment either in England or Ireland unless he be ranked among the faithful, that is, professes himself a member of the Church of England. This reason (which carries mathematical evidence with it) has converted such numbers of Dissenters of all persuasions, that not a twentieth part of the nation is out of the pale of the Established Church. The English clergy have retained a great number of the Romish ceremonies, and especially that of receiving, with a most scrupulous attention, their tithes. They also have the pious ambition to aim at superiority.

Moreover, they inspire very religiously their flock with a holy zeal against Dissenters of all denominations. This zeal was pretty violent under the Tories in the four last years of Queen Anne; but was productive of no greater mischief than the breaking the windows of some meeting-houses and the demolishing of a few of them. For religious rage ceased in England with the civil wars, and was no more under Queen Anne than the hollow noise of a sea whose billows still heaved, though so long after the storm when the Whigs and Tories laid waste their native country, in the same manner as the Guelphs and Ghibellines formerly did theirs. It was absolutely necessary for both parties to call in religion on this occasion; the Tories declared for Episcopacy, and the Whigs, as some imagined, were for abolishing it; however, after these had got the upper hand, they contented themselves with only abridging it.

At the time when the Earl of Oxford and the Lord Bolingbroke used to drink healths to the Tories, the Church of England considered those noblemen as the defenders of its holy privileges. The lower House of Convocation (a kind of House of Commons) composed wholly of the clergy, was in some credit at that time; at least the members of it had the liberty to meet, to dispute on ecclesiastical matters, to sentence impious books from time to time to the flames, that is, books written against themselves. The Ministry which is now composed of Whigs does not so much as allow those gentlemen to assemble, so that they are at this time reduced (in the obscurity of their respective parishes) to the melancholy occupation of praying for the prosperity of the Government whose tranquillity they would willingly disturb. With regard to the bishops, who are twenty-six in all, they still have seats in the House of Lords in spite of the Whigs, because the ancient abuse of considering them as barons subsists to this day. There is a clause, however, in the oath which the

Government requires from these gentlemen, that puts their Christian patience to a very great trial, viz., that they shall be of the Church of England as by law established. There are few bishops, deans, or other dignitaries but imagine they are so *jure divino;* it is consequently a great mortification to them to be obliged to confess that they owe their dignity to a pitiful law enacted by a set of profane laymen. A learned monk (Father Courayer) wrote a book lately to prove the validity and succession of English ordinations. This book was forbid in France, but do you believe that the English Ministry were pleased with it? Far from it. Those damned Whigs don't care a straw whether the episcopal succession among them hath been interrupted or not, or whether Bishop Parker was consecrated (as it is pretended) in a tavern or a church; for these Whigs are much better pleased that the Bishops should derive their authority from the Parliament than from the Apostles. The Lord Bolingbroke observed that this notion of divine right would only make so many tyrants in lawn sleeves, but that the laws made so many citizens.

With regard to the morals of the English clergy, they are more regular than those of France, and for this reason. All the clergy (a very few excepted) are educated in the Universities of Oxford or Cambridge, far from the depravity and corruption which reign in the capital. They are not called to dignities till very late, at a time of life when men are sensible of no other passion but avarice, that is, when their ambition craves a supply. Employments are here bestowed both in the Church and the army, as a reward for long services; and we never see youngsters made bishops or colonels immediately upon their laying aside the academical gown; and besides most of the clergy are married. The stiff and awkward air contracted by them at the University, and the little familiarity the men of this country have with the ladies, commonly oblige a bishop to confine himself to, and rest contented with, his own. Clergymen sometimes take a glass at the tavern, custom giving them a sanction on this occasion; and if they fuddle themselves it is in a very serious manner, and without giving the least scandal.

That fable-mixed kind of mortal (not to be defined), who is neither of the clergy nor of the laity; in a word, the thing called *Abbé* in France; is a species quite unknown in England. All the clergy here are very much upon the reserve, and most of them pedants. When these are told that in France young fellows famous for their dissoluteness, and raised to the highest dignities of the Church by female intrigues, address the fair publicly in an amorous way, amuse themselves in writing tender love songs, entertain their friends very splendidly every night at their own houses, and after the banquet is ended withdraw to invoke the assistance of the Holy Ghost, and call themselves boldly the successors of the Apostles, they bless God for their being Protestants. But these are shameless heretics, who deserve to be blown hence through the flames to old Nick, as Rabelais says, and for this reason I don't trouble myself about them. (Letter V)

On the Presbyterians

The Church of England is confined almost to the kingdom whence it received its name, and to Ireland, for Presbyterianism is the established religion in Scotland. This Presbyterianism is directly the same with Calvinism, as it was established in France, and is now professed at Geneva. As the priests of this sect receive but very inconsiderable stipends from their churches, and consequently cannot emulate the splendid luxury of bishops, they exclaim very naturally against honours which they can never attain to. Figure to yourself the haughty Diogenes trampling under foot the pride of Plato. The Scotch Presbyterians are not very unlike that proud though tattered reasoner. Diogenes did not use Alexander half so impertinently as these treated King Charles II; for when they took up arms in his cause in opposition to Oliver, who had deceived them, they forced that poor monarch to undergo the hearing of three or four sermons every day, would not suffer him to play, reduced him to a state of penitence and mortification, so that Charles soon grew sick of these pedants, and accordingly eloped from them with as much joy as a youth does from school.

A Church of England minister appears as another Cato in presence of a juvenile, sprightly French graduate, who bawls for a whole morning together in the divinity schools, and hums a song in chorus with ladies in the evening; but this Cato is a very spark when before a Scotch Presbyterian. The latter affects a serious gait, puts on a sour look, wears a vastly broad-brimmed hat and a long cloak over a very short coat, preaches through the nose, and gives the name of the whore of Babylon to all churches where the ministers are so fortunate as to enjoy an annual revenue of five or six thousand pounds, and where the people are weak enough to suffer this, and to give them the titles of my lord, your lordship, or your eminence.

These gentlemen, who have also some churches in England, introduced there the mode of grave and severe exhortations. To them is owing the sanctification of Sunday in the three kingdoms. People are there forbidden to work or take any recreation on that day, in which the severity is twice as great as that of the Romish Church. No operas, plays, or concerts are allowed in London on Sundays, and even cards are so expressly forbidden that none but persons of quality, and those we call the genteel, play on that day; the rest of the nation go either to church, to the tavern, or to see their mistresses.

Though the Episcopal and Presbyterian sects are the two prevailing ones in Great Britain, yet all others are very welcome to come and settle in it, and live very sociably together, though most of their preachers hate one another almost as cordially as a Jansenist damns a Jesuit.

Take a view of the Royal Exchange in London, a place more venerable than many courts of justice, where the representatives of all nations meet for the benefit of mankind. There the Jew, the Mahometan, and the Christian transact together, as though they all professed the same religion, and give the name of infidel to none but bankrupts. There the Presbyterian confides in the Anabaptist, and the Churchman depends on the Quaker's word. At the breaking up of this pacific and free assembly, some withdraw to the synagogue, and others to take a glass. This man goes and is baptized in a great tub, in the name of the Father, Son and Holy Ghost: that man has his son's foreskin cut off, whilst a set of Hebrew words (quite unintelligible to him) are mumbled over his child. Others retire to their churches, and there wait for the inspiration of heaven with their hats on, and all are satisfied.

If one religion only were allowed in England, the Government would very possibly become arbitrary; if there were but two, the people would cut one another's throats; but as there are such a multitude, they all live happy and in peace. (Letter VI)

On the Socinians, or Arians, or Antitrinitarians

There is a little sect here composed of clergymen, and of a few very learned persons among the laity, who, though they don't call themselves Arians or Socinians, do yet dissent entirely from St. Athanasius with regard to their notions of the Trinity, and declare very frankly that the Father is greater than the Son.

Do you remember what is related of a certain orthodox bishop, who in order to convince an emperor of the reality of consubstantiation put his hand under the chin of the monarch's son, and took him by the nose in presence of his sacred majesty? The emperor was going to order his attendants to throw the bishop out of the window, when the good old man gave him this handsome and convincing reason: "Since your majesty," said he, "is angry when your son has not due respect shown him, what punishment do you think will God the Father inflict on those who refuse His Son Jesus the titles due to Him?" The persons I just now mentioned declare that the holy bishop took a very wrong step, that his argument was inconclusive, and that the emperor should have answered him thus: "Know that there are two ways by which men may be wanting in respect to me—first, in not doing honor sufficient to my son; and, secondly, in paying him the same honor as to me."

Be this as it will, the principles of Arius began to revive, not only in England, but in Holland and Poland. The celebrated Sir Isaac Newton honored this opinion so far as to countenance it. This philosopher thought that the Unitarians argued more mathematically than we do. But the most sanguine stickler for Arianism is the illustrious Dr. Clark. This man is rigidly virtuous, and of a mild disposition, is more fond of his tenets than desirous of propagating them, and absorbed so entirely in problems and calculations that he is a mere reasoning machine.

It is he who wrote a book which is much esteemed and little understood, on the existence of God, and another, more intelligible, but pretty much contemned, on the truth of the Christian religion. He never engaged in scholastic disputes, which our friend calls venerable trifles. He only published a work containing all the testimonies of the primitive ages for and against the Unitarians, and leaves to the reader the counting of the voices and the liberty of forming a judgment. This book won the doctor a great number of partisans, and lost him the See of Canterbury but, in my humble opinion, he was out in his calculation, and had better have been Primate of all England than merely an Arian parson.

You see that opinions are subject to revolutions as well as empires. Arianism, after having triumphed during three centuries, and been forgot twelve, rises at last out of its own ashes; but it has chosen a very improper season to make its appearance in, the present age being quite cloyed with disputes and sects. The members of this sect are, besides, too few to be indulged the liberty of holding public assemblies, which, however, they will, doubtless, be permitted to do in case they spread considerably. But people are now so very cold with respect to all things of this kind, that there is little probability any new religion, or old one, that may be revived, will meet with favour. Is it not whimsical enough that Luther, Calvin, and Zuinglius, all of 'em wretched authors, should have founded sects which are now spread over a great part of Europe, that Mahomet, though so ignorant, should have given a religion to Asia and Africa, and that Sir Isaac Newton, Dr. Clark, Mr. Locke, Mr. Le Clerc, etc., the greatest philosophers, as well as the ablest writers of their ages, should scarce have been able to raise a little flock, which even decreases daily.

This it is to be born at a proper period of time. Were Cardinal de Retz to return again into the world neither his eloquence nor his intrigues would draw together ten women in Paris. Were Oliver Cromwell, he who beheaded his sovereign, and seized upon the kingly dignity, to rise from the dead, he would be a wealthy City trader, and no more. (Letter VII)

On Government

. . . There is no such thing here as *haute*, *moyenne*, and *basse justice*—that is, a power to judge in all matters civil and criminal; nor a right or privilege of hunting in the grounds of a citizen, who at the same time is not permitted to fire a gun in his own field.

No one is exempted in this country from paying certain taxes because he is a nobleman or a priest. All duties and taxes are settled by the House of Commons, whose power is greater than that of the Peers, though inferior to it in dignity. The spiritual as well as temporal Lords have the liberty to reject a Money Bill brought in by the Commons; but they are not allowed to alter anything in it, and must either pass or throw it out without restriction. When the Bill has passed the Lords and is signed by the king, then the whole nation pays, every man in proportion to his revenue or estate, not according to his title, which would be absurd. There is no such thing as an arbitrary subsidy or poll-tax, but a real tax on the lands, of all which an estimate was made in the reign of the famous King William III.

The land-tax continues still upon the same foot, though the revenue of the lands is increased. Thus no one is tyrannised over, and every one is easy. The feet of the peasants are not bruised by wooden shoes; they eat white bread, are well clothed, and are not afraid of increasing their stock of cattle, nor of tiling their houses, from any apprehension that their taxes will be raised the year following. The annual income of the estates of a great many commoners in England amounts to two hundred thousand livres, and yet these do not think it beneath them to plough the lands which enrich them, and on which they enjoy their liberty. (Letter IX)

On Trade

As trade enriched the citizens in England, so it contributed to their freedom, and this freedom on the other side extended their commerce, whence arose the grandeur of the State. Trade raised by insensible degrees the naval power, which gives the English a superiority over the seas, and they now are masters of very near two hundred ships of war. Posterity will very probably be surprised to hear that an island whose only produce is a little lead, tin, fuller's-earth, and coarse wool, should become so powerful by its commerce, as to be able to send, in 1723, three fleets at the same time to three different and far distanced parts of the globe. One before Gibraltar, conquered and still possessed by the English; a second to Porto Bello, to dispossess the King of Spain of the treasures of the West Indies; and a third into the Baltic, to prevent the Northern Powers from coming to an engagement.

At the time when Louis XIV made all Italy tremble, and that his armies, which had already possessed themselves of Savoy and Piedmont, were upon the point of taking Turin; Prince Eugene was obliged to march from the middle of Germany in order to succor Savoy. Having no money, without which cities cannot be either taken or defended, he addressed himself to some English merchants. These, at an hour and a half's warning, lent him five millions, whereby he was enabled to deliver Turin, and to beat the French; after which he wrote the following short letter to the persons who had disbursed him the above-mentioned sums: "Gentlemen, I received your money, and flatter myself that I have laid it out to your satisfaction." Such a circumstance as this raises a just pride in an English merchant, and makes him presume (not without some reason) to compare himself to a Roman citizen; and, indeed, a peer's brother does not think traffic beneath him. When the Lord Townshend was Minister of State, a brother of his was content to be a City merchant; and at the time that the Earl of Oxford governed Great Britain, his younger brother was no more than a factor in Aleppo, where he chose to live, and where he died. This custom, which begins, however, to be laid aside, appears monstrous to Germans, vainly puffed up with their extraction. These think it morally impossible that the son of an English peer should be no more than a rich and powerful citizen, for all are princes in Germany. There have been thirty highnesses of the same name, all whose patrimony consisted only in their escutcheons and their pride.

In France the title of marquis is given gratis to any one who will accept of it; and whosoever arrives at Paris from the midst of the most remote provinces with money in his purse, and a name terminating in *ac* or *ille*, may strut about, and cry, "Such a man as I! A man of my rank and figure!" and may look down upon a trader with sovereign contempt; whilst the trader on the other side, by thus often hearing his profession treated so disdainfully, is fool enough to blush at it. However, I need not say which is most useful to a nation; a lord, powdered in the tip of the mode, who knows exactly at what o'clock the king rises and goes to bed, and who gives himself airs of grandeur and state, at the same time that he is acting the slave in the ante-chamber of a prime minister; or a merchant, who enriches his country, despatches orders from his counting-house to Surat and Grand Cairo, and contributes to the felicity of the world. (Letter X)

On Mr. Locke

Perhaps no man ever had a more judicious or more methodical mind, or was a more acute logician than Mr. Locke, and yet he was not a great mathematician. He could never subject himself to the tedious fatigue of calculations, nor to the dry pursuit of mathematical truths, which do not at first present any tangible objects to the mind; and no one has ever given better proofs than he, that it is possible for a man to have a geometrical head without the assistance of geometry. Before his time, several great philosophers had declared, in the most positive terms, what the soul of man is; but as these knew absolutely nothing about it, they might very well be allowed to differ entirely in opinion from one another.

In Greece, the cradle of arts and of errors, where the grandeur as well as the folly of the human mind went to such prodigious lengths, the people used to reason about the soul in the very same manner as we do.

The divine Anaxagoras, in whose honor an altar was erected for his having taught mankind that the sun was greater than Peloponnesus, that snow was black, and that the heavens were of stone, affirmed that the soul was an aërial spirit, but at the same time immortal. Diogenes (not he who was a cynical philosopher after having coined base money) declared that the soul was a portion of the substance of God: an idea which we must confess was very sublime. Epicurus maintained that it was composed of parts in the same manner as the body.

Aristotle, who has been explained in a thousand ways because he was unintelligible, was of the opinion, according to some of his disciples, that the understanding in all men is one and the same substance. The divine Plato, master of the divine Aristotle—and the divine Socrates, master of the divine Plato—used to say that the soul was corporeal and eternal. No doubt but the demon of Socrates had instructed him in the nature of it. Some people, indeed, pretended that a man who boasted his being attended by a familiar genius must infallibly be either a knave or a madman, but this kind of people are just too hard to please.

As for our Church Fathers, several in the primitive ages believed that the soul was human, and the angels and God corporeal. Men naturally improve upon every system. St. Bernard, as Father Mabillon confesses, taught that the soul after death did not behold God in the celestial regions, but conversed with Christ's human nature only. However, he was not believed this time on his bare word; the adventure of the crusade having a little discredited his oracles. Afterwards a thousand Schoolmen arose, such as the Irrefragable Doctor, the Subtile Doctor, the Angelic Doctor, the Seraphic Doctor, the Cherubic Doctor, who were all sure that they had a very clear and distinct idea of the soul, and yet wrote in such a manner that one would conclude they were resolved no one should understand a word in their writings. Our Descartes, born to discover the errors of antiquity, and at the same time to substitute his own, and carried away by that systematic spirit which throws a cloud over the minds of the greatest men, thought he had demonstrated that the soul is the same thing as thought, in the same manner that matter, in his opinion, is the same as extension. He asserted that man thinks eternally and that the soul, at its coming into the body, is informed with the whole series of metaphysical notions: knowing God, infinite space, possessing all abstract ideas—in a word, completely endued with the most sublime lights, which it unhappily forgets at its issuing from the womb.

Father Malebranche, the Oratorian, in his sublime illusions, not only admitted innate ideas, but did not doubt of our living wholly in God, and that God is, as it were, our soul.

Such a multitude of reasoners having written the romance of the soul, a sage at last arose, who gave very modestly its history. Mr. Locke has displayed the human soul in the same manner as an excellent anatomist explains the springs of the human body. He everywhere takes the light of physics for his guide. He sometimes presumes to speak affirmatively, but then he presumes also to doubt. Instead of concluding at once what we know not, he examines gradually what we want to know. He takes an infant at the instant of his birth; he traces step by step the progress of his understanding; examines what things he has in common with brutes, and what he possesses above them. Above all, he consults his own experience, the awareness of his own thought.

"I shall leave," says he, "to those who know more of this matter than I, the examining whether the soul exists before or after the organization of our bodies. But I confess that it is my lot to be animated with one of those heavy souls which do not always think; and I am even so unhappy as not to conceive how it is more necessary that the soul should think perpetually than that bodies should be forever in motion."

With regard to myself, I shall boast that I have the honor to be as stupid in this particular as Mr. Locke. No one shall ever make me believe that I always think: and I am as little inclined as he could be to fancy that some weeks after I was conceived I was a very learned soul; knowing at that time a thousand things which I forgot at my birth; and possessing when in the womb (though to no manner of purpose) knowledge which I lost the instant I had occasion for it; and which I have never since been able to recover perfectly.

Mr. Locke, after having destroyed innate ideas; after having fully renounced the vanity of believing that we always think; after having laid down, from the most solid principles, that ideas enter the mind through the senses; having examined our simple and complex ideas; having traced the human mind through its several operations; having shown that all the languages in the world are imperfect, and the great abuse that is made of words every moment, he at last comes to consider the extent or rather the narrow limits of human knowledge. It is in this chapter that he presumed to advance, but very modestly, the following words: "We shall perhaps never be capable of knowing whether a being, purely material, thinks or not." This sage assertion was, by more divines than one, looked upon as a scandalous declaration that the soul is material and mortal. Some Englishmen, devout after their way, sounded the alarm. The superstitious are the same in society as cowards in the army; they themselves are seized with a panic fear and communicate it to others. It was loudly exclaimed that Mr. Locke intended to destroy religion; nevertheless, religion had nothing to do with the business, it being a question purely philosophical, altogether independent of faith and revelation. Mr. Locke's opponents needed but to examine, calmly and impartially, whether the declaring that matter can think implies a contradiction; and whether God is able to communicate thought to matter. But divines are too apt to begin their declarations by saying that God is offended when people differ from them in opinion; in which they too much resemble the bad poets, who used to declare publicly that Boileau spoke irreverently of Louis XIV, because he ridiculed their stupid productions. Bishop Stillingfleet got the reputation of being a calm and unprejudiced divine because he did not expressly make use of injurious terms in his dispute with Mr. Locke. That divine entered the lists against him, but he was defeated; for he argued as a Schoolman, and Locke as a philosopher, who was perfectly acquainted with the strong as well as the weak side of the human mind and fought with weapons whose temper he knew.

If I might presume to give my opinion on so delicate a subject after Mr. Locke, I would say that men have long disputed on the nature and the immortality of the soul. With regard to its immortality, it is impossible to give a demonstration of it, since its nature is still the subject of controversy; which, however, must be thoroughly understood before a person can be able to determine whether it is immortal or not. Human reason is so little able by itself to demonstrate the immortality of the soul, that it was absolutely necessary for religion to reveal it to us. It is of advantage to society in general, that mankind should believe the soul to be immortal; faith commands us to do this; nothing more is required, and the matter is cleared up at once. But it is otherwise with respect to its nature; it is of little importance to religion, which only requires the soul to be virtuous, whatever substance it may be made of. It is a clock which is given us to regulate, but the artisan has not told us of what materials the spring of this clock is composed. . . .

Besides, we must not be apprehensive that any philosophical opinion will ever harm the religion of a country. Though our demonstrations clash directly with our mysteries, that is nothing to the purpose, for the latter are not less revered upon that account by our Christian philosophers, who know very well that the objects of reason and those of faith are of a very different nature. Philosophers will never form a religious sect, the reason of which is, their writings are not calculated for the common people, and they themselves are free from enthusiasm. If we divide mankind into twenty parts, it will be found that nineteen of these consist of persons employed in manual labor, who will never know that such a man as Mr. Locke existed. In the remaining twentieth part how few are readers? And among such as are so, twenty amuse themselves with romances to one who studies philosophy. The thinking part of mankind is confined to a very small number, and these will never disturb the peace and tranquillity of the world.

Neither Montaigne, Locke, Bayle, Spinoza, Hobbes, Lord Shaftesbury, Collins, nor Toland, lighted up the firebrand of discord in their countries; this has generally been the work of divines, who being at first puffed up with the ambition of becoming chiefs of a sect, grew very desirous of being the head of a party. But what do I say? All the works of the modern philosophers put together will never raise so much commotion as did the dispute among the Franciscans, over the form of their sleeves and cowls. (Letter XIII)

Later Economical Reflections

Luxury

Men have declaimed against luxury for two thousand years in verse and in prose, and yet they have always liked it.

What have they not said about the early Romans? When these brigands ravished and pillaged the harvests; when, to enlarge their little village, they destroyed the little villages of the Volsci and the Samnites, they were unselfish and virtuous men: they had not yet been able to steal gold or silver or precious stones, because there was none in the towns that they plundered. Their woods and their swamps produced no partridges nor pheasants, and yet their temperance is praised.

When little by little they had pillaged and robbed everything from the head of the Adriatic Sea to the Euphrates and had intelligence enough to enjoy the fruits of their rapine; when they cultivated the arts, enjoyed all pleasures and even made the vanquished enjoy them, then they ceased, we are told, to be wise and good.

All this declamation proves only that a thief should never eat the dinner he has seized, nor wear the coat he has pilfered nor adorn himself with the ring he has stolen. All that should be thrown in the river, it is said, if we want to live like honest people; it would be better to say that we should not steal. Condemn brigands when they pillage, but do not condemn them as fools when they enjoy their plunder. In all good faith, when a great many English sailors became rich at the capture of Pondicherry and of Havana, were they wrong in enjoying pleasure afterwards in London to pay for the trouble they had had way off in Asia and America?

The declaimers would like to see buried the wealth piled up through the fortune of war, through agriculture, commerce, and industry. They cite Lacedemonia; why do they not also cite the republic of San Marino? What good did Sparta do Greece? Did she produce a Demosthenes, a Sophocles, an Apelles, or a Phidias? The luxury of Athens produced great men in all walks of life. Sparta had a few captains, and even these were fewer than in the other cities. But all the better if a small republic like Lacedemonia maintains its poverty. One arrives at death just as surely whether he lacks everything or whether he enjoys those things that make life agreeable. The Canadian savage subsists and attains old age as surely as the English citizen who has fifty guineas income. But who will ever compare the country of the Iroquois with England? . . .

If by luxury you mean excess, it is well known that excess of all kinds is pernicious: in abstinence as well as in gluttony; in frugality as in liberality. I don't know how it happens that in my villages, where the soil is ungrateful, the taxes heavy, and the law against exporting one's own wheat intolerable, yet there is hardly a planter who does not own a good woolen coat, and who is not well shod and well nourished. If this planter should work his fields in his fine coat and white linen, with his hair curled and powdered, that would indeed be the greatest and most impertinent of luxuries; but for a Paris or London bourgeois to appear at a play dressed like this peasant, that is the coarsest and most ridiculous parsimony. . . .

At the time of the invention of scissors, which are certainly not of the highest antiquity, what was not said against those who first pared their nails and cut off a part of their hair, which was hanging down over their noses? They were doubtless called fops and spendthrifts who paid excessively for an instrument of vanity in order to spoil the work of the Creator. What a terrible sin to shorten the horn that God brought forth on the ends of our fingers! It was an outrage against the Divinity. And it was much worse when shirts and socks were invented. It is well known with what fury the old councillors, who never wore any, cried out against the young magistrates who yielded to this fatal luxury.

Note. If by luxury one means everything over and above the necessities of life, then luxury is the natural consequence of the progress of the human race; and to reason consistently, every enemy of luxury must believe with Rousseau that the state of happiness and virtue for man is not that of the savage but that of the orang-outang. It would be manifestly absurd to regard as evil conveniences which all men enjoy: so in general the name of luxury is given only to the superfluities which only a small number of individuals can enjoy. In this sense, luxury is a necessary consequence of property, without which no state can subsist, and of a great inequality in wealth, which is the consequence, not of the right of property, but of bad laws. Luxury arises then from bad laws, and good laws can destroy it. Moralists should address their sermons to the legislators, and not to private individuals, because it is within the realm of possibility that a virtuous and enlightened man might have the power of making reasonable laws, and because it is not in human nature that all the rich of a country should renounce through virtue the satisfactions of pleasure or vanity which they can afford to buy for themselves.

Equality

All the poor are not unhappy. Most of them are born in poverty, and constant toil keeps them from feeling too keenly their situation. But when they do feel it then there are wars, such as that of the popular party against the senatorial party at Rome, and those of the peasants in Germany, England and France. All these wars end sooner or later with the subjection of the people, because those in power have money, and money is sole master in a state: I say in a state, because it is not true between nations. The nation which makes the best use of the sword will always subjugate the nation which has more gold and less courage.

Every man is born with a rather violent propensity for domination, wealth and pleasure, and with a strong taste for idleness; consequently every man would like to have the money and the wives or daughters of other men, to be their master, to subject them to his every caprice, and to do nothing, or at least to do nothing but what is most agreeable. It is easily seen that with these handsome propensities it is as impossible for men to be equal as it is impossible for two preachers or two professors of theology not to be jealous of each other.

The human race such as it is cannot subsist unless there

is an infinite number of useful men who possess nothing at all: for certainly a man in easy circumstances will not leave his land to come and plough yours; and if you need a pair of shoes, it will not be the judge of petitions who will make them for you. Equality is therefore at the same time most natural and most chimerical.

As men are excessive in everything when they are able, this inequality has been carried too far; it has been claimed in several countries that it was not permissible for a citizen to leave the land where he chanced to be born: the meaning of such a law is visibly this: "This country is bad and so poorly governed that we forbid any man to leave it, for fear lest everyone leave it." Do better than that: instil in all your subjects the desire to stay in your country, and in foreigners the desire to come there.

Every man in the depth of his heart has the right to consider himself equal to other men: it does not follow from that that the cardinal's cook should order his master to prepare his dinner; the cook may say: "I am a man like my master: I was born like him in tears; he will die like me with the same anguish and the same ceremonies. We both of us perform the same animal functions. If the Turks take possession of Rome and if then I am cardinal and my master is cook, I will take him into my service." This language is entirely reasonable and just: but while waiting for the Grand Turk to take possession of Rome, the cook should do his duty, or all human society is subverted.

In regard to the man who is neither cardinal's cook nor invested with any other office in the state; in regard to a private citizen who has no connections but who is vexed at being received everywhere with an air of protection or contempt, who sees clearly that several *monsignori* have no more knowledge nor intelligence nor virtue than he, and who dislikes to be waiting sometimes in their antechambers, what is he to do about it? He has only to go away.

Montesquieu
1689-1755

BORN ON the family estate of La Brède near Bordeaux and accorded the sound classical education that was customary among the sons of the nobility, Charles Louis de Secondat, later to be called Baron de Montesquieu, studied law and was admitted in 1708 to the bar of his native province. Less interested in the practice of law than in its theory, he went to Paris and lived for four years in Parisian society. His critical mind and observing eye were here at work collecting material for his immensely popular *Persian Letters.* In 1713, he returned to Bordeaux, became the head of his family upon his father's death, and married a Protestant wife, whose dowry helped to rehabilitate the family fortune. In 1716, he inherited the title by which he has since been known and the office of President of the Parlement de Bordeaux.

After the publication of the *Persian Letters* in 1721 (it was soon known, but could not be said, that he was the author of that boldly satirical work), he made frequent trips to Paris and associated with many of the younger *philosophes* and scientists of the age. His scientific interests and analytical mind had already produced papers on anatomy and physics read at the Bordeaux Academy of Science, of which he was a member. In 1726 he sold his office, returned to Paris, and was elected to the French Academy. The major preoccupation of the rest of his life was his great work on the theory of law and political science. The collection of material led him first to visit many countries in continental Europe and to spend two years of study and observation in England. Completed and published in 1748, *The Spirit of Laws* was extraordinarily well received, and much discussed and admired throughout the civilized world. The task, however, had ruined the author's health and eyesight. He died and was buried in Paris, in 1755.

The notebooks and the catalogue of his library at La Brède, which have been recently published, give ample evidence of his great passion for books: "Study," he wrote, "has been for me the sovereign remedy for life's unpleasantnesses, for I have never felt a sorrow that an hour's reading did not dissipate." Other jottings from his *Cahiers*, or notebooks, reveal his philosophy of life: "Let us try to adapt ourselves to this life; it is not up to this life to adapt itself to us."

"I awake in the morning with a secret joy: I see the light of day with a kind of rapture. The rest of the day I am happy. I sleep through the night without awaking; and when I go to bed, a sort of drowsiness keeps me from reflection."

The sheer joy of existence should not be forgotten: "happiness is this very moment which we would not exchange for non-existence." All unhappy people, he adds, have recourse to God, often for very human reasons.

Like many another *philosophe* who had not lost his faith in man, Montesquieu wasted no time in despairing over the human condition or musing upon the absurdity of man's existence. He accepted life on its own terms, fully and completely, and with it life's inevitable companion, death. Towards the end it was only a question of *savoir-faire:* "I have only two matters left to attend to: one, to know how to be ill, the other, to know how to die."

The world-citizen is apparent in the following extracts: "If I knew something useful to my nation, but ruinous to another nation, I would not propose it to my ruler, because I am a man before I am a Frenchman, or rather because I am man by necessity and Frenchman only by chance of birth."

"If I knew something useful to my country, but prejudicial to Europe, or useful to Europe but prejudicial to the human race, I would consider it a crime."

The final appeal of many a chapter of the *Persian Letters* and *The Spirit of Laws* is to humanity.

Persian Letters
(1721)

When Louis XIV died—at last—in 1715, the glory of France's classic age as well as his own military glory was long since past. There was a tremendous sigh of relief un-

derlying the customary cry: "The king is dead; long live the king." For the glory of his house the old king would have liked to be succeeded by his grandson, Philip V, bigoted king of inquisitorial Spain, but in France the scientific and philosophical movements were already too far advanced to make such a regressive solution acceptable. Many heirs to the throne had died, three of them between 1712 and 1714, leaving the succession to a great-grandson, Louis XV, then a five-year-old boy, under the regency of Philippe d'Orléans. Philippe's generally sound plans for reform were met by overwhelming opposition on the part of the princes and nobles of high rank, who were determined to maintain their accustomed privileges. Philippe himself was successfully debauched, and his Regency went down in history as a period of uneasiness and general dissolution. A momentary relaxation in the censorship permitted in 1721 the publication of Montesquieu's Persian Letters, *a surprisingly audacious satire of French institutions and the Parisian life of the second decade of the century. The tremendous popularity of his work, the urbanity of his good-natured satire, and his noble birth, all saved the author from the serious embarrassment that might, at another moment, have resulted from the charges of impiety that were leveled against him.*

Montesquieu's excuse lay in the technique and general plan of the "novel." Two Persians, Usbek and his friend Rhedi, were portrayed as visiting Paris and relating their impressions in the form of letters written to each other and to friends at home. (Also included were letters received from the wives and eunuchs of Usbek's harem.) To the Persian visitors, for example, it was perfectly natural that the king and the pope should appear to be magicians. Few aspects of the French official and social scene escaped the barbs of Montesquieu's wit. At the same time the picture of the life and customs of the Persians represents serious study and voracious reading of all available accounts of travelers to the Middle East.

Besides the genuine literary merits of the portraits and satire and the informal, yet polished style, the Persian Letters *are of interest to the modern reader as a foretaste of the author's liberal views, especially his ideas of justice and penology, which were to be developed at greater length in* The Spirit of Laws.

Persian Letters

If there is a God, my dear Rhedi, he must necessarily be just; for if he were not, he would be the most wicked and imperfect of all beings.

Justice is a true relation between two things: this relation is always the same, no matter who examines it, whether it be God, or an angel, or lastly, man himself.

It is true that men do not always perceive these relations; often even when they do perceive them, they turn away from them, and their self-interest is what they perceive most clearly. Justice cries aloud, but her voice can hardly be heard above the tumult of the passions.

Men can commit unjust acts because it is to their advantage to do so and because they prefer their own contentment to that of others. They always act from selfish motives: no man is evil gratuitously: there must be a determining cause, and that cause is always selfishness.

But God cannot possibly commit an unjust act: once we assume that he perceives what is just he must of necessity act accordingly, for since he is self-sufficient and in need of nothing, he would otherwise be the most wicked of beings, since he has no selfish interests.

Thus if there were no God, we would still be obliged to venerate justice, that is, we should do everything possible to resemble that being of whom we have such an exalted notion and who, if he exists, would necessarily be just. Free though we might be from the yoke of religion, we should never be free from the bonds of equity.

That, Rhedi, is what makes me think that justice is eternal and does not depend on human conventions. And if it did depend on them, that would be a terrible fact that we should hide from ourselves.

We are surrounded by men stronger than we are: they can harm us in a thousand different ways; three times out of four, they can do it with impunity. What a relief for us to know that there is in the hearts of all men an inner principle fighting in our behalf and protecting us from their attempts.

Without that principle, we could live only in a state of constant alarm; we would walk among men as among lions; and we could never be assured for a moment of our goods, our honor, or our lives.

These thoughts always stir me up against those theologians who represent God as a being who makes tyrannical use of his power; who make him do things that we would not do for fear of offending him; who burden him with all the imperfections that he punishes us for: and represent him, quite contradictorily, sometimes as an evil being, sometimes as a being who hates evil and punishes it.

When a man looks within himself, what a satisfaction it is for him to find that his heart is just! This pleasure, no matter how austere, should delight him: he sees himself as far above those lacking in this quality as he is above tigers and bears. Yes, Rhedi, if I were always sure of following inviolably the justice that I perceive, I would consider myself the first among men. (Letter no. 83)

* * *

You know, Mirza, that a number of ministers of Shah-Soliman had formed the project of forcing all the Armenians in Persia to leave the realm or become Mohammedans, with the idea that our empire would be polluted as long as it kept these infidels in our midst.[1]

That would have meant the end of the grandeur of Persia, if blind devotion had been heeded on this occasion.

It is not known why the project failed. Neither those who proposed it nor those who rejected it knew what the consequences thereof would have been: chance played the part of reason and policy and saved the empire from a risk greater than it could have run from the loss of a battle and the capture of two cities.

[1] This is, of course, a transparent reference to the revocation in 1685 of the Edict of Nantes, promulgated in 1598, and the subsequent persecution and flight of the Protestants.

By proscribing the Armenians, the ministers were on the verge of destroying in a single day all the merchants and nearly all the artisans of the kingdom. I am sure that the great Shah-Abbas would have preferred to cut off his two arms rather than sign such an order, and that by sending to the Mogul and other kings of India his most industrious subjects, he would have believed he was giving away half of his States.

The persecutions that our zealous Mohammedans have inflicted upon the Parsees obliged a multitude of them to flee into India and deprived Persia of a population devoted to agriculture which alone was capable by dint of labor to overcome the sterility of our soil.

Religious devotees had only to make a second attempt and ruin industry; as a result of which the empire would have toppled, and with it, as a matter of course, the very religion that they had sought to strengthen.

All prejudice aside, I do not know, Mirza, if it is not a good thing to have several religions in a State.

It is notable that those who adhere to tolerated religions ordinarily render more useful services to their country than do those who are members of the dominant religion, because, since they are kept from honored positions and can gain distinction only through opulence, they are led to acquire wealth by their toil and embrace the most arduous of society's tasks.

Besides, since all religions entertain socially useful precepts, it is good to have them zealously observed. And what is more apt than a multiplicity of religions to inspire zeal?

Rival religions grant each other nothing. Their jealousy is shared by their individual members: all are on their guard and are afraid of doing things that would dishonor their sect and expose it to the contempt and unpardonable censure of the opposite sect.

It has also always been observed that the introduction of a new sect into a State has been the surest means of correcting the abuses of the older sect.

In vain we say that it is not in the interests of the prince to tolerate several religions within his State: even if all the sects in the world should happen to be brought together, no harm would result, because there is not one of them which does not prescribe obedience and preach submission.

I confess that histories are replete with religious wars: but on close examination, it is apparent that they were caused, not by a multiplicity of religions, but by the spirit of intolerance that ran rife in the religion that considered itself dominant.

The cause was that spirit of proselytism which the Jews took over from the Egyptians and which passed from them, like a common epidemic disease, to Mohammedans and Christians.

It was indeed a kind of madness, the progress of which can be looked upon only as a total eclipse of human reason.

For even if it were not inhuman to afflict the consciences of other peoples, even if there were none of the evil results that are counted by the thousands, it would be madness even to consider it. The man who wants to make me change my religion surely does so only because he would not change his, even if forced: he thinks it strange, then, that I do not do something he would not do himself perhaps for the whole world. (Letter no. 85)

The Spirit of Laws
(1748)

This widely read and influential book was the result of almost a lifetime of arduous labor. Great pains were taken by the author to enliven his subject matter by striking stylistic effects, frequent chapter and section divisions, changes of tone from serious to ironic, and a multiplicity of examples, often exotic, derived from a comprehensive reading of histories and travelogues. He was, of course, well acquainted with the political philosophies and customs of the Greek republics and the legalistic writings of the Romans. His readings and observations during his English sojourn (1729-1731) left a vivid mark upon his work and in considerable measure changed its direction.

The complexity of the organization of Montesquieu's abundant material can be attributed to a duality of sources and method: on the one hand, deductive reasoning, based on the natural, universal law of equity and reason; on the other, inductive generalizations derived from historical and geographical investigations of the variety and relativity of positive laws and customs. The appeal to natural law is balanced by an appeal to experience. With the gradually developing sense of equity, positive laws were written, but must have been preceded by the feeling that there ought to be a law. Justice was Montesquieu's supreme political virtue (see above, Persian Letters, *no. 83) and the criterion of superior political institutions and civilizations.*

A very one-sided view of The Spirit of Laws *has branded Montesquieu as conservative and reactionary. It is true that for various reasons his governmental pattern for France was a constitutional monarchy, in which the nobles, descendants, like the author, of the Frankish feudal barons, should constitute a House of Lords to balance the power of the king. Because of his mistaken notion that English liberties originated among the Anglo-Saxons, the final chapters of his work are devoted to the origins of French feudal institutions. This explains the criticisms of his work by Helvetius, Voltaire, and other* philosophes. *Diderot, however, attended Montesquieu's funeral as a final tribute to a fellow-*philosophe, *and Voltaire proclaimed that "the human race had lost its titles and Montesquieu restored them."*

The mighty liberalizing impact of Montesquieu on America and on many European countries is a matter of history. Even in France, before the uprising of the masses and the reign of terror, he was the spirit behind the Constitution of 1791 and of many of the articles of its preamble, the Declaration of the Rights of Man and the Citizen. The sole aim of laws was for him the liberty and security of the citizen and the prosperity of the nation, and, as for Voltaire, freedom meant dependence on nothing but law. He courageously attacked the atrocities of the legal procedure of his day and the cruelty of the laws and their application. The Italian nobleman Beccaria declared that Montesquieu was the instigator of his Essay on Crimes and Punishments, *a work which was translated in many languages and, often with Voltaire's commentary, was a major influence in eighteenth-century penal reform. Montesquieu also insisted on the underlying principle, where laws were concerned, of the separation of Church and State: the civil power should not be used to punish men for heresy, sorcery or witchcraft. Even Catherine the Great confessed, as she made a vain effort to recodify Russian law, that Montesquieu and Beccaria were her chief guides.*

The founders of the American Commonwealth, especially Franklin, Jefferson and Madison, were imbued with the principles of The Spirit of Laws. *The theory of the balance and separation of powers between the executive, legislative and judicial found ready soil in the American colonial system and became an essential principle of the American constitution of 1789. Before then, Montesquieu's liberalizing influence had been felt in state constitutions, such as Franklin's in Pennsylvania and Jefferson's in Virginia, especially in matters of penology and civil liberties, and from these were derived the amendments or Bill of Rights of 1791. Montesquieu's work is a monument to the progressive rise of the human spirit, to faith in the power of reason to overcome abuses in the direction of justice and humanity. Also, whether or not he had a theoretical preference for the democratic way of life, he greatly strengthened the democratic principles of freedom of worship, freedom of thought, freedom from fear, and freedom from want.*

Of Laws Directly Derived from the Nature of Government

Of the Nature of Three Different Governments

There are three species of government: republican, monarchical, and despotic. In order to discover their nature, it is sufficient to recollect the common notion, which supposes three definitions, or rather three facts:

that a republican government is that in which the body, or only a part of the people, is possessed of the supreme power; monarchy, that in which a single person governs by fixed and established laws; a despotic government, that in which a single person directs everything by his own will and caprice.

This is what I call the nature of each government; we must now inquire into those laws which directly conform to this nature, and consequently are the fundamental institutions. (II, 1)

Of the Republican Government, and the Laws in Relation to Democracy

When the body of the people is possessed of the supreme power, it is called a democracy. When the supreme power is lodged in the hands of a part of the people, it is then an aristocracy.

In a democracy the people are in some respects the sovereign, and in others the subject.

There can be no exercise of sovereignty but by their suffrages, which are their own will; now, the sovereign's will is the sovereign himself. The laws, therefore, which establish the right of suffrage are fundamental to this government. And indeed it is as important to regulate in a republic, in what manner, by whom, to whom, and concerning what suffrages are to be given, as it is in a monarchy to know who is the prince, and after what manner he ought to govern. . . .

It is an essential point to fix the number of citizens who are to form the public assemblies; otherwise it would be uncertain whether the whole or only a part of the people had given their votes. At Sparta the number was fixed at ten thousand. But Rome, designed by Providence to rise from the weakest beginnings to the highest pitch of grandeur; Rome, doomed to experience all the vicissitudes of fortune; Rome, who had sometimes all her inhabitants without her walls, and sometimes all Italy and a considerable part of the world within them; Rome, I say, never fixed the number; and this was one of the principal causes of her ruin.

MONTESQUIEU.

The people, in whom the supreme power resides, ought to have the management of everything within their reach: that which exceeds their abilities must be conducted by their ministers.

But they cannot properly be said to have their ministers, without the power of nominating them: it is, therefore, a fundamental maxim in this government, that the people should choose their ministers—that is, their magistrates.

They have occasion, as well as monarchs, and even more so, to be directed by a council or senate. But to have a proper confidence in these, they should have the choosing of the members; whether the election be made by themselves, as at Athens, or by some magistrate deputed for that purpose, as on certain occasions was customary at Rome.

The people are extremely well qualified for choosing those whom they are to intrust with part of their authority. They have only to be determined by things to which they cannot be strangers, and by facts that are obvious to sense. They can tell when a person has fought many battles, and been crowned with success; they are, therefore, capable of electing a general. They can tell when a judge is assiduous in his office, gives general satisfaction, and has never been charged with bribery: this is sufficient for choosing a prætor. They are struck with the magnificence or riches of a fellow-citizen; no more is requisite for electing an edile. These are facts of which they can have better information in a public forum than a monarch in his palace. But are they capable of conducting an intricate affair, of seizing and improving the opportunity and critical moment of action? No; this surpasses their abilities. . . .

As most citizens have sufficient ability to choose, though unqualified to be chosen, so the people, though capable of calling others to an account for their administration, are incapable of conducting the administration themselves.

The public business must be carried on with a certain motion, neither too quick nor too slow. But the motion of the people is always either too remiss or too violent. Sometimes with a hundred thousand arms they overturn all before them; and sometimes with a hundred thousand feet they creep like insects. . . .

It is likewise a fundamental law in democracies, that the people should have the sole power to enact laws. And yet there are a thousand occasions on which it is necessary the senate should have the power of decreeing; nay, it is frequently proper to make some trial of a law before it is established. The constitutions of Rome and Athens were excellent—the decrees of the senate had the force of laws for the space of a year, but did not become perpetual till they were ratified by the consent of the people. (II, 2)

Of the Principles of the Three Kinds of Government

Of the Principle of Democracy

There is no great share of probity necessary to support a monarchical or despotic government. The force of laws in one, and the prince's arm in the other, are sufficient to direct and maintain the whole. But in a popular state, one spring more is necessary, namely, virtue.

What I have here advanced is confirmed by the unanimous testimony of historians, and is extremely agreeable to the nature of things. For it is clear that in a monarchy, where he who commands the execution of the laws generally thinks himself above them, there is less need of virtue than in a popular government, where the person intrusted with the execution of the laws is sensible of his being subject to their direction.

Clear is it also that a monarch who, through bad advice or indolence, ceases to enforce the execution of the laws, may easily repair the evil; he has only to follow other advice, or to shake off this indolence. But when, in a popular government, there is a suspension of the laws, as this can proceed only from the corruption of the republic, the state is certainly undone. . . .

When virtue is banished, ambition invades the minds of those who are disposed to receive it, and avarice possesses the whole community. The objects of their desires are changed; what they were fond of before has become indifferent; they were free while under the restraint of laws, but they would fain now be free to act against law; and as each citizen is like a slave who has run away from his master, that which was a maxim of equity he calls rigor; that which was a rule of action he styles constraint; and to precaution he gives the name of fear. Frugality, and not the thirst of gain, now passes for avarice. Formerly the wealth of individuals constituted the public treasure; but now this has become the patrimony of private persons. The members of the commonwealth riot on the public spoils, and its strength is only the power of a few, and the license of many. . . . (III, 3)

Of Education in a Republican Government

It is in a republican government that the whole power of education is required. The fear of despotic governments naturally arises of itself amidst threats and punishments; the honor of monarchies is favored by the passions, and favors them in its turn; but virtue is a self-renunciation, which is ever arduous and painful.

This virtue may be defined as the love of the laws and of our country. As such love requires a constant preference of public to private interest, it is the source of all private virtues; for they are nothing more than this very preference itself.

This love is peculiar to democracies. In these alone the government is intrusted to private citizens. Now, a government is like every thing else: to preserve it we must love it.

Has it ever been known that kings were not fond of monarchy, or that despotic princes hated arbitrary power?

Every thing, therefore, depends on establishing this love in a republic; and to inspire it ought to be the principal business of education: but the surest way of instilling it into children is for parents to set them an example.

People have it generally in their power to communicate their ideas to their children; but they are still better able to transfuse their passions.

If it happens otherwise, it is because the impressions made at home are effaced by those they have received abroad.

It is not the young people that degenerate; they are not spoiled till those of maturer age are already sunk into corruption. (IV, 5)

Of the Power of Punishments

. . . Mankind must not be governed with too much severity; we ought to make a prudent use of the means which nature has given us to conduct them. If we inquire into the cause of all human corruptions, we shall find that they proceed from the impunity of criminals, and not from the moderation of punishments.

Let us follow nature, who has given shame to man for his scourge; and let the heaviest part of the punishment be the infamy attending it.

But if there be some countries where shame is not a consequence of punishment, this must be owing to tyranny, which has inflicted the same penalties on villains and honest men.

And if there are others where men are deterred only by cruel punishments, we may be sure that this must, in a great measure, arise from the violence of the government which has used such penalties for slight transgressions.

It often happens that a legislator, desirous of remedying an abuse, thinks of nothing else; his eyes are open only to this object, and shut to its inconveniences. When the abuse is redressed, you see only the severity of the legislator; yet there remains an evil in the state that has sprung from this severity; the minds of the people are corrupted, and become habituated to despotism. . . .

There are two sorts of corruptions—one when the people do not observe the laws; the other when they are corrupted by the laws: an incurable evil, because it is in the very remedy itself. (VI, 12)

Of the Rack

The wickedness of mankind makes it necessary for the law to suppose them better than they really are. Hence the deposition of two witnesses is sufficient in the punishment of all crimes. The law believes them, as if they spoke by the mouth of truth. Thus we judge that every child conceived in wedlock is legitimate; the law having a confidence in the mother, as if she were chastity itself. But the use of the rack against criminals cannot be defended on a like plea of necessity.

We have before us the example of a nation blessed with an excellent civil government [England], where without any inconvenience the practice of racking criminals is rejected. It is not, therefore, in its own nature necessary.

So many men of learning and genius have written against the custom of torturing criminals, that after them I dare not presume to meddle with the subject. I was going to say that it might suit despotic states, where whatever inspires fear is the fittest spring of government. I was going to say that the slaves among the Greeks and Romans—but nature cries out aloud, and asserts her rights. (VI, 17)

Of the Corruption of the Principles of Democracy

The principle of democracy is corrupted not only when the spirit of equality is extinct, but likewise when they fall into a spirit of extreme equality, and when each citizen would fain be upon a level with those whom he has chosen to command him. Then the people, incapable of bearing the very power they have delegated, want to manage everything themselves, to debate for the senate, to execute for the magistrate, and to decide for the judges.

When this is the case, virtue can no longer subsist in the republic. The people are desirous of exercising the functions of the magistrates, who cease to be revered. The deliberations of the senate are slighted; all respect is then laid aside for the senators, and consequently for old age. If there is no more respect for old age, there will be none presently for parents; deference to husbands will be likewise thrown off, and submission to masters. This license will soon become general, and the trouble of command be as fatiguing as that of obedience. Wives, children, slaves will shake off all subjection. No longer will there be any such thing as manners, order, or virtue. . . .

Democracy has, therefore, two excesses to avoid—the spirit of inequality, which leads to aristocracy or monarchy, and the spirit of extreme equality, which leads to despotic power, as the latter is completed by conquest. . . . (VIII, 2)

Of the Spirit of Extreme Equality

As distant as heaven is from earth, so is the true spirit of equality from that of extreme equality. The former does not imply that everybody should command, or that no one should be commanded, but that we obey or command our equals. It endeavors not to shake off the authority of a master, but that its masters should be none but its equals.

In the state of nature, indeed, all men are born equal, but they cannot continue in this equality. Society makes them lose it, and they recover it only by the protection of the laws.

Such is the difference between a well-regulated democracy and one that is not so, that in the former men are equal only as citizens, but in the latter they are equal also as magistrates, as senators, as judges, as fathers, as husbands, or as masters.

The natural place of virtue is near to liberty; but it is not nearer to excessive liberty than to servitude. (VIII, 3)

Distinctive Properties of a Republic

It is natural for a republic to have only a small territory; otherwise it cannot long subsist. In an extensive republic there are men of large fortunes, and consequently of less moderation; there are trusts too considerable to be placed in any single subject; he has interests of his own; he soon begins to think that he may be happy and glorious by oppressing his fellow-citizens, and that he may raise himself to grandeur on the ruins of his country.

In an extensive republic the public good is sacrificed to a thousand private views; it is subordinate to exceptions, and depends on accidents. In a small one, the interest of the public is more obvious, better understood, and more within the reach of every citizen; abuses have less extent, and, of course, are less protected.

The long duration of the republic of Sparta was owing to her having continued in the same extent of territory after all her wars. The sole aim of Sparta was liberty; and the sole advantage of her liberty, glory.

It was the spirit of the Greek republics to be as contented with their territories as with their laws. Athens was first fired with ambition and gave it to Lacedæmon; but it was an ambition rather of commanding a free people than of governing slaves; rather of directing than of breaking the union. All was lost upon the starting up of monarchy—a government whose spirit is more turned to increase of dominion. . . . (VIII, 16)

In What Manner Republics Provide for Their Safety

If a republic be small, it is destroyed by a foreign force; if it be large, it is ruined by an internal imperfection.

To this twofold inconvenience democracies and aristocracies are equally liable, whether they be good or bad. The evil is in the very thing itself, and no form can redress it.

It is, therefore, very probable that mankind would have been, at length, obliged to live constantly under the government of a single person, had they not contrived a kind of constitution that has all the internal advantages of a republican, together with the external force of a monarchical, government. I mean a confederate republic.

This form of government is a convention by which several petty states agree to become members of a larger one, which they intend to establish. It is a kind of assemblage of societies, that constitute a new one, capable of increasing by means of further associations, till they arrive at such a degree of power as to be able to provide for the security of the whole body.

It was these associations that so long contributed to the prosperity of Greece. By these the Romans attacked the whole globe, and by these alone the whole globe withstood them; for when Rome had arrived at her highest pitch of grandeur, it was the associations beyond the Danube and the Rhine—associations formed by the terror of her arms—that enabled the barbarians to resist her.

Hence it proceeds that Holland, Germany, and the Swiss cantons are considered in Europe as perpetual republics.

The associations of cities were formerly more necessary than in our times. A weak, defenceless town was exposed to greater danger. By conquest it was deprived not only of the executive and legislative power, as at present, but, moreover, of all human property.

A republic of this kind, able to withstand an external force, may support itself without any internal corruption; the form of this society prevents all manner of inconveniences.

If a single member should attempt to usurp the supreme power, he could not be supposed to have an equal authority and credit in all the confederate states. Were he to have too great an influence over one, this would alarm the rest; were he to subdue a part, that which would still remain free might oppose him with forces independent of those which he had usurped, and overpower him before he could be settled in his usurpation.

Should a popular insurrection happen in one of the confederate states, the others are able to quell it. Should abuses creep into one part, they are reformed by those that remain sound. The state may be destroyed on one side, and not on the other; the confederacy may be dissolved, and the confederates preserve their sovereignty.

As this government is composed of petty republics, it enjoys the internal happiness of each; and with regard to its external situation, by means of the association, it possesses all the advantages of large monarchies. (IX, 1)

That a Confederate Government Ought to be Composed of States of the Same Nature, Especially of the Republican Kind

The Canaanites were destroyed by reason that they were petty monarchies that had had no union or confederacy for their common defence; and, indeed, a confederacy is not agreeable to the nature of petty monarchies.

As the confederate republic of Germany consists of free cities, and of petty states subject to different princes, experience shows us that it is much more imperfect than that of Holland and Switzerland.

The spirit of monarchy is war and enlargement of dominion: peace and moderation are the spirit of a republic. These two kinds of government cannot naturally subsist in a confederate republic.

Thus we observe, in the Roman history, that when the Veientes had chosen a king, they were immediately abandoned by all the other petty republics of Tuscany. Greece was undone as soon as the kings of Macedon obtained a seat among the Amphictyons.

The confederate republic of Germany, composed of princes and free towns, subsists by means of a chief who is, in some respects, the magistrate of the union, in others the monarch. (IX, 2)

In What Liberty Consists

It is true that in democracies the people seem to act as they please; but political liberty does not consist in an unlimited freedom. In governments, that is, in societies directed by laws, liberty can consist only in the power of doing what we ought to will, and in not being constrained to do what we ought not to will.

We must have continually present to our minds the difference between independence and liberty. Liberty is a right of doing whatever the laws permit, and if a citizen could do what they forbid he would be no longer possessed of liberty, because all his fellow-citizens would have the same power.

Democratic and aristocratic states are not in their own nature free. Political liberty is to be found only in moderate governments; and even in these it is not always found. It is there only when there is no abuse of power. But constant experience shows us that every man invested with power is apt to abuse it, and to carry his authority as far as it will go. Is it not strange, though true, to say that virtue itself has need of limits?

To prevent this abuse, it is necessary from the very

nature of things that power should be a check to power. A government may be so constituted, as no man shall be compelled to do things to which the law does not oblige him, nor forced to abstain from things which the law permits. (XI, 3, 4)

Of the Constitution of England [1]

In every government there are three sorts of power: the legislative; the executive in respect to things dependent on the law of nations; and the executive in regard to matters that depend on the civil law.

By virtue of the first, the prince or magistrate enacts temporary or perpetual laws, and amends or abrogates those that have been already enacted. By the second, he makes peace or war, sends or receives embassies, establishes the public security, and provides against invasions. By the third, he punishes criminals, or determines the disputes that arise between individuals. The latter we shall call the judiciary power, and the other simply the executive power of the state.

The political liberty of the subject is a tranquillity of mind arising from the opinion each person has of his safety. In order to have this liberty, it is requisite the government be so constituted as one man need not be afraid of another.

When the legislative and executive powers are united in the same person, or in the same body of magistrates, there can be no liberty; because apprehensions may arise, lest the same monarch or senate should enact tyrannical laws, to execute them in a tyrannical manner.

Again, there is no liberty, if the judiciary power be not separated from the legislative and executive. Were it joined with the legislative, the life and liberty of the subject would be exposed to arbitrary control; for the judge would be then the legislator. Were it joined to the executive power, the judge might behave with violence and oppression.

[1] The greater part of the principles produced in this chapter by Montesquieu are derived from Locke's "Treatise upon Civil Government," XII.

There would be an end of everything, were the same man or the same body, whether of the nobles or of the people, to exercise those three powers, that of enacting laws, that of executing the public resolutions, and of trying the causes of individuals.

Most kingdoms in Europe enjoy a moderate government because the prince who is invested with the two first powers leaves the third to his subjects. In Turkey, where these three powers are united in the Sultan's person, the subjects groan under the most dreadful oppression.

In the republics of Italy, where these three powers are united, there is less liberty than in our monarchies. Hence their government is obliged to have recourse to as violent methods for its support as even that of the Turks; witness the state inquisitors, and the lion's mouth[1] into which every informer may at all hours throw his written accusations.

In what a situation must the poor subject be in those republics! The same body of magistrates are possessed, as executors of the laws, of the whole power they have given themselves in quality of legislators. They may plunder the state by their general determinations; and as they have likewise the judiciary power in their hands, every private citizen may be ruined by their particular decisions.

The whole power is here united in one body; and though there is no external pomp that indicates a despotic sway, yet the people feel the effects of it every moment.

Hence it is that many of the princes of Europe, whose aim has been levelled at arbitrary power, have constantly set out with uniting in their own persons all the branches of magistracy, and all the great offices of state.

I allow indeed that the mere hereditary aristocracy of the Italian republics does not exactly answer to the despotic power of the Eastern princes. The number of magistrates sometimes moderate the power of the magistracy; the whole body of the nobles do not always concur in

[1] A famous drop for anonymous denunciations in the Venetian Republic.

the same design; and different tribunals are erected, that temper each other. Thus at Venice the legislative power is in the council, the executive in the *pregadi*, and the judiciary in the *quarantia*. But the mischief is, that these different tribunals are composed of magistrates all belonging to the same body; which constitutes almost one and the same power.

The judiciary power ought not to be given to a standing senate; it should be exercised by persons taken from the body of the people at certain times of the year, and consistently with a form and manner prescribed by law, in order to erect a tribunal that should last only so long as necessity requires.

By this method the judicial power, so terrible to mankind, not being annexed to any particular state or profession, becomes, as it were, invisible. People have not then the judges continually present to their view; they fear the office, but not the magistrate.

In accusations of a deep and criminal nature, it is proper the person accused should have the privilege of choosing, in some measure, his judges, in concurrence with the law; or at least he should have a right to except against so great a number that the remaining part may be deemed his own choice.

The other two powers may be given rather to magistrates or permanent bodies, because they are not exercised on any private subject; one being no more than the general will of the state, and the other the execution of that general will.

But though the tribunals ought not to be fixed, the judgments ought; and to such a degree as to be ever conformable to the letter of the law. Were they to be the private opinion of the judge, people would then live in society without exactly knowing the nature of their obligations.

The judges ought likewise to be of the same rank as the accused, or, in other words, his peers, to the end that he may not imagine he is fallen into the hands of persons inclined to treat him with rigor.

If the legislature leaves the executive power in possession of a right to imprison those subjects who can give security for their good behavior, there is an end of liberty; unless they are taken up in order to answer without delay to a capital crime, in which case they are really free, being subject only to the power of the law.

But should the legislature think itself in danger by some secret conspiracy against the state, or by a correspondence with a foreign enemy, it might authorize the executive power, for a short and limited time, to imprison suspected persons, who in that case would lose their liberty only for a while, to preserve it forever.

And this is the only reasonable method that can be substituted to the tyrannical magistracy of the Ephori, and to the state inquisitors of Venice, who are also despotic.

As in a country of liberty, every man who is supposed a free agent ought to be his own governor; the legislative power should reside in the whole body of the people. But since this is impossible in large states, and in small ones is subject to many inconveniences, it is fit the people should transact by their representatives what they cannot transact by themselves.

The inhabitants of a particular town are much better acquainted with its wants and interests than with those of other places; and are better judges of the capacity of their neighbors than of that of the rest of their countrymen. The members, therefore, of the legislature should not be chosen from the general body of the nation; but it is proper that in every considerable place a representative should be elected by the inhabitants.

The great advantage of representatives is their capacity of discussing public affairs. For this the people collectively are extremely unfit, which is one of the chief inconveniences of a democracy.

It is not at all necessary that the representatives who have received a general instruction from their constituents should wait to be directed on each particular affair, as is practised in the diets of Germany. True it is that by this way of proceeding the speeches of the deputies might with greater propriety be called the voice of the nation; but, on the other hand, this would occasion infinite delays; would give each deputy a power of controlling the assembly; and, on the most urgent and pressing occasions, the wheels of government might be stopped by the caprice of a single person.

When the deputies, as Mr. Sidney well observes, represent a body of people, as in Holland, they ought to be accountable to their constituents; but it is a different thing in England, where they are deputed by boroughs.

All the inhabitants of the several districts ought to have a right of voting at the election of a representative, except such as are in so mean a situation as to be deemed to have no will of their own.

One great fault there was in most of the ancient republics, that the people had a right to active resolutions, such as require some execution, a thing of which they are absolutely incapable. They ought to have no share in the government but for the choosing of representatives, which is within their reach. For though few can tell the exact degree of men's capacities, yet there are none but are capable of knowing in general whether the person they choose is better qualified than most of his neighbors.

Neither ought the representative body to be chosen for the executive part of government, for which it is not so fit; but for the enacting of laws, or to see whether the laws in being are duly executed, a thing suited to their abilities, and which none indeed but themselves can properly perform.

In such a state there are always persons distinguished by their birth, riches, or honors: but were they to be confounded with the common people, and to have only the weight of a single vote like the rest, the common liberty would be their slavery, and they would have no interest in supporting it, as most of the popular resolutions would be against them. The share they have, therefore, in the legislature ought to be proportioned to their other advantages in the state; which happens only when they form a body that has a right to check the licentiousness of the people, as the people have a right to oppose any encroachment of theirs.

The legislative power is therefore committed to the body of the nobles, and to that which represents the people, each having their assemblies and deliberations apart, each their separate views and interests.

Of the three powers above mentioned, the judiciary is in some measure next to nothing: there remain, therefore, only two; and as these have need of a regulating power to moderate them, the part of the legislative body composed of the nobility is extremely proper for this purpose.

The body of the nobility ought to be hereditary. In the first place it is so in its own nature; and in the next there must be a considerable interest to preserve its privileges —privileges that in themselves are obnoxious to popular envy, and of course in a free state are always in danger.

But as a hereditary power might be tempted to pursue its own particular interests, and forget those of the people, it is proper that where a singular advantage may be gained by corrupting the nobility, as in the laws relating to the supplies, they should have no other share in the legislation than the power of rejecting, and not that of resolving.

By the power of resolving I mean the right of ordaining by their own authority, or of amending what has been ordained by others. By the power of rejecting I would be understood to mean the right of annulling a resolution taken by another; which was the power of the tribunes at Rome. And though the person possessed of the privilege of rejecting may likewise have the right of approving, yet this approbation passes for no more than a declaration, that he intends to make no use of his privilege of rejecting, and is derived from that very privilege.

The executive power ought to be in the hands of a monarch, because this branch of government, having need of despatch, is better administered by one than by many: on the other hand, whatever depends on the legislative power is oftentimes better regulated by many than by a single person.

But if there were no monarch, and the executive power

should be committed to a certain number of persons selected from the legislative body, there would be an end then of liberty; by reason the two powers would be united, as the same persons would sometimes possess, and would be always able to possess, a share in both.

Were the legislative body to be a considerable time without meeting, this would likewise put an end to liberty. For of two things one would naturally follow: either that there would be no longer any legislative resolutions, and then the state would fall into anarchy; or that these resolutions would be taken by the executive power, which would render it absolute.

It would be needless for the legislative body to continue always assembled. This would be troublesome to the representatives, and, moreover, would cut out too much work for the executive power, so as to take off its attention to its office, and oblige it to think only of defending its own prerogatives, and the right it has to execute.

Again, were the legislative body to be always assembled, it might happen to be kept up only by filling the places of the deceased members with new representatives; and in that case, if the legislative body were once corrupted, the evil would be past all remedy. When different legislative bodies succeed one another, the people who have a bad opinion of that which is actually sitting may reasonably entertain some hopes of the next: but were it to be always the same body, the people upon seeing it once corrupted would no longer expect any good from its laws; and of course they would either become desperate or fall into a state of indolence.

The legislative body should not meet of itself. For a body is supposed to have no will but when it is met; and besides, were it not to meet unanimously, it would be impossible to determine which was really the legislative body; the part assembled, or the other. And if it had a right to prorogue itself, it might happen never to be prorogued; which would be extremely dangerous, in case it should ever attempt to encroach on the executive power. Besides, there are seasons, some more proper than others, for assembling the legislative body: it is fit, therefore, that the executive power should regulate the time of meeting, as well as the duration of those assemblies, according to the circumstances and exigencies of a state known to itself.

Were the executive power not to have a right of restraining the encroachments of the legislative body, the latter would become despotic; for as it might arrogate to itself what authority it pleased, it would soon destroy all the other powers.

But it is not proper, on the other hand, that the legislative power should have a right to stay the executive. For as the execution has its natural limits, it is useless to confine it; besides, the executive power is generally employed in momentary operations. The power, therefore, of the Roman tribunes was faulty, as it put a stop not only to the legislation, but likewise to the executive part of government; which was attended with infinite mischief.

But if the legislative power in a free state has no right to stay the executive, it has a right and ought to have the means of examining in what manner its laws have been executed; an advantage which this government has over that of Crete and Sparta, where the Cosmi and the Ephori gave no account of their administration.

But whatever may be the issue of that examination, the legislative body ought not to have a power of arraigning the person, nor, of course, the conduct, of him who is intrusted with the executive power. His person should be sacred, because as it is necessary for the good of the state to prevent the legislative body from rendering themselves arbitrary, the moment he is accused or tried there is an end of liberty. . . .

The executive power, pursuant of what has been already said, ought to have a share in the legislature by the power of rejecting; otherwise it would soon be stripped of its prerogative. But should the legislative power usurp a share of the executive, the latter would be equally undone.

If the prince were to have a part in the legislature by the power of resolving, liberty would be lost. But as it is necessary he should have a share in the legislature for the support of his own prerogative, this share must consist in the power of rejecting.

The change of government at Rome was owing to this, that neither the senate, who had one part of the executive power, nor the magistrates, who were intrusted with the other, had the right of rejecting, which was entirely lodged in the people.

Here, then, is the fundamental constitution of the government we are treating of. The legislative body being composed of two parts, they check one another by the mutual privilege of rejecting. They are both restrained by the executive power, as the executive is by the legislative.

These three powers should naturally form a state of repose or inaction. But as there is a necessity for movement in the course of human affairs, they are forced to move, but still in concert.

As the executive power has no other part in the legislative than the privilege of rejecting, it can have no share in the public debates. It is not even necessary that it should propose, because as it may always disapprove of the resolutions that shall be taken, it may likewise reject the decisions on those proposals which were made against its will.

In some ancient commonwealths, where public debates were carried on by the people in a body, it was natural for the executive power to propose and debate in conjunction with the people, otherwise their resolutions must have been attended with a strange confusion.

Were the executive power to determine the raising of public money, otherwise than by giving its consent, liberty would be at an end; because it would become legislative in the most important point of legislation.

If the legislative power was to settle the subsidies, not from year to year, but forever, it would run the risk of losing its liberty, because the executive power would be no longer dependent; and when once it was possessed of such a perpetual right, it would be a matter of indifference whether it held it of itself or of another. The same may be said if it should come to a resolution of intrusting, not an annual, but a perpetual command of the fleets and armies to the executive power. . . .

In perusing the admirable treatise of Tacitus "On the Manners of the Germans," we find it is from that nation the English have borrowed the idea of their political government. This beautiful system was invented first in the woods.

As all human things have an end, the state we are speaking of will lose its liberty, will perish. Have not Rome, Sparta and Carthage perished? It will perish when the legislative power shall be more corrupt than the executive.

It is not my business to examine whether the English actually enjoy this liberty or not. Sufficient it is for my purpose to observe that it is established by their laws; and I inquire no further.

Neither do I pretend by this to undervalue other governments, nor to say that this extreme political liberty ought to give uneasiness to those who have only a moderate share of it. How should I have any such design, I who think that even the highest refinement of reason is not always desirable, and that mankind generally find their account better in mediums than in extremes? . . . (XI, 6)

Of the Laws That Form Political Liberty, in Relation to the Subject

It is not sufficient to have treated of political liberty in relation to the constitution; we must examine it likewise in the relation it bears to the subject.

We have observed that in the former case it arises from a certain distribution of the three powers; but in the latter, we must consider it in another light. It consists in security, or in the opinion people have of their security.

The constitution may happen to be free, and the subject not. The subject may be free, and not the constitution. In those cases, the constitution will be free by right, and not in fact; the subject will be free in fact, and not by right.

It is the disposition only of the laws, and even of the fundamental laws, that constitutes liberty in relation to the constitution. But as it regards the subject: manners, customs, or received examples may give rise to it, and particular civil laws may encourage it, as we shall presently observe.

Further, as in most states liberty is more checked or depressed than their constitution requires, it is proper to treat of the particular laws that in each constitution are apt to assist or check the principle of liberty which each state is capable of receiving. (XII, 1)

Of the Liberty of the Subject

Philosophic liberty consists in the free exercise of the will; or at least, if we must speak agreeably to all systems, in an opinion that we have the free exercise of our will. Political liberty consists in security, or, at least, in the opinion that we enjoy security.

This security is never more dangerously attacked than in public or private accusations. It is, therefore, on the goodness of criminal laws that the liberty of the subject principally depends. . . .

The knowledge already acquired in some countries, or that may be hereafter attained in others, concerning the surest rules to be observed in criminal judgments, is more interesting to mankind than any other thing in the world.

Liberty can be founded on the practice of this knowledge only; and supposing a state to have the best laws imaginable in this respect, a person tried under that state, and condemned to be hanged the next day, would have much more liberty than a pasha enjoys in Turkey.

Those laws which condemn a man to death on the deposition of a single witness are fatal to liberty. In reason there should be two, because a witness who affirms, and the accused who denies, make an equal balance, and a third must decline the scale. (XII, 2, 3)

Of Certain Accusations that Require Particular Moderation and Prudence

It is an important maxim, that we ought to be very circumspect in the prosecution of witchcraft and heresy. The accusation of these two crimes may be vastly injurious to liberty, and productive of infinite oppression, if the legislator knows not how to set bounds to it. For as it does not directly point at a person's actions, but at his character, it grows dangerous in proportion to the ignorance of the people; and then a man is sure to be always in danger, because the most exceptional conduct, the purest morals, and the constant practice of every duty in life are not a sufficient security against the suspicion of his being guilty of the like crimes. . . .

Under the reign of Philip the Long, the Jews were expelled from France, being accused of having poisoned the springs with their lepers. So absurd an accusation ought to make us doubt all those that are founded on public hatred.

I have not here asserted that heresy ought not to be punished; I said only that we ought to be extremely circumspect in punishing it. (XII, 5)

Of Indiscreet Speeches

Nothing renders the crime of high treason more arbitrary than declaring people guilty of it for indiscreet speeches. Speech is so subject to interpretation; there is so great a difference between indiscretion and malice; and frequently so little is there of the latter in the freedom of expression, that the law can hardly subject people to a capital punishment for words unless it expressly declares what words they are.

Words do not constitute an overt act; they remain only in idea. When considered by themselves, they have generally no determinate signification; for this depends on the tone in which they are uttered. It often happens that in repeating the same words they have not the same meaning; this depends on their connection with other things, and sometimes more is signified by silence than by any expression whatever. Since there can be nothing so equivocal and ambiguous as all this, how is it possible to convert it into a crime of high treason? Wherever this law is established, there is an end not only of liberty, but even of its very shadow. . . . (XII, 12)

Of Writings

In writings there is something more permanent than in words, but when they are in no way preparative to high treason they cannot amount to that charge. . . .

Satirical writings are hardly known in despotic governments, where dejection of mind on the one hand, and ignorance on the other, afford neither abilities nor will to write. In democracies they are not hindered, for the very same reason which causes them to be prohibited in monarchies; being generally levelled against men of power and authority, they flatter the malignancy of the people, who are the governing party. In monarchies they are forbidden, but rather as a subject of civil animadversion than as a capital crime. They may amuse the general malevolence, please the malcontents, diminish the envy against public employments, give the people patience to suffer, and make them laugh at their sufferings. . . . (XII, 13)

Of the General Spirit of Mankind

Mankind are influenced by various causes: by the climate, by the religion, by the laws, by the maxims of government, by precedents, morals, and customs; whence is formed a general spirit of nations.

In proportion as, in every country, any one of these causes acts with more force, the others in the same degree are weakened. Nature and the climate rule almost alone over the savages; customs govern the Chinese; the laws tyrannize in Japan; morals had formerly all their influence at Sparta; maxims of government, and the ancient simplicity of manners, once prevailed at Rome. (XIX, 4)

How Far We Should Be Attentive Lest the General Spirit of a Nation Be Changed [*France*]

Should there happen to be a country whose inhabitants were of a social temper, open-hearted, cheerful, endowed with taste and a facility in communicating their thoughts; who were sprightly and agreeable; sometimes imprudent, often indiscreet; and besides had courage, generosity, frankness, and a certain notion of honor, no one ought to endeavor to restrain their manners by laws, unless he would lay a constraint on their virtues. If in general the character be good, the little foibles that may be found in it are of small importance.

They might lay a restraint upon women, enact laws to reform their manners and to reduce their luxury, but who knows but that by these means they might lose that peculiar taste which would be the source of the wealth of the nation, and that politeness which would render the country frequented by strangers?

It is the business of the legislature to follow the spirit of the nation, when it is not contrary to the principles of government; for we do nothing so well as when we act with freedom, and follow the bent of our natural genius.

If an air of pedantry be given to a nation that is naturally gay, the state will gain no advantage from it, either at home or abroad. Leave it to do frivolous things in the most serious manner, and with gayety the things most serious. (IX, 5)

That Everything Ought Not To Be Corrected

Let them but leave us as we are, said a gentleman of a nation which had a very great resemblance to that we have been describing, and nature will repair whatever is amiss. She has given us a vivacity capable of offending and hurrying us beyond the bounds of respect: this same vivacity is corrected by the politeness it procures, inspiring us with a taste of the world, and, above all, for the conversation of the fair sex.

Let them leave us as we are; our indiscretions joined

to our good nature would make the laws which should constrain our sociability not at all proper for us. (XIX, 6)

Of Hospitals

A man is not poor because he has nothing, but because he does not work. The man who without any degree of wealth has an employment is as much at his ease as he who without labor has an income of a hundred crowns a year. He who has no substance, and yet has a trade, is not poorer than he who, possessing ten acres of land, is obliged to cultivate it for his subsistence. The mechanic who gives his art as an inheritance to his children has left them a fortune, which is multiplied in proportion to their number. It is not so with him who, having ten acres of land, divides it among his children.

In trading countries, where many men have no other subsistence but from the arts, the state is frequently obliged to supply the necessities of the aged, the sick and the orphan. A well-regulated government draws this support from the arts themselves. It gives to some such employment as they are capable of performing; others are taught to work, and this teaching of itself becomes an employment.

The alms given to a naked man in the street do not fulfil the obligations of the state, which owes to every citizen a certain subsistence, a proper nourishment, convenient clothing, and a kind of life not incompatible with health. . . .

The riches of the state suppose great industry. Amidst the numerous branches of trade it is impossible but that some must suffer, and consequently the mechanics must be in a momentary necessity.

Whenever this happens, the state is obliged to lend them a ready assistance, whether it be to prevent the sufferings of the people, or to avoid a rebellion. In this case hospitals, or some equivalent regulations, are necessary to prevent this misery.

But when the nation is poor, private poverty springs from the general calamity, and is, if I may so express myself, the general calamity itself. All the hospitals in the world cannot cure this private poverty; on the contrary, the spirit of indolence, which it constantly inspires, increases the general and consequently the private misery. . . .

I have observed that wealthy nations have need of hospitals, because fortune subjects them to a thousand accidents; but it is plain that transient assistances are much better than perpetual foundations. The evil is momentary; it is necessary, therefore, that the succor should be of the same nature, and that it be applied to particular accidents. (XXIII, 29)

A Most Humble Remonstrance to the Inquisitors of Spain and Portugal

A Jewess of eighteen years of age, who was burned at Lisbon at the last *auto-da-fé*, gave occasion to the following little piece, the most idle, I believe, that ever was written. When we attempt to prove things so evident, we are sure never to convince.

The author declares, that though a Jew he has a respect for the Christian religion; and that he should be glad to take away from the princes who are not Christians a plausible pretence for persecuting this religion.

"You complain," says he to the Inquisitors, "that the Emperor of Japan caused all the Christians in his dominions to be burned by a slow fire. But he will answer, we treat you who do not believe like us, as you yourselves treat those who do not believe like you; you can only complain of your weakness, which has hindered you from exterminating us, and which has enabled us to exterminate you.

"But it must be confessed, that you are much more cruel than this emperor. You put us to death who believe only what you believe, because we do not believe all that you believe. We follow a religion which you yourselves know to have been formerly dear to God. We think that God loves it still, and you think that he loves it no more: and because you judge thus, you make those suffer by sword and fire who hold an error so pardonable as to believe that God still loves what he once loved.

"If you are cruel to us, you are much more so to our children; you cause them to be burned because they follow the inspirations given them by those whom the law of nature and the laws of all nations teach them to regard as gods.

"You deprive yourselves of the advantage you have over the Mahommedans, with respect to the manner in which their religion was established. When they boast of the number of their believers, you tell them that they have obtained them by violence, and that they have extended their religion by the sword; why then do you establish yours by fire?

"When you would bring us over to you, we object to a source from which you glory to have descended. You reply to us that though your religion is new, it is divine; and you prove it from its growing amidst the persecutions of pagans, and when watered by the blood of your martyrs; but at present you play the part of the Diocletians, and make us take yours.

"We conjure you, not by the mighty God whom both you and we serve, but by that Christ, who, you tell us, took upon him a human form, to propose himself as an example for you to follow; we conjure you to behave to us as he himself would behave were he upon earth. You would have us become Christians, and you will not be so yourselves.

"But if you will not be Christians, be at least men; treat us as you would, if having only the weak light of justice which nature bestows, you had not a religion to conduct, and a revelation to enlighten you.

"If Heaven has had so great a love for you as to make you see the truth, you have received a singular favor; but is it for children who have received the inheritance of their father, to hate those who have not?

"If you have this truth, hide it not from us by the manner in which you propose it. The characteristic of truth is its triumph over hearts and minds, and not that impotency which you confess when you would force us to receive it by tortures.

"If you were wise, you would not put us to death for no other reason than because we are unwilling to deceive you. If your Christ is the son of God, we hope he will reward us for being so unwilling to profane his mysteries; and we believe that the God whom both you and we serve will not punish us for having suffered death for a religion which he formerly gave us, only because we believe that he still continues to give it.

"You live in an age in which the light of nature shines more brightly than it has ever done; in which philosophy has enlightened human understandings; in which the morality of your gospel has been better known; in which the respective rights of mankind with regard to each other and the empire which one conscience has over another are best understood. If you do not, therefore, shake off your ancient prejudices, which, whilst unregarded, mingle with your passions, it must be confessed that you are incorrigible, incapable of any degree of light or instruction; and a nation must be very unhappy that gives authority to such men.

"Would you have us frankly tell you our thoughts? You consider us rather as your enemies than as the enemies of your religion; for if you loved your religion you would not suffer it to be corrupted by such gross ignorance.

"It is necessary that we should warn you of one thing, that is, if any one in times to come shall dare to assert that in the age in which we live the people of Europe were civilized, you will be cited to prove that they were barbarians; and the idea they will have of you will be such as will dishonor your age, and spread hatred over all your contemporaries." (XXV, 13)

Rousseau

1712-1778

Born of Protestant parents in Calvinist Geneva and deprived of his mother at birth, Rousseau received a very haphazard early education. After an unhappy experience as apprentice, he took to the road and at Turin was converted somewhat halfheartedly to Catholicism. Many years were spent in vagabondage and adventure before he settled down in earnest to educate himself. This seemed an inauspicious beginning for a man who was to become a dominant influence in literature and in educational and political theory for generations to come. For he has been called, with considerable justification, the father of Romanticism and of the French Revolution, and grandfather of the Russian Revolution.

At the age of thirty, he came to Paris and made the acquaintance of Diderot, for whose *Encyclopedia* he was later to write the essentially sound articles on music. Both men were leading a precarious existence on the fringe of intellectual society and of greatness. Rousseau was the first to achieve fame, with his prize-winning *Discourse on the Arts and Sciences* (1749). In it, he took the unpopular side and tried to prove that not only the revival of learning but all progress in the arts and sciences had contributed to the moral corruption of man. The discourse was rhetorical and not to be taken too seriously in all aspects. It did, however, persuade his readers that he was a primitivist, preaching a return to nature. This impression was strengthened by a second discourse, *On the Origins of Inequality among Men* (1755), and is true to the extent that he saw the Golden Age in the past, as opposed to the idea of progress upheld by Voltaire and Condorcet.

His very real appreciation of nature and the simpler pleasures of country life is revealed, in often lyrically refreshing prose, in an epistolary novel, *La Nouvelle Héloïse* (1761), the *Confessions*, begun some years later and published posthumously, and his final work, the *Rêveries d'un promeneur solitaire*. In these works his romantic sensibilities are given free play in idyllic descriptions of the beauty of the country side, with its trees and flowers, and of the

Swiss lakes and foothills of the Alps. A constitutional malformation, accompanied by frequent attacks of uremic poisoning, undoubtedly contributed to the keenness of his sensibilities and artistic genius, as well as to the many eccentricities and paranoia that caused him to break with his former friends, Diderot and Voltaire in particular, and Hume, who invited him to England and tried in vain to befriend him. His *Emile* (1762), a very influential treatise, in which he preached a practical education based on activities rather than books, contained a section on religion which brought about his banishment from France. The work was also burned in Geneva where, having returned to the Protestant fold, he hoped to have his citizenship reinstated. His mania thus had considerable foundation in reality. He was allowed, however, to pass his final years unmolested in Paris and its environs.

Rousseau's greatest influence on the modern world has been in the field of political thought, especially in the *Discourse on the Origins of Inequality* and *The Social Contract* (1762). In spite of, or perhaps because of, the ambiguity of many of his political ideas, they have dominated political theorizing down to the present day.

A Discourse on the Origin of Inequality (1755)

This work, like the later Social Contract, *has been the subject of various interpretations ever since its publication. Its main themes, however, are not difficult to establish.*

Part I deals with the ascent of man, in three well-defined stages. In earliest times, man was little more than a healthy, non-moral, good-natured brute. To this stage only can be applied the much quoted phrase: "The man who meditates is a depraved animal." The second stage presents an evolutionary conception of human development through countless centuries, a view that reflects the mid-century evolutionary interests of Diderot, Maupertuis and Buffon in his recently published volume of Natural History. *The period was marked by the discovery of fire and the inven-*

tion and use of language. Only in the third, idyllic stage are primitive societies formed and with them moral man, whose social virtues still outweigh his social vices.

Having shown the ascent of man from brute, Rousseau shows man's subsequent degradation as population increases and social institutions become more complex. The author's own anti-social proclivities guide his pen. He assumes the presence of a radically evil element in human nature, which develops as society progresses and makes men proud, ambitious, self-seeking, vindictive and warlike. This state represents the first fall from grace. With rhetorical flourish Rousseau condemns first the institution of private property and then the division of labor consequent to the discovery of wheat and iron. Wealth and the competitive spirit reduced men to anarchy and the Hobbesian state of war. It was then that political institutions were devised by the wealthy to usurp power and enslave the workers, who had nothing to lose but their chains, "in order that a privileged few should gorge themselves with superfluities, while the starving multitude are in want of the bare necessities of life."

It is difficult not to see in the ending of the Discourse a diatribe against the capitalist state, the early murmurings of the class struggle, and a thoroughly pessimistic view of the human predicament, in which man, though natively good, is inevitably corrupted by society. In The Social Contract, *Rousseau will seek an escape from the dilemma.*

The First Part

Important as it may be, in order to judge rightly of the natural state of man, to consider him from his origin, and to examine him, as it were, in the embryo of his species, I shall not follow his organization through its successive developments, nor shall I stay to inquire what his animal system must have been at the beginning, in order to become at length what it actually is. I shall not ask whether his long nails were at first, as Aristotle supposes, only crooked talons; whether his whole body, like that of a bear, was covered with hair; or whether the fact that he walked upon all fours, with his looks directed toward the earth, confined to a horizon of a few paces, did not at once point out the nature and limits of his ideas. On this subject I could form none but vague and almost imaginary conjectures. Comparative anatomy has as yet made too little progress, and the observations of naturalists are too uncertain, to afford an adequate basis for any solid reasoning. So that, without having recourse to the supernatural information given us on this head, or paying any regard to the changes which must have taken place in the internal, as well as the external, conformation of man, as he applied his limbs to new uses, and fed himself on new kinds of food, I shall suppose his conformation to have been at all times what it appears to us at this day; that he always walked on two legs, made use of his hands as we do, directed his looks over all nature, and measured with his eyes the vast expanse of Heaven.

If we strip this being, thus constituted, of all the supernatural gifts he may have received, and all the artificial faculties he can have acquired only by a long process; if we consider him, in a word, just as he must have come from the hands of nature, we behold in him an animal weaker than some, and less agile than others; but, taking him all round, the most advantageously organized of any. I see him satisfying his hunger at the first oak, and slaking his thirst at the first brook; finding his bed at the foot of the tree which afforded him a repast; and, with that, all his wants supplied.

While the earth was left to its natural fertility and covered with immense forests, whose trees were never mutilated by the axe, it would present on every side both sustenance and shelter for every species of animal. Men, dispersed up and down among the rest, would observe and imitate their industry, and thus attain even to the instinct of the beasts, with the advantage that, whereas every species of brutes was confined to one particular instinct, man, who perhaps has not any one peculiar to himself, would appropriate them all, and live upon most of those different foods, which other animals shared among themselves; and thus would find his subsistence much more easily than any of the rest.

Accustomed from their infancy to the inclemencies of the weather and the rigor of the seasons, inured to fatigue, and forced, naked and unarmed, to defend themselves and their prey from other ferocious animals, or to escape them by flight, men would acquire a robust and almost unalterable constitution. The children, bringing with them into the world the excellent constitution of their parents, and fortifying it by the very exercises which first produced it, would thus acquire all the vigor of which the human frame is capable. Nature in this case treats them exactly as Sparta treated the children of her citizens: those who come well formed into the world she renders strong and robust, and all the rest she destroys; differing in this respect from our modern communities, in which the State, by making children a burden to their parents, kills them indiscriminately before they are born. . . .

We should beware, therefore, of confounding the savage man with the men we have daily before our eyes. Nature treats all the animals left to her care with a predilection that seems to show how jealous she is of that right. The horse, the cat, the bull, and even the ass are generally of greater stature, and always more robust, and have more vigor, strength and courage, when they run wild in the forests than when bred in the stall. By becoming domesticated, they lose half these advantages; and it seems as if all our care to feed and treat them well serves only to deprave them. It is thus with man also: as he becomes sociable and a slave, he grows weak, timid and servile; his effeminate way of life totally enervates his strength and courage. To this it may be added that there is still a greater difference between savage and civilized man than between wild and tame beasts: for men and brutes having been treated alike by nature, the several conveniences in which men indulge themselves still more than they do their beasts are so many additional causes of their deeper degeneracy.

It is not therefore so great a misfortune to these primitive men, nor so great an obstacle to their preservation, that they go naked, have no dwellings, and lack all the superfluities which we think so necessary. If their skins are not covered with hair, they have no need of such covering in warm climates, and in cold countries they soon learn to appropriate the skins of the beasts they have overcome. If they have but two legs to run with, they have two arms to defend themselves with and to provide for their wants. Their children are slowly and with difficulty taught to walk; but their mothers are able to carry them with ease; an advantage which other animals lack, as the mother, if pursued, is forced either to abandon her young, or to regulate her pace by theirs. Unless, in short, we suppose a singular and fortuitous concurrence of circumstances of which I shall speak later, and which would be unlikely to exist, it is plain in every state of the case, that the man who first made himself clothes or a dwelling was furnishing himself with things not at all necessary; for he had till then done without them, and there is no reason why he should not have been able to put up in manhood with the same kind of life as had been his in infancy. . . .

Savage man, left by nature solely to the direction of instinct, or rather indemnified for what he may lack by faculties capable at first of supplying its place, and afterwards of raising him much above it, must accordingly begin with purely animal functions: thus seeing and feeling must be his first condition, which would be common to him and all other animals. To will, and not to will, to desire and to fear, must be the first, and almost the only operations of his soul, till new circumstances occasion new developments of his faculties.

Whatever moralists may hold, the human understanding is greatly indebted to the passions which, it is universally allowed, are also much indebted to the understanding. It is by the activity of the passions that our reason is improved, for we desire knowledge only because we wish to enjoy; and it is impossible to conceive any reason why a person who has neither fears nor desires should give himself the trouble of reasoning. The passions, again, originate in our wants, and their progress depends on that of our knowledge; for we cannot desire or fear anything, except from the idea we have of it, or from the simple impulse of nature. Now savage man, being destitute of every species of intelligence, can have no passions save those of the latter kind: his desires never go beyond his physical wants. The only goods he recognizes in the universe are food, a female, and sleep: the only evils he fears are pain and hunger. I say pain, and not death: for no animal can know what it is to die, the knowledge of death and its terrors being one of the first acquisitions made by man in departing from an animal state. . . .

Let it be considered how many ideas we owe to the use of speech, how far grammar exercises the understanding and facilitates its operations. Let us reflect on the inconceivable pains and the infinite space of time that the first invention of languages must have cost. To these reflections add what preceded, and then judge how many thousand ages must have elapsed in the successive development in the human mind of those operations of which it is capable. . . .

The first language of mankind, the most universal and vivid, in a word the only language man needed, before he had occasion to exert his eloquence to persuade assembled multitudes, was the simple cry of nature. But as this was excited only by a sort of instinct on urgent occasions, to implore assistance in case of danger, or relief in case of suffering, it could be of little use in the ordinary course of life, in which more moderate feelings prevail. When the ideas of men began to expand and multiply, and closer communication took place among them, they strove to invent more numerous signs and a more copious language. They multiplied the inflexions of the voice, and added gestures, which are in their own nature more expressive, and depend less for their meaning on a prior determination. Visible and movable objects were therefore expressed by gestures, and audible ones by imitative sounds: but, as hardly anything can be indicated by gestures, except objects actually present or easily described, and visible actions; as they are not universally useful—for darkness or the interposition of a material object destroys their efficacy—and as besides they rather request than secure our attention; men at length bethought themselves of substituting for them the articulate sounds of the voice which, without bearing the same relation to any particular ideas, are better calculated to express them all as conventional signs. Such an institution could only be made by common consent, and must have been effected in a manner not very easy for men whose gross organs had not been accustomed to any such exercise. It is also in itself still more difficult to conceive, since such a common agreement must have had motives, and speech seems to have been highly necessary to establish the use of it.

It is reasonable to suppose that the words first made use of by mankind had a much more extensive signification than those used in languages already formed, and that ignorant as they were of the division of discourse into its constituent parts, they at first gave every single word the sense of a whole proposition. When they began to distinguish subject and attribute, and noun and verb, which was itself no common effort of genius, substantives were at first only so many proper names; the present infinitive was the only tense of verbs; and the very idea of adjectives must have been developed with great difficulty; for every adjective is an abstract idea, and abstractions are painful and unnatural operations. . . .

It appears, at first view, that men in a state of nature, having no moral relations or determinate obligations one with another, could not be either good or bad, virtuous or vicious; unless we take these terms in a physical sense, and call, in an individual, those qualities vices which may be injurious to his preservation, and those virtues which contribute to it; in which case, he would have to be accounted most virtuous who put least check on the pure impulses of nature. But without deviating from the ordinary sense of the words, it will be proper to suspend the judgment we might be led to form on such a state, and be on our guard against our prejudices, till we have weighed the matter in the scales of impartiality, and seen whether virtues or vices preponderate among civilized men: and whether their virtues do them more good than their vices do harm; till we have discovered whether the progress of the sciences sufficiently indemnifies them for the mischiefs they do one another, in proportion as they are better informed of the good they ought to do; or whether they would not be, on the whole, in a much happier condition if they had nothing to fear or to hope from any one than as they are, subjected to universal dependence and obliged to take everything from those who engage to give them nothing in return.

Above all, let us not conclude, with Hobbes, that because man has no idea of goodness, he must be naturally wicked; that he is vicious because he does not know virtue; that he always refuses to do his fellow-creatures services which he does not think they have a right to demand; or that by virtue of the right he truly claims everything he needs, he foolishly imagines himself the sole proprietor of the whole universe. Hobbes had seen clearly the defects of all the modern definitions of natural right: but the consequences which he deduces from his own show that he understands it in an equally false sense. In reasoning on the principles he lays down, he ought to have said that the state of nature, being that in which the care for our own preservation is the least prejudicial to that of others, was consequently the best calculated to promote peace, and the most suitable for mankind. He does say the exact opposite, in consequence of having improperly admitted, as a part of savage man's care for self-preservation, the gratification of a multitude of passions which are the work of society, and have made laws necessary. A bad man, he says, is a robust child. But it remains to be proved whether man in a state of nature is this robust child: and, should we grant that he is, what would he infer? Why truly, that if this man, when robust and strong, were dependent on others as he is when feeble, there is no extravagance he would not be guilty of; that he would beat his mother when she was too slow in giving him her breast; that he would strangle one of his younger brothers, if he should be troublesome to him, or bite the arm of another, if he put him to any inconvenience. But that man in the state of nature is both strong and dependent involves two contrary suppositions. Man is weak when he is dependent, and is his own master before he comes to be strong. . . .

Having proved that the inequality of mankind is hardly felt, and that its influence is next to nothing in a state of nature, I must next show its origin and trace its progress in the successive developments of the human mind. Having shown that human *perfectibility*, the social virtues, and the other faculties which natural man potentially possessed, could never develop of themselves, but must require the fortuitous concurrence of many foreign causes that might never arise, and without which he would have remained for ever in his primitive condition, I must now collect and consider the different accidents which may have improved the human understanding while depraving the species, and made man wicked while making him sociable; so as to bring him and the world from that distant period to the point at which we now behold them. . . .

The Second Part

The first man who, having enclosed a piece of ground, bethought himself of saying "This is mine," and found people simple enough to believe him, was the real founder of civil society. From how many crimes, wars and murders, from how many horrors and misfortunes might not any one have saved mankind, by pulling up the stakes, or filling up the ditch, and crying to his fellows: "Beware of listening to this impostor; you are undone if you once forget that the fruits of the earth belong to us all, and the earth itself to nobody." But there is great probability that things had then already come to such a pitch that they could no longer continue as they were; for the idea of property depends on many prior ideas which could only be acquired successively, and cannot have been formed all at once in the human mind. Mankind must have made very considerable progress, and acquired considerable knowledge and industry which they must also have transmitted and increased from age to age, before they arrived at this last point of the state of nature. Let us then go farther back, and endeavor to unify under a single point of view that slow succession of events and discoveries in the most natural order.

Man's first feeling was that of his own existence, and his first care that of self-preservation. The produce of the earth furnished him with all he needed, and instinct told him how to use it. Hunger and other appetites made him at various times experience various modes of existence; and among these was one which urged him to propagate his species—a blind propensity that, having nothing to do with the heart, produced a merely animal act. The want once gratified, the two sexes knew each other no more; and even the offspring was nothing to its mother, as soon as it could do without her.

Such was the condition of infant man; the life of an animal limited at first to mere sensations, and hardly profiting by the gifts nature bestowed on him, much less capable of entertaining a thought of forcing anything from her. But difficulties soon presented themselves, and it became necessary to learn how to surmount them: the height of the trees, which prevented him from gathering their fruits, the competition of other animals desirous of the same fruits, and the ferocity of those who needed them for their own preservation, all obliged him to apply himself to bodily exercises. He had to be active, swift of foot, and vigorous in fight. Natural weapons, stones and sticks, were easily found: he learnt to surmount the obstacles of nature, to contend in case of necessity with other animals and to dispute for the means of subsistence even with other men, or to indemnify himself for what he was forced to give up to a stronger.

In proportion as the human race grew more numerous, men's cares increased. The difference of soils, climates and seasons must have introduced some differences into their manner of living. Barren years, long and sharp winters, scorching summers which parched the fruits of the earth, must have demanded a new industry. On the seashore and the banks of rivers, they invented the hook and line, and became fishermen and eaters of fish. In the forests they made bows and arrows, and became huntsmen and warriors. In cold countries they clothed themselves with the skins of the beasts they had slain. The lightning, a volcano, or some lucky chance acquainted them with fire, a new resource against the rigors of winter: they next learned how to preserve this element, then how to reproduce it, and finally how to prepare with it the flesh of animals which before they had eaten raw.

This repeated relevance of various beings to himself, and one to another, would naturally give rise in the human mind to the perceptions of certain relations between them. Thus the relations which we denote by the terms great, small, strong, weak, swift, slow, fearful, bold, and the like, almost insensibly compared at need, must have at length produced in him a kind of reflection, or rather a mechanical prudence, which would indicate to him the precautions most necessary to his security.

The new intelligence which resulted from this development increased his superiority over other animals, by making him sensible of it. He would now endeavor, therefore, to ensnare them, would play them a thousand tricks, and though many of them might surpass him in swiftness or in strength, would in time become the master of some and the scourge of others. Thus, the first time he looked into himself, he felt the first emotion of pride; and, at a time when he scarce knew how to distinguish the different orders of beings, by looking upon his species as of the highest order, he prepared the way for assuming pre-eminence as an individual. . . .

Taught by experience that the love of well-being is the sole motive of human actions, he found himself in a position to distinguish the few cases, in which mutual interest might justify him in relying upon the assistance of his fellows; and also the still fewer cases in which a conflict of interests might give cause to suspect them. In the former case, he joined in the same herd with them, or at most in some kind of loose association, that laid no restraint on its members, and lasted no longer than the transitory occasion that formed it. In the latter case, every one sought his own private advantage, either by open force, if he thought himself strong enough, or by address and cunning, if he felt himself the weaker. . . .

Hurried on by the rapidity of time, by the abundance of things I have to say, and by the almost insensible progress of things in their beginnings, I pass over in an instant a multitude of ages; for the slower the events were in their succession, the more rapidly may they be described.

These first advances enabled men to make others with greater rapidity. In proportion as they grew enlightened, they grew industrious. They ceased to fall asleep under the first tree, or in the first cave that afforded them shelter; they invented several kinds of implements of hard and sharp stones, which they used to dig up the earth, and to cut wood; they then made huts out of branches, and afterwards learnt to plaster them over with mud and clay. This was the epoch of a first revolution, which established and distinguished families, and introduced a kind of property, in itself the source of a thousand quarrels and conflicts. As, however, the strongest were probably the first to build themselves huts which they felt themselves able to defend, it may be concluded that the weak found it much easier and safer to imitate, than to attempt to dislodge them: and of those who were once provided with huts, none could have any inducement to appropriate that of his neighbor; not indeed so much because it did not belong to him, as because it could be of no use, and he could not make himself master of it without exposing himself to a desperate battle with the family which occupied it.

The first expansions of the human heart were the effects of a novel situation, which united husbands and wives, fathers and children, under one roof. The habit of living together soon gave rise to the finest feelings known to humanity, conjugal love and paternal affection. Every family became a little society, the more united because liberty and reciprocal attachment were the only bonds of its union. The sexes, whose manner of life had been hitherto the same, began now to adopt different ways of living. The women became more sedentary, and accustomed themselves to mind the hut and their children, while the men went abroad in search of their common subsistence. From living a softer life, both sexes also began to lose something of their strength and ferocity: but, if individuals became to some extent less able to encounter wild beasts separately, they found it, on the other hand, easier to assemble and resist in common.

The simplicity and solitude of man's life in this new condition, the paucity of his wants, and the implements he had invented to satisfy them, left him a great deal of leisure, which he employed to furnish himself with many conveniences unknown to his fathers: and this was the first yoke he inadvertently imposed on himself, and the first source of the evils he prepared for his descendants. For, besides continuing thus to enervate both body and mind, these conveniences lost with use almost all their power to please, and even degenerated into real needs, till the want of them became far more disagreeable than the possession of them had been pleasant. Men would have been unhappy at the loss of them, though the possession did not make them happy. . . .

As ideas and feelings succeeded one another, and heart and head were brought into play, men continued to lay aside their original wildness; their private connections became every day more intimate as their limits extended. They accustomed themselves to assemble before their huts round a large tree; singing and dancing, the true offspring of love and leisure, became the amusement, or rather the occupation, of men and women thus assembled together with nothing else to do. Each one began to consider the rest, and to wish to be considered in turn; and thus a value came to be attached to public esteem. Whoever sang or danced best, whoever was the handsomest, the strongest, the most dexterous, or the most eloquent, came to be of most consideration; and this was the first step towards inequality, and at the same time towards vice. From these first distinctions arose on the one side vanity and contempt and on the other shame and envy: and the fermentation caused by these new leavens ended by producing combinations fatal to innocence and happiness. . . .

But it must be remarked that the society thus formed, and the relations thus established among men, required of them qualities different from those which they possessed from their primitive constitution. Morality began to appear in human actions, and every one, before the institution of law, was the only judge and avenger of the injuries done him, so that the goodness which was suitable in the pure state of nature was no longer proper in the new-born state of society. Punishments had to be made more severe, as opportunities of offending became more frequent, and the dread of vengeance had to take the place of the rigor of the law. Thus, though men had become less patient, and their natural compassion had already suffered some diminution, this period of expansion of the human faculties, keeping a just mean between the indolence of the primitive state and the petulant activity of our egoism, must have been the happiest and most stable of epochs. The more we reflect on it, the more we shall find that this state was the least subject to revolutions, and altogether the very best man could experience; so that he can have departed from it only through some fatal accident, which, for the public good, should never have happened. The example of savages, most of whom have been found in this state, seems to prove that men were meant to remain in it, that it is the real youth of the world, and that all subsequent advances have been apparently so many steps towards the perfection of the individual, but in reality towards the decrepitude of the species.

So long as men remained content with their rustic huts, so long as they were satisfied with clothes made of the skins of animals and sewn together with thorns and fishbones, adorned themselves only with feathers and shells, and continued to paint their bodies different colors, to improve and beautify their bows and arrows, and to make with sharp-edged stones fishing boats or clumsy musical instruments; in a word, so long as they undertook only what a single person could accomplish, and confined themselves to such arts as did not require the joint labor of several hands, they lived free, healthy, honest and happy lives, so long as their nature allowed, and as they continued to enjoy the pleasures of mutual and independent intercourse. But from the moment one man began to stand in need of the help of another; from the moment it appeared advantageous to any one man to have enough provisions for two, equality disappeared, property was introduced, work became indispensable, and vast forests became smiling fields, which man had to water with the sweat of his brow, and where slavery and misery were soon seen to germinate and grow up with the crops.

Metallurgy and agriculture were the two arts which produced this great revolution. The poets tell us it was gold and silver, but for the philosophers it was iron and corn which first civilized men and ruined humanity. Thus both were unknown to the savages of America, who for that reason are still savage: the other nations also seem to have continued in a state of barbarism while they practised only one of these arts. One of the best reasons, perhaps, why Europe has been, if not longer, at least more constantly and highly civilized than the rest of the world, is that it is at once the most abundant in iron and the most fertile in corn. . . .

No sooner were artificers wanted to smelt and forge iron, than others were required to maintain them; the more hands that were employed in manufactures, the fewer were left to provide for the common subsistence, though the number of mouths to be furnished with food remained the same: and as some required commodities in exchange for their iron, the rest at length discovered the method of making iron serve for the multiplication of commodities. By this means the arts of husbandry and agriculture were established on the one hand, and the art of working metals and multiplying their uses on the other. . . .

Behold then all human faculties developed, memory and imagination in full play, egoism interested, reason active, and the mind almost at the highest point of its perfection. Behold all the natural qualities in action, the rank and condition of every man assigned him; not merely his share of property and his power to serve or injure others, but also his wit, beauty, strength or skill, merit or talents: and these being the only qualities capable of commanding respect, it soon became necessary to possess or to affect them.

It now became the interest of men to appear what they really were not. To be and to seem became two totally different things; and from this distinction sprang insolent pomp and cheating trickery, with all the numerous vices that go in their train. On the other hand, free and independent as men were before, they were now, in consequence of a multiplicity of new wants, brought into subjection, as it were, to all nature, and particularly to one another; and each became in some degree a slave even in becoming the master of other men: if rich, they stood in need of the services of others; if poor, of their assistance; and even a middle condition did not enable them to do without one another. Man must now, therefore, have been perpetually employed in getting others to interest themselves in his lot, and in making them, apparently at least, if not really, find their advantage in promoting his own. Thus he must have been sly and artful in his behavior to some, and imperious and cruel to others; being under a kind of necessity to ill-use all the persons of whom he stood in need, when he could not frighten them into compliance, and did not judge it his interest to be useful to them. Insatiable ambition, the thirst of raising their respective fortunes, not so much from real want as from the desire to surpass others, inspired all men with a vile propensity to injure one another, and with a secret jealousy, which is the more dangerous, as it puts on the mask of benevolence, to carry its point with greater security. In a word, there arose rivalry and competition on the one hand, and conflicting interests on the other, together with a secret desire on both of profiting at

J. J. ROUSSEAU.

the expense of others. All these evils were the first effects of property, and the inseparable attendants of growing inequality.

Before the invention of signs to represent riches, wealth could hardly consist in anything but lands and cattle, the only real possessions men can have. But, when inheritances so increased in number and extent as to occupy the whole of the land, and to border on one another, one man could aggrandize himself only at the expense of another; at the same time the supernumeraries, who had been too weak or too indolent to make such acquisitions, and had grown poor without sustaining any loss, because, while they saw everything change around them, they remained still the same, were obliged to receive their subsistence, or steal it, from the rich; and this soon bred, according to their different characters, dominion and slavery, or violence and rapine. The wealthy, on their part, had no sooner begun to taste the pleasure of command than they disdained all others, and, using their old slaves to acquire new, thought of nothing but subduing and enslaving their neighbors, like ravenous wolves which, having once tasted human flesh, despise every other food and thenceforth seek only men to devour.

Thus, as the most powerful or the most miserable considered their might or misery as a kind of right to the possessions of others, equivalent, in their opinion, to that of property, the destruction of equality was attended by the most terrible disorders. Usurpations by the rich, robbery by the poor, and unbridled passions of both, suppressed the cries of natural compassion and the still feeble voice of justice, and filled men with avarice, ambition and vice. Between the title of the strongest and that of the first occupier, there arose perpetual conflicts, which never ended but in battles and bloodshed. The new-born state of society thus gave rise to a horrible state of war; men thus harassed and depraved were no longer capable of retracing their steps or renouncing the fatal acquisitions they had made, but, laboring by the abuse of the faculties which do them honor, merely to their own confusion, brought themselves to the brink of ruin.

Attonitus novitate mali, divesque miserque,
Effugere optat opes; et quae modo voverat odit.[1]

It is impossible that men should not at length have reflected on so wretched a situation, and on the calamities that overwhelmed them. The rich, in particular, must have felt how much they suffered by a constant state of war, of which they bore all the expense; and in which, though all risked their lives, they alone risked their property. Besides, however speciously they might disguise their usurpations, they knew that they were founded on precarious and false titles; so that, if others took from them by force what they themselves had gained by force, they would have no reason to complain. Even those who had been enriched by their own industry, could hardly base their proprietorship on better claims. It was in vain to repeat: "I built this well; I gained this spot by my industry." Who gave you your standing, it might be answered, and what right have you to demand payment of us for doing what we never asked you to do? Do you not know that numbers of your fellow-creatures are starving, for want of what you have too much of? You ought to have had the express and universal consent of mankind, before appropriating more of the common subsistence than you needed for your own maintenance. Destitute of valid reasons to justify and sufficient strength to defend himself, able to crush individuals with ease, but easily crushed himself by a troop of bandits, one against all, and incapable, on account of mutual jealousy, of joining with his equals against numerous enemies united by the common hope of plunder, the rich man, thus urged by necessity, conceived at length the profoundest plan that ever entered the mind of man: this was to employ in his favor the forces of those who attacked him, to make allies of his adversaries, to inspire them with different maxims, and to give them other institutions as favorable to himself as the law of nature was unfavorable.

[1] Ovid, *Metamorphoses,* XI, 127.
Rich and yet poor, shocked at his new-found ills,
He would fly from wealth, and hates what he had sought.

With this view, after having represented to his neighbors the horror of a situation which armed every man against the rest, and made their possessions as burdensome to them as their wants, and in which no safety could be expected either in riches or in poverty, he readily devised plausible arguments to make them close with his design. "Let us join," said he, "to guard the weak from oppression, to restrain the ambitious, and secure to every man the possession of what belongs to him: let us institute rules of justice and peace, to which all without exception may be obliged to conform; rules that may in some measure make amends for the caprices of fortune, by subjecting equally the powerful and the weak to the observance of reciprocal obligations. Let us, in a word, instead of turning our forces against ourselves, collect them in a supreme power which may govern us by wise laws, protect and defend all the members of the association, repulse their common enemies, and maintain eternal harmony among us."

Far fewer words to this purpose would have been enough to impose on men so barbarous and easily seduced; especially as they had too many disputes among themselves to do without arbitrators, and too much ambition and avarice to go long without masters. All ran headlong to their chains, in hopes of securing their liberty; for they had just wit enough to perceive the advantages of political institutions, without experience enough to enable them to foresee the dangers. The most capable of foreseeing the dangers were the very persons who expected to benefit by them; and even the most prudent judged it not inexpedient to sacrifice one part of their freedom to ensure the rest; as a wounded man has his arm cut off to save the rest of his body.

Such was, or may well have been, the origin of society and law, which bound new fetters on the poor, and gave new powers to the rich; which irretrievably destroyed natural liberty, eternally fixed the law of property and inequality, converted clever usurpation into unalterable right, and, for the advantage of a few ambitious individuals, subjected all mankind to perpetual labor, slavery and wretchedness. It is easy to see how the establishment of one community made that of all the rest necessary, and how, in order to make head against united forces, the rest of mankind had to unite in turn. . . .

I have endeavored to trace the origin and progress of inequality, and the institution and abuse of political societies, as far as these are capable of being deduced from the nature of man merely by the light of reason, and independently of those sacred dogmas which give the sanction of divine right to sovereign authority. It follows from this survey that, as there is hardly any inequality in the state of nature, all the inequality which now prevails owes its strength and growth to the development of our faculties and the advance of the human mind, and becomes at last permanent and legitimate by the establishment of property and laws. Secondly, it follows that moral inequality, authorized by positive right alone, clashes with natural right, whenever it is not proportionate to physical inequality—a distinction which sufficiently determines what we ought to think of that species of inequality which prevails in all civilized countries; since it is plainly contrary to the law of nature, however defined, that children should command old men, fools wise men, and that the privileged few should gorge themselves with superfluities while the starving multitude are in want of the bare necessities of life.

The Social Contract (1762)

In this work Rousseau explains theoretically how natural man may be denaturalized and remolded into civil man, how civil liberty may be substituted for natural liberty, and how equality may be regained through a society founded on the general will of a sovereign people. The social contract, logical basis of all legitimate authority, is the fundamental (if sometimes forgotten) implication of every political institution.

Rousseau deals in the first book with the general principles of the social contract. No man has any natural authority over his fellow-men, no king rules by divine right. The individual as the basic political unit surrenders his natural rights to the State, in which he is both sovereign and subject. The concept of civil rights supplants that of natural forces. Might does not make right, which remains always as a supreme court of appeal and justifies revolution against tyranny or the usurpation of political powers.

The general subject of the second book is the sovereignty of the people, an inalienable right fundamental to all legitimate government. Rousseau's conception of the general will is a quite debatable abstraction, which degenerates perforce into the will of the majority. But to Rousseau, the body politic was a personal organism whose general will was more than the sum of separate wills and was called the voice of the people, or, since it could not err, the voice of God.

In the third book, Rousseau treats three possible forms of government, democratic, aristocratic, and monarchic. Sharing Plato's distrust of democratic forms, he admits, like Montesquieu, that the machinery of government for any given people should be determined by practical as well as by moral and theoretical factors.

In the fourth book, Rousseau establishes a civic profession of faith and concludes that all minorities must conform to the general will or be banished from the State. An ardent individualist in his other writings, he reveals himself in The Social Contract *as a no less thoroughgoing collectivist. A fundamental clause of the contract: "the total abandonment of each associate of all his rights to the community as a whole," sounds a note of absolutism or totalitarianism.*

It is especially true of Rousseau that what he meant to say has been of less importance historically than what subsequent generations have believed that he said. Partly because of his very oscillations and ambiguities, he has exercised a tremendous dual influence on political thinking. His defense of the inalienable rights of man and of the sovereignty of the people were echoed in the American

Declaration of Independence and the French Declaration of the Rights of Man and of the Citizen. His individualistic tendencies appealed to such writers as John Stuart Mill, Emerson, Thoreau and Whitman. The collectivistic aspects were developed by Kant, Hegel, Fichte and Marx.

The Social Contract or Principles of Political Right

I mean to inquire if, in the civil order, there can be any sure and legitimate rule of administration, men being taken as they are and laws as they might be. In this inquiry I shall endeavor always to unite what right sanctions with what is prescribed by interest, in order that justice and utility may in no case be divided.

I enter upon my task without proving the importance of the subject. I shall be asked if I am a prince or a legislator, to write on politics. I answer that I am neither, and that is why I do so. If I were a prince or a legislator, I should not waste time in saying what wants doing; I should do it, or hold my peace.

As I was born a citizen of a free State, and a member of the Sovereign, I feel that, however feeble the influence my voice can have on public affairs, the right of voting on them makes it my duty to study them: and I am happy, when I reflect upon governments, to find my inquiries always furnish me with new reasons for loving that of my own country.

Subject of the First Book

Man was born free; and everywhere he is in chains. One thinks himself the master of others, and still remains a greater slave than they. How did this change come about? I do not know. What can make it legitimate? That question I think I can answer.

If I took into account only force, and the effects derived from it, I should say: "As long as a people is compelled to obey, and obeys, it does well; as soon as it can shake off the yoke, and shakes it off, it does still better; for, regaining its liberty by the same right as took it away, either it is justified in resuming it, or there was no justification for those who took it away." But the social order is a sacred right which is the basis of all rights. Nevertheless, this right does not come from nature, and must therefore be founded on conventions. Before coming to that, I have to prove what I have just asserted. (I, 1)

The Right of the Strongest

The strongest is never strong enough to be always the master, unless he transforms strength into right, and obedience into duty. Hence the right of the strongest, which, though to all seeming meant ironically, is really laid down as a fundamental principle. But are we never to have an explanation of this phrase? Force is a physical power, and I fail to see what moral effect it can have. To yield to force is an act of necessity, not of will—at the most, an act of prudence. In what sense can it be a duty?

Suppose for a moment that this so-called "right" exists. I maintain that the sole result is a mass of inexplicable nonsense. For, if force creates right, the effect changes with the cause: every force that is greater than the first succeeds to its right. As soon as it is possible to disobey with impunity, disobedience is legitimate; and, the strongest being always in the right, the only thing that matters is to act so as to become the strongest. But what kind of right is that which perishes when force fails? If we must obey perforce, there is no need to obey because we ought; and if we are not forced to obey, we are under no obligation to do so. Clearly, the word "right" adds nothing to force: in this connection, it means absolutely nothing.

Obey the powers that be. If this means yield to force, it is a good precept, but superfluous: I can answer for its never being violated. All power comes from God, I admit; but so does all sickness: does that mean that we are forbidden to call in the doctor? A brigand surprises me at the edge of a wood: must I not merely surrender my purse on compulsion; but, even if I could withhold it, am

I in conscience bound to give it up? For certainly the pistol he holds is also a power.

Let us then admit that force does not create right, and that we are obliged to obey only legitimate powers. In that case, my original question recurs. . . . (I, 3)

Slavery

Since no man has a natural authority over his fellow, and force creates no right, we must conclude that conventions form the basis of all legitimate authority among men.

If an individual, says Grotius, can alienate his liberty and make himself the slave of a master, why could not a whole people do the same and make itself subject to a king? There are in this passage plenty of ambiguous words which would need explaining; but let us confine ourselves to the word *alienate*. To alienate is to give or to sell. Now, a man who becomes the slave of another does not give himself; he sells himself, at the least for his subsistence: but for what does a people sell itself? A king is so far from furnishing his subjects with their subsistence that he gets his own only from them; and, according to Rabelais, kings do not live on nothing. Do subjects then give their persons on condition that the king takes their goods also? I fail to see what they have left to preserve.

It will be said that the despot assures his subjects civil tranquillity. Granted; but what do they gain, if the wars his ambition brings down upon them, his insatiable avidity, and the vexatious conduct of his ministers press harder on them than their own dissensions would have done? What do they gain, if the very tranquillity they enjoy is one of their miseries? Tranquillity is found also in dungeons; but is that enough to make them desirable places to live in? The Greeks imprisoned in the cave of the Cyclops lived there very tranquilly, while they were awaiting their turn to be devoured.

To say that a man gives himself gratuitously is to say what is absurd and inconceivable; such an act is null and illegitimate, from the mere fact that he who does it is out of his mind. To say the same of a whole people is to suppose a people of madmen; and madness creates no right.

Even if each man could alienate himself, he could not alienate his children: they are born men and free; their liberty belongs to them, and no one but they has the right to dispose of it. Before they come to years of discretion, the father can, in their name, lay down conditions for their preservation and well-being, but he cannot give them irrevocably and without conditions: such a gift is contrary to the ends of nature, and exceeds the rights of paternity. It would therefore be necessary, in order to legitimize an arbitrary government, that in every generation the people should be in a position to accept or reject it; but, were this so, the government would be no longer arbitrary.

To renounce liberty is to renounce being a man, to surrender the rights of humanity and even its duties. For him who renounces everything no indemnity is possible. Such a renunciation is incompatible with man's nature; to remove all liberty from his will is to remove all morality from his acts. Finally, it is an empty and contradictory convention that sets up, on the one side, absolute authority, and, on the other, unlimited obedience. Is it not clear that we can be under no obligation to a person from whom we have the right to exact everything? Does not this condition alone, in the absence of equivalence or exchange, in itself involve the nullity of the act? For what right can my slave have against me, when all that he has belongs to me, and, his right being mine, this right of mine against myself is a phrase devoid of meaning? . . . (I, 4)

That We Must Always Go Back to a First Convention

Even if I granted all that I have been refuting, the friends of despotism would be no better off. There will always be a great difference between subduing a multitude and ruling a society. Even if scattered individuals were successively enslaved by one man, however numerous they might be, I still see no more than a master and his slaves, and certainly not a people and its ruler; I see what may be termed an aggregation, but not an association; there is as yet neither public good nor body politic. The man in question, even if he has enslaved half the world, is still only an individual; his interest, apart from that of others, is still a purely private interest. If this same man comes to die, his empire, after him, remains scattered and without unity, as an oak falls and dissolves into a heap of ashes when the fire has consumed it.

A people, says Grotius, can give itself to a king. Then according to Grotius, a people is a people before it gives itself. The gift is itself a civil act, and implies public deliberation. It would be better, before examining the act by which a people gives itself to a king, to examine that by which it has become a people; for this act, being necessarily prior to the other, is the true foundation of society. . . . (I, 5)

The Social Compact

I suppose men to have reached the point at which the obstacles in the way of their preservation in the state of nature show their power of resistance to be greater than the resources at the disposal of each individual for his maintenance in that state. That primitive condition can then subsist no longer; and the human race would perish unless it changed its manner of existence.

But, as men cannot engender new forces, but only unite and direct existing ones, they have no other means of preserving themselves than the formation, by aggregation, of a sum of forces great enough to overcome the resistance. These they have to bring into play by means of a single motive power, and cause to act in concert.

This sum of forces can arise only where several persons come together: but, as the force and liberty of each man are the chief instruments of his self-preservation, how can he pledge them without harming his own interests, and neglecting the care he owes to himself? This difficulty, in its bearing on my present subject, may be stated in the following terms:

"The problem is to find a form of association which will defend and protect with the whole common force the person and goods of each associate, and in which each, while uniting himself with all, may still obey himself alone, and remain as free as before." This is the fundamental problem of which the *Social Contract* provides the solution.

The clauses of this contract are so determined by the nature of the act that the slightest modification would make them vain and ineffective; so that, although they have perhaps never been formally set forth, they are everywhere the same and everywhere tacitly admitted and recognized, until, on the violation of the social compact, each regains his original rights and resumes his natural liberty, while losing the conventional liberty in favor of which he renounced it.

These clauses, properly understood, may be reduced to one—the total alienation of each associate, together with all his rights, to the whole community; for, in the first place, as each gives himself absolutely, the conditions are the same for all; and, this being so, no one has any interest in making them burdensome to others.

Moreover, the alienation being without reserve, the union is as perfect as it can be, and no associate has anything more to demand: for, if the individuals retained certain rights, as there would be no common superior to decide between them and the public, each, being on one point his own judge, would ask to be so on all; the state of nature would thus continue, and the association would necessarily become inoperative or tyrannical.

Finally, each man, in giving himself to all, gives himself to nobody; and as there is no associate over which he does not acquire the same right as he yields others over himself, he gains an equivalent for everything he loses, and an increase of force for the preservation of what he has.

If then we discard from the social compact what is not

of its essence, we shall find that it reduces itself to the following terms:

"*Each of us puts his person and all his power in common under the supreme direction of the general will, and, in our corporate capacity, we receive each member as an indivisible part of the whole.*"

At once, in place of the individual personality of each contracting party, this act of association creates a moral and collective body, composed of as many members as the assembly contains voters, and receiving from this act its unity, its common identity, its life, and its will. This public person, so formed by the union of all other persons, formerly took the name of *city*, and now takes that of *Republic* or *body politic;* it is called by its members *State* when passive, *Sovereign* when active, and *Power* when compared with others like itself. Those who are associated in it take collectively the name of *people*, and severally are called *citizens*, as sharing in the sovereign power, and *subjects*, as being under the laws of the State. But these terms are often confused and taken one for another: it is enough to know how to distinguish them when they are being used with precision. (I, 6)

The Civil State

The passage from the state of nature to the civil state produces a very remarkable change in man, by substituting justice for instinct in his conduct, and giving his actions the morality they had formerly lacked. Then only, when the voice of duty takes the place of physical impulses and right of appetite, does man, who so far had considered only himself, find that he is forced to act on different principles, and to consult his reason before listening to his inclinations. Although, in this state, he deprives himself of some advantages which he got from nature, he gains in return others so great, his faculties are so stimulated and developed, his ideas so extended, his feelings so ennobled, and his whole soul so uplifted, that, did not the abuses of this new condition often degrade him below that which he left, he would be bound to bless continually the happy moment which took him from it for ever, and, instead of a stupid and unimaginative animal, made him an intelligent being and a man.

Let us draw up the whole account in terms easily commensurable. What man loses by the social contract is his natural liberty and an unlimited right to everything he tries to get and succeeds in getting; what he gains is civil liberty and the proprietorship of all he possesses. If we are to avoid mistake in weighing one against the other, we must clearly distinguish natural liberty, which is bounded only by the strength of the individual, from civil liberty, which is limited by the general will; and possession, which is merely the effect of force or the right of the first occupier, from property, which can be founded only on a positive title.

We might, over and above all this, add, to what man acquires in the civil state, moral liberty, which alone makes him truly master of himself; for the mere impulse of appetite is slavery, while obedience to a law which we prescribe to ourselves is liberty. But I have already said too much on this head, and the philosophical meaning of the word liberty does not concern us here. (I, 8)

That Sovereignty Is Inalienable

The first and most important deduction from the principles we have so far laid down is that the general will alone can direct the State according to the object for which it was instituted, i.e. the common good: for if the clashing of particular interests made the establishment of societies necessary, the agreement of these very interests made it possible. The common element in these different interests is what forms the social tie; and, were there no point of agreement between them all, no society could exist. It is solely on the basis of this common interest that every society should be governed.

I hold then that Sovereignty, being nothing less than the exercise of the general will, can never be alienated, and that the Sovereign, who is no less than a collective being, cannot be represented except by himself: the power indeed may be transmitted, but not the will.

In reality, if it is not impossible for a particular will to agree on some point with the general will, it is at least impossible for the agreement to be lasting and constant; for the particular will tends, by its very nature, to partiality, while the general will tends to equality. It is even more impossible to have any guarantee of this agreement; for even if it should always exist, it would be the effect not of art, but of chance. The Sovereign may indeed say: "I now will actually what this man wills, or at least what he says he wills"; but it cannot say: "What he wills to-morrow, I too shall will" because it is absurd for the will to bind itself for the future, nor is it incumbent on any will to consent to anything that is not for the good of the being who wills. If then the people promises simply to obey, by that very act it dissolves itself and loses what makes it a people; the moment a master exists, there is no longer a Sovereign, and from that moment the body politic has ceased to exist.

This does not mean that the commands of the rulers cannot pass for general wills, so long as the Sovereign, being free to oppose them, offers no opposition. In such a case, universal silence is taken to imply the consent of the people. This will be explained at greater length. (II, 1)

Whether the General Will Is Fallible

It follows from what has gone before that the general will is always right and tends to the public advantage; but it does not follow that the deliberations of the people are always equally correct. Our will is always for our own good, but we do not always see what that is; the people is never corrupted, but it is often deceived, and on such occasions only does it seem to will what is bad.

There is often a great deal of difference between the will of all and the general will; the latter considers only the common interest, while the former takes private interest into account, and is no more than a sum of particular wills: but take away from these same wills the pluses and minuses that cancel one another, and the general will remains as the sum of the differences. . . . (II, 3)

The Limits of the Sovereign Power

If the State is a moral person whose life is in the union of its members, and if the most important of its cares is the care for its own preservation, it must have a universal and compelling force, in order to move and dispose each part as may be most advantageous to the whole. As nature gives each man absolute power over all his members, the social compact gives the body politic absolute power over all its members also; and it is this power which, under the direction of the general will, bears, as I have said, the name of Sovereignty.

But, besides the public person, we have to consider the private persons composing it, whose life and liberty are naturally independent of it. We are bound then to distinguish clearly between the respective rights of the citizens and the Sovereign, and between the duties the former have to fulfil as subjects, and the natural rights they should enjoy as men.

Each man alienates, I admit, by the social compact, only such part of his powers, goods and liberty as it is important for the community to control; but it must also be granted that the Sovereign is sole judge of what is important.

Every service a citizen can render the State he ought to render as soon as the Sovereign demands it; but the Sovereign, for its part, cannot impose upon its subjects any fetters that are useless to the community, nor can it even wish to do so; for no more by the law of reason than by the law of nature can anything occur without a cause.

The undertakings which bind us to the social body are obligatory only because they are mutual; and their nature is such that in fulfilling them we cannot work for others without working for ourselves. Why is it that the general will is always in the right, and that all continually will the happiness of each one, unless it is because there is not a man who does not think of "each" as meaning him, and consider himself in voting for all? This proves that equality of rights and the idea of justice which such equality creates originate in the preference each man gives to himself, and accordingly in the very nature of man. It proves that the general will, to be really such, must be general in its object as well as its essence; that it must both come from all and apply to all; and that it loses its natural rectitude when it is directed to some particular and determinate object, because in such a case we are judging of something foreign to us, and have no true principle of equity to guide us. . . .

We can see from this that the sovereign power, absolute, sacred and inviolable as it is, does not and cannot exceed the limits of general conventions, and that every man may dispose at will of such goods and liberty as these conventions leave him; so that the Sovereign never has a right to lay more charges on one subject than on another, because, in that case, the question becomes particular, and ceases to be within its competency.

When these distinctions have once been admitted, it is seen to be so untrue that there is, in the social contract, any real renunciation on the part of the individuals, that the position in which they find themselves as a result of the contract is really preferable to that in which they were before. Instead of a renunciation, they have made an advantageous exchange: instead of an uncertain and precarious way of living they have got one that is better and more secure; instead of natural independence they have got liberty, instead of the power to harm others security for themselves, and instead of their strength, which others might overcome, a right which social union makes invincible. Their very life, which they have devoted to the State, is by it constantly protected; and when they risk it in the State's defence, what more are they doing than giving back what they have received from it? What are they doing that they would not do more often and with greater danger in the state of nature, in which they would inevitably have to fight battles at the peril of their lives in defence of that which is the means of their preservation? All have indeed to fight when their country needs them; but then no one has ever to fight for himself. Do we not gain something by running, on behalf of what gives us our security, only some of the risks we should have to run for ourselves, as soon as we lost it? (II, 4)

The Right of Life and Death

The question is often asked how individuals, having no right to dispose of their own lives, can transfer to the Sovereign a right which they do not possess. The difficulty of answering this question seems to me to lie in its being wrongly stated. Every man has a right to risk his own life in order to preserve it. Has it ever been said that a man who throws himself out of the window to escape from a fire is guilty of suicide? Has such a crime ever been laid to the charge of him who perishes in a storm because, when he went on board, he knew of the danger?

The social treaty has for its end the preservation of the contracting parties. He who wills the end wills the means also, and the means must involve some risks, and even some losses. He who wishes to preserve his life at others' expense should also, when it is necessary, be ready to give it up for their sake. Furthermore, the citizen is no longer the judge of the dangers to which the law desires him to expose himself; and when the prince says to him: "It is expedient for the State that you should die," he ought to die, because it is only on that condition that he has been living in security up to the present, and because his life is no longer a mere bounty of nature, but a gift made conditionally by the State.

The death-penalty inflicted upon criminals may be looked on in much the same light: it is in order that we may not fall victims to an assassin that we consent to die if we ourselves turn assassins. In this treaty, so far from disposing of our own lives, we think only of securing them, and it is not to be assumed that any of the parties then expects to get hanged. . . . (II, 5)

Law

By the social compact we have given the body politic existence and life; we have now by legislation to give it movement and will. For the original act by which the body is formed and united still in no respect determines what it ought to do for its preservation.

Laws are, properly speaking, only the conditions of civil association. The people, being subject to the laws, ought to be their author: the conditions of the society ought to be regulated solely by those who come together to form it. But how are they to regulate them? Is it to be by common agreement, by a sudden inspiration? Has the body politic an organ to declare its will? Who can give it the foresight to formulate and announce its acts in advance? Or how is it to announce them in the hour of need? How can a blind multitude, which often does not know what it wills, because it rarely knows what is good for it, carry out for itself so great and difficult an enterprise as a system of legislation? Of itself the people wills always the good, but of itself it by no means always sees it. The general will is always in the right, but the judgment which guides it is not always enlightened. It must be got to see objects as they are, and sometimes as they ought to appear to it; it must be shown the good road it is in search of, secured from the seductive influences of individual wills, taught to see times and spaces as a series, and made to weigh the attractions of present and sensible advantages against the danger of distant and hidden evils. The individuals see the good they reject; the public wills the good it does not see. All stand equally in need of guidance. The former must be compelled to bring their wills into conformity with their reason; the latter must be taught to know what it wills. If that is done, public enlightenment leads to the union of understanding and will in the social body: the parts are made to work exactly together, and the whole is raised to its highest power. This makes a legislator necessary. (II, 6)

The Legislator

In order to discover the rules of society best suited to nations, a superior intelligence beholding all the passions of men without experiencing any of them would be needed. This intelligence would have to be wholly unrelated to our nature, while knowing it through and through; its happiness would have to be independent of us, and yet ready to occupy itself with ours; and lastly, it would have, in the march of time, to look forward to a distant glory, and, working in one century, to be able to enjoy in the next. It would take gods to give men laws. . . .

He who dares to undertake the making of a people's institutions ought to feel himself capable, so to speak, of changing human nature, of transforming each individual, who is by himself a complete and solitary whole, into part of a greater whole from which he in a manner receives his life and being; of altering man's constitution for the purpose of strengthening it; and of substituting a partial and moral existence for the physical and independent existence nature has conferred on us all. He must, in a word, take away from man his own resources and give him instead new ones alien to him, and incapable of being made use of without the help of other men. The more completely these natural resources are annihilated, the greater and the more lasting are those which he acquires, and the more stable and perfect the new institutions; so that if each citizen is nothing and can do nothing without the rest, and the resources acquired by the whole are equal or superior to the aggregate of the resources of all the individuals, it may be said that legislation is at the highest possible point of perfection.

The legislator occupies in every respect an extraordinary position in the State. If he should do so by reason of his genius, he does so no less by reason of his office, which is neither magistracy, nor Sovereignty. This office, which sets up the Republic, nowhere enters into its constitution; it is an individual and superior function, which has nothing in common with human empire; for if he who holds command over men ought not to have command over the laws, he who has command over the laws ought not any more to have it over men; or else his laws would be the ministers of his passions and would often merely serve to perpetuate his injustices: his private aims would inevitably mar the sanctity of his work. . . . (II, 7)

Voting

. . . There is but one law which, from its nature, needs unanimous consent. This is the social compact; for civil association is the most voluntary of all acts. Every man being born free and his own master, no one, under any pretext whatsoever, can make any man subject without his consent. To decide that the son of a slave is born a slave is to decide that he is not born a man.

If then there are opponents when the social compact is made, their opposition does not invalidate the contract, but merely prevents them from being included in it. They are foreigners among citizens. When the State is instituted, residence constitutes consent; to dwell within its territory is to submit to the Sovereign.

Apart from this primitive contract, the vote of the majority always binds all the rest. This follows from the contract itself. But it is asked how a man can be both free and forced to conform to wills that are not his own. How are the opponents at once free and subject to laws they have not agreed to?

I retort that the question is wrongly put. The citizen gives his consent to all the laws, including those which are passed in spite of his opposition, and even those which punish him when he dares to break any of them. The constant will of all the members of the State is the general will; by virtue of it they are citizens and free. When in the popular assembly a law is proposed, what the people is asked is not exactly whether it approves or rejects the proposal, but whether it is in conformity with the general will, which is their will. Each man, in giving his vote, states his opinion on that point; and the general will is found by counting votes. When therefore the opinion that is contrary to my own prevails, this proves neither more nor less than that I was mistaken, and that what I thought to be the general will was not so. If my particular opinion had carried the day I should have achieved the opposite of what was my will; and it is in that case that I should not have been free.

This presupposes, indeed, that all the qualities of the general will still reside in the majority: when they cease to do so, whatever side a man may take, liberty is no longer possible. . . .

There are two general rules that may serve to regulate this relation. First, the more grave and important the questions discussed, the nearer should the opinion that is to prevail approach unanimity. Secondly, the more the matter in hand calls for speed, the smaller the prescribed difference in the numbers of votes may be allowed to become: where an instant decision has to be reached, a majority of one vote should be enough. The first of these two rules seems more in harmony with the laws, and the second with practical affairs. In any case, it is the combination of them that gives the best proportions for determining the majority necessary. (IV, 2)

Civil Religion

. . . The right which the social compact gives the Sovereign over the subjects does not, we have seen, exceed the limits of public expediency. The subjects then owe the Sovereign an account of their opinions only to such an extent as they matter to the community. Now, it matters very much to the community that each citizen should have a religion. That will make him love his duty; but the dogmas of that religion concern the State and its members only so far as they have reference to morality and to the duties which he who professes them is bound to do to others. Each man may have, over and above, what opinions he pleases, without its being the Sovereign's business to take cognizance of them; for, as the Sovereign has no authority in the other world, whatever the lot of its subjects may be in the life to come, that is not its business, provided they are good citizens in this life.

There is therefore a purely civil profession of faith of which the Sovereign should fix the articles, not exactly as religious dogmas, but as social sentiments without which a man cannot be a good citizen or a faithful subject. While it can compel no one to believe them, it can banish from the State whoever does not believe them—it can banish him, not for impiety, but as an anti-social being, incapable of truly loving the laws and justice, and of sacrificing, at need, his life to his duty. If any one, after publicly recognizing these dogmas, behaves as if he does not believe them, let him be punished by death: he has committed the worst of all crimes, that of lying before the law.

The dogmas of civil religion ought to be few, simple and exactly worded, without explanation or commentary. The existence of a mighty, intelligent and benficent Divinity, possessed of foresight and providence, the life to come, the happiness of the just, the punishment of the wicked, the sanctity of the social contract and the laws: these are its positive dogmas. Its negative dogmas I confine to one, intolerance, which is a part of the cults we have rejected.

Those who distinguish civil from theological intolerance are, to my mind, mistaken. The two forms are inseparable. It is impossible to live at peace with those we regard as damned; to love them would be to hate God who punishes them: we positively must either reclaim or torment them. Wherever theological intolerance is admitted, it must inevitably have some civil effect; and as soon as it has such an effect, the Sovereign is no longer

Sovereign even in the temporal sphere: thenceforth priests are the real masters, and kings only their ministers.

Now that there is and can be no longer an exclusive national religion, tolerance should be given to all religions that tolerate others, so long as their dogmas contain nothing contrary to the duties of citizenship. But whoever dares to say "Outside the Church is no salvation," ought to be driven from the State, unless the State is the Church, and the prince the pontiff. Such a dogma is good only in a theocratic government; in any other, it is fatal. . . . (IV, 8)

Emile: A Treatise on Education (1762)

Close association with the wealthy D'Epinay family in Paris in the middle fifties aroused Rousseau's interest in education. The private school attended by the son in the family had been so psychologically unsound in its educational methods that the boy was put in the hands of a private tutor. This aristocratic background explains much of the artificiality of Rousseau's system. Emile *remains, however, as the fountainhead of modern educational theory and marks a great advance in educational psychology.*

In natural or "progressive" education, the question of timing is paramount. Rousseau divides the child's life roughly into four periods, or ages. In infancy, children should not be too tightly swaddled, and mothers should nurse their children for their mutual physical and mental health. Children learn by experience, not by precept. Rousseau writes an impassioned manifesto in favor of childhood as an end in itself, at a time when infant mortality was deplorably high.

The years from three to twelve, Rousseau calls the age of sensation, when education should be almost entirely negative. Emile at the age of twelve is thus a natural healthy savage, without prejudices or bookish learning. Having now reached the age of reason, he studies history, the heroics of Plutarch's Lives, *and the practical sciences. A strongly developed social conscience, quite remarkable for the times, led Rousseau to recommend that Emile learn a trade in order to become self-reliant and self-sufficient in the service of society.*

For Rousseau, the age of sentiment, or feeling, succeeds the age of reason and makes of Emile a loving, sensitive, moral and religious being. Against the objections of the philosophes, *which reason was unable to answer, he ended his work with the sentimental, but quite unorthodox, affirmation of his belief in God and of his Christian sympathies, which led to his banishment.*

The rhetorical flourish at the beginning of Emile: *"Everything is good as it comes from the hand of the Creator; everything degenerates in the hands of man," absolves God from the evil inherent in man as a social animal and also means that nothing should interfere with the normal stages of the child's natural development. Following nature now also means following the dictates of the divinely inspired voice of conscience, the voice of the soul as opposed to the call of the body.*

Emile

. . . Nothing is more uncertain than the life span of individual man; very few men reach old age. The greatest risks are incurred at the beginning of life: the less we have lived the less we may expect to live. Of the children that are born half at most grow to adolescence; thus it is probable that your pupil will not attain the age of manhood.

What must we think then of the barbarous education which sacrifices the present for an uncertain future, which surrounds a child with all sorts of fetters and begins by making him wretched in order to prepare him for a hypothetical future happiness that he will probably never live to enjoy? Even if I supposed this educational objective to be reasonable, how could I behold without indignation poor unfortunates bowed beneath an insupportable yoke and condemned like galley-slaves to perpetual labor, with no assurance that all this attention will ever be of service to them? The age of gayety is passed over amid tears, chastisement, threats and slavery. We torment the poor child for his own good and do not see that we are summoning death, which will seize him in the midst of this sad business. Who knows how many children perish the victims of a father's or tutor's extravagant wisdom? Happy to escape their cruelty, the only advantage children derive from the ills they have been made to suffer is to die without regretting life, of which they have tasted only the sorrows.

Men, be humane, that is your first duty: be so for all conditions, all ages, all that is germane to man. What does wisdom avail you except as it concerns humanity? Cherish childhood, look with favor on its games, its pleasures, its friendly instincts. Who of you has not at times longed for that age when laughter is always bursting forth and the soul is ever at peace? Why do you want to rob these young innocents of the pleasures of such brief and fleeting hours and of such precious gifts, which they are too young to misuse? Why wish to fill with bitterness and grief these early years that pass so quickly and will not return for them any more than for us? Fathers, do you know the moment that death awaits your child? Do not prepare for yourselves a life of sorrow by robbing them of the brief moment that nature gives them: as soon as they are able to sense the pleasure of existing, see to it that they enjoy themselves, see to it that at whatever hour God calls them, they do not die without having tasted of life. . . .

Let us not forget our human condition and pursue idle fancies. Humanity has its place in the general order; childhood, too, in the span of human life; we must look upon man in manhood and the child in childhood. To assign to each one his place and establish him in it, to order the human passions in accordance with man's constitution, that is all we can do for his well being. The rest depends on extraneous circumstances that are beyond our power to control. . . .

May I venture to state here that the greatest, most important, and most useful rule of all education is not to save time, but to lose it? Gentle reader, pardon my paradoxes: they follow necessarily upon reflection; and whatever you may say, I would rather be paradoxical than prejudiced. The most dangerous period of human life extends from birth to the age of twelve. That is the time when error and vice take root before there is any counteracting faculty; and when that faculty develops, the roots are so deep that it is too late to pull them up. If children jumped suddenly from the breast to the age of reason, the education that they now receive would suffice; but in the natural process of growth, they need an entirely different one. Their minds should be left uncultivated until all their faculties have developed; for until then it is impossible for them to see the light that you offer as a guide or to follow, in the immense realm of ideas, a path that reason traces ever so faintly even for the trained eye.

Early education should therefore be purely negative. It consists, not in teaching virtue or truth, but in protecting the heart from vice and the mind from error. If you could let your pupil alone and see that he is left alone; if you could bring him up sane and sound to the age of twelve, without his being able to tell his right hand from his left, then from his very first lessons, the eyes of his understanding would be open to reason; free from all prejudices and preconceptions, his mind would present no obstacle to the full effect of your teaching; and from a purely negative beginning, you would achieve an educational prodigy.

Proceed counter to customary practice and you will almost always be right. By trying to make a learned man out of a child, fathers and tutors begin all too soon tormenting, correcting, reprimanding, flattering, threatening, bribing, instructing, and reasoning. Rather than that, be reasonable and never reason with your pupil, especially when you want to make him change his dislikes; for by dragging reason into unpleasant matters you make it distasteful to him and discredit it early in a mind that is not ready to understand it. . . . (Bk. II)

You put your trust in the present order of society without thinking that this order is subject to inevitable revolutions and that you cannot possibly foresee or provide against the society with which your children may have to deal. The great become small, the rich become poor, the monarch a subject; are these strokes of fortune so rare that you can count on immunity? We are approaching a crisis and the age of revolutions. Who can guarantee what will become of you then? Everything men have made, men can destroy: nature's characters alone are ineffaceable; and nature forms no princes, no rich men, or men of high degree. . . .

Man as citizen, whoever he may be, has no property to invest in society but himself; all his other goods are there in spite of himself; and when a man is rich, either he does not profit from his wealth or the public profits too. In the former case, he steals from others what he denies himself; and in the second case, he gives them nothing that is not theirs. Thus he remains entirely in debt to society as long as he contributes only his goods. "But my father, in acquiring it, performed a social service." Agreed: he paid his debt, but not yours. You owe more to others than if you had been born without wealth, since you were born favored. It is not just that the service one man has rendered to society should discharge another man's debt; for each person, being completely indebted himself, can pay only for himself, and no father can transmit to his son the right to be useless to his fellow men: but, you say, that is just what he does when he transmits his wealth, which is the proof and the reward of his labor. The man who consumes in idleness what he has not himself earned is a thief; and a bondholder whom the State pays for doing nothing differs little, as I see it, from a highway robber who lives at the expense of travelers. A man isolated from society, owing nothing to anyone, has a right to live as he pleases; but in society where he has to live at others' expense, he owes in labor the price of his keep; and that is without exception. Work, then, is an indispensable social obligation. Rich or poor, powerful or weak, every idle citizen is a thief.

Now of all the occupations that can give a man a livelihood, the one that brings him closest to the state of nature is the work of his hands; of all stations in life the one depending least on chance and men is that of the artisan. The artisan depends only on his work; he is free, as free as the agricultural laborer is a slave; for the laborer is held to his field, the harvesting of which is dependent on others. An enemy, the prince, a powerful neighbor, a law suit, can take his field away from him; it can cause him a multitude of vexations; but wherever an artisan suffers vexation, his goods are soon packed up: he has his hands, and with those he goes away. Nevertheless agriculture is man's first trade; the most honest, the most useful, and consequently the noblest that he can undertake. I do not say to Emile: Learn agriculture, for he is already familiar with it. All rustic labors are well-known to him; he began with them, and to them he keeps returning. So I say to him: Cultivate the heritage of your fathers. But if you lose that heritage, or if you have none, what is to be done? Learn a trade.

A trade for my son! my son an artisan! Sir, what are you thinking of? I am thinking of better things for him than you, madam, who are trying to reduce him to a state of never being able to become anything but a lord, a marquis, or a prince, and perhaps some day less than nothing at all; whereas I want to raise him to a rank that he cannot lose, a rank which will do him honor at all times; I want to raise him to the estate of manhood and whatever you may say of that, he will have fewer equals with that title than with all those you will bestow upon him.

The letter kills, but the spirit quickens. It is less a matter of learning a trade for the sake of a trade than of overcoming the prejudice that looks down on it. You will never be reduced to working for a living. Well, so much the worse, so much the worse for you! But no matter, work anyway, not because you have to, but for the glory of it. . . .

Remember I am asking of you not a talent, but a trade, a real trade, a purely mechanical art, which calls for the work of the hands more than of the head, and which does not lead to fortune, but which makes fortune unnecessary. . . .

Instead of resorting for a livelihood to higher learning, which provides nourishment for the soul rather than the body, if you depend in case of need on your hands and your handiwork, all difficulties disappear, all intrigue becomes useless; you are ready for any emergency; probity and honor no longer present an obstacle to life; you need no longer be cowardly and mendacious with the great, supple and abject with rascals, a toady to the whole world, a borrower or a thief, for that amounts to the same thing when you are destitute: others' opinions do not trouble you; you have to pay court to no one, you have no fool to flatter, no doorman to bribe, no woman to pay off, or worse still, to burn incense to. It does not matter to you if rascals are in charge of affairs of state; that will not keep you, in the obscurity of your life, from being an honest man and earning a living. You enter the first shop of the trade that you have learned. "Master, I need work.—Comrade, take your place there and work." Before the dinner hour, you have earned your dinner; if you are diligent and sober, before a week has passed, you will have enough to live on for another week; you will have lived a free, healthy, authentic, laborious and just life. Time is not wasted when you are thus rewarded. . . . (Bk. III)

La Mettrie
1709-1751

THE CONTRIBUTION of Julien Offray de La Mettrie to the advancement of science has not yet received full recognition. Early in life he abandoned a religious career for medicine and studied anatomy at Leyden under the renowned Boerhaave, many of whose medical works he translated into French. In his *Natural History of the Soul* (1745), he indulged in philosophical speculations which received further development in his most celebrated work, *Man a Machine* (1747). These works and pungent satires against French doctors and the French Faculty of Medicine aroused such hostility among priests and doctors that he was lucky to find refuge in Berlin, as a member of Frederick the Great's newly established Academy of Sciences. In further tracts on happiness and Epicureanism, he urged the futility and harmfulness of feelings of guilt and remorse. This proved to be too strong medicine for his fellow philosophers, especially Voltaire and Diderot, for whom it was important not to be associated with such a pronounced miscreant.

Man a Machine
(1747)

As an example of the great strides taken by science in the middle years of the eighteenth century, La Mettrie's Man a Machine *was certainly the most notorious, and, along with the volumes of Buffon's* Natural History, *which began to appear in 1749, among the most influential. In his separation of science from theology, Descartes had attempted to prove that animals, as distinct from man, were automatons or pure machines. La Mettrie accepted the proof and went a step further by applying it to man. His studies with Boerhaave, the greatest physician of the age, and his medical experience in the army, convinced him of the close correlation between the mind and the body, of which he gives many examples. With complete acceptance of the scientific method, he developed a materialistic philosophy of science and a mechanistic psychology which is a direct ancestor of the neurophysiological theories that underly present-day cybernetics and the mechanical brain.*

Man a Machine *was written with the recklessness and brashness of tone that characterize much of La Mettrie's work. It greatly influenced Diderot and Cabanis, who, however, were quite unwilling to recognize their debt to their ill-reputed forbear.*

The mind, or the soul, for La Mettrie, is an abstraction which represents nothing more than the brain functioning: "an empty word, of which no one has any idea, and which an enlightened man should use only to signify the part in us that thinks." The dominant faculty of the mind is the imagination, which is inseparably bound up with physical or bodily change. La Mettrie was far from naive, however, and less dogmatic than he sounds. If man is a machine, as he must be from a strictly scientific point of view, he is nevertheless such a complex machine that his essence and the motives of his acts will probably never be completely understood.

A wise man should do more than study nature and truth; he should dare state the truth for the benefit of the few who are willing and able to think. As for the rest, who are the willing slaves of prejudice, they can no more attain truth than frogs can fly.

I reduce to two the systems of philosophers on the subject of man's soul. The first and older system is materialism; the second is spiritualism.

The metaphysicians who hinted that matter may well be endowed with the faculty of thought did not perhaps reason too badly. Why? Because they had the very real advantage in this case of not expressing their true meaning. For to ask whether matter can think, without considering it otherwise than in itself, is like asking whether matter can tell time. It may be foreseen that we shall avoid this reef on which Locke had the bad luck to founder.

The Leibnitzians with their monads set up an unintelligible hypothesis. They rather spiritualized matter than materialized the soul. How can we define a being whose nature is absolutely unknown to us?

Descartes and all the Cartesians, among whom the followers of Malebranche have long been numbered, made the same mistake. They recognized two distinct substances in man, as if they had seen them, and actually counted them. . . .

Experience and observation should here be our only guides. They are to be found throughout the records of physicians who were philosophers, and not in the works of philosophers who were not physicians. The former have traveled through and illuminated the labyrinth of man; they alone have exposed for us those vital elements hidden beneath the skin, which hides from us so many wonderful things. They alone, tranquilly contemplating our soul, have surprised it, a thousand times, both in its wretchedness and its glory, and have no more despised it in the first state, than admired it in the second. Once again we see that only physicians have the right to speak on this subject. What could the others, especially the theologians, have to tell us? Is it not ridiculous to hear them shamelessly dogmatize on a subject which lies completely out of their province and from which on the contrary they have been completely turned aside by obscure studies that have led them to a thousand prejudiced opinions, in a word, to fanaticism, which only increases their ignorance of the mechanism of the body?

But even though we have chosen the best guides, we shall still find many thorns and obstructions in our path.

Man is such a complicated machine that it is impossible to form a clear idea of it beforehand, and hence impossible to define it. For this reason, all the investigations which the greatest philosophers have conducted *a priori,* that is to say, by attempting in a way to use the wings of the spirit, have been fruitless. Thus it is only *a posteriori* or by seeking to discover the soul through the organs of the body, so to speak, that we can reach the highest probability concerning man's own nature, even though one can not discover with certainty what that nature is.

Let us lean then on the staff of experience and pay no attention to the history of all idle philosophical theories. To be blind and to think that we can do without this staff is the worst kind of blindness. How truly a modern writer has said that through vanity alone do we fail to draw from secondary causes the same conclusions as from primary causes! We even should admire all these fine geniuses in their most useless works, Descartes, Malebranche, Leibnitz, Wolff, and the rest, but what profit, I ask, has anyone gained from their profound meditations, and from all their works? Let us start afresh then and discover not what has been thought, but what must be thought for the sake of repose in life.

There are as many different minds, characters, and customs, as there are different temperaments. Even Galen knew this truth, which Descartes carried so far as to claim that medicine alone could change minds and morals, along with bodies. It is true that melancholy, bile, phlegm, blood, etc., and the nature, abundance and diverse combinations of these humors, make one man different from another.

In disease the soul is sometimes hidden, showing no sign of life; sometimes it is so inflamed by fury that it seems to be doubled; sometimes imbecility vanishes and convalescence turns a fool into a wit. Sometimes the greatest genius becomes imbecile and no longer recognizable. Farewell then to all that fine knowledge, acquired at so high a price, and with so much trouble! Here is a paralytic, who asks if his leg is in bed with him; there is a soldier, who thinks he still has the arm which has been cut off. The memory of his old sensations, and of the place to which they were referred by his soul, is the cause of his illusion and kind of delirium. The mere mention of the member which he has lost is enough to make him remember and feel all its motions; and this produces an indefinable and inexpressible kind of imaginary suffering.

This man cries like a child at death's approach, while this other jests. What was needed to change the bravery of Caius Julius, Seneca or Petronius into faintheartedness or cowardice? An obstruction in the spleen, in the liver, an impediment in the portal vein. Why? Because the imagination is obstructed along with the viscera, and this gives rise to all those strange phenomena of hysteria and hypochondria.

What could I add to what has been told of those who imagine themselves transformed into wolf-men, cocks or vampires, or those who think that the dead suck their blood? Why should I stop to speak of those who imagine that their noses or some other members are made of glass and who must be advised to sleep on straw to keep from breaking them, so that they may recover the use of their flesh-and-blood organs by setting the straw afire and scaring them—a fright that has sometimes cured paralysis? I must not tarry over facts that are common knowledge.

Nor shall I dwell at length on the effects of sleep. Take this tired soldier. He snores in a trench, to the sound of a hundred cannon. His soul hears nothing; his sleep is perfect apoplexy. A bomb is about to wipe him out. He will feel the shock less perhaps than an insect under his foot.

On the other hand, this man who is devoured by jealousy, hatred, avarice, or ambition, can never find any rest. The most peaceful spot, the coolest and most calming drinks, all have no effect on a man whose heart is a prey to the torment of passion.

The soul and the body fall asleep together. As the pulse gradually slows down, a sweet feeling of peace and quiet spreads throughout the whole machine. The soul feels itself gently sinking along with the eyelids and relaxing along with the fibers of the brain; thus little by little it becomes as if paralyzed along with all the muscles of the body. These can no longer sustain the weight of the head, and the soul can no longer bear the burden of thought; in sleep it is as if it did not exist.

Is the pulse too quick? the soul cannot sleep. Is the soul too agitated? the pulse cannot be quieted: the blood gallops through the veins with an audible murmur. Such are the two interacting causes of insomnia. A simple fright in our dreams makes the heart beat twice as fast and snatches us from needed or delightful repose, as a sharp pain or dire necessity would do. Lastly, just as the cessation of the functions of the soul induces sleep, the mind, even when we are awake (or in this case half awake), takes very frequent short naps, or day dreams, which show that the soul does not always wait for the body to sleep. For if the soul is not fast asleep, it surely is almost so, since it cannot point out a single object to which it has paid attention, among the countless confused ideas which, like so many clouds, so to speak, fill the atmosphere of our brains. . . .

The human body is a machine which winds itself up, the living image of perpetual motion. Food nourishes the movements which fever excites. Without food, the soul pines away, goes mad, and dies exhausted. It is a candle whose light flares up the moment before it goes out. But nourish the body, pour into its veins invigorating juices and strong liquors; then the soul, taking on their strength, arms itself with a proud courage, and the soldier whom water would have made flee, now made bold, runs joyously to death to the sound of drums. Thus a warming drink excites the blood which a cold drink would have calmed.

What power there is in a meal! Joy is born again in a sad heart; it infects the souls of table-companions, who burst into the friendly songs in which the French excel. The melancholy man alone is dejected, and the studious man is likewise out of place. . . .

In general, the form and structure of the brains of quadrupeds are almost the same as in man; the same shape, the same arrangement everywhere, but with this essential difference, that of all the animals man has the largest brain, and, in proportion to its mass, the brain with the most convolutions. Then comes the monkey, the beaver, the elephant, the dog, the fox, the cat, etc., animals which are the most like man; for among them, too, the same progressive analogy can be seen in relation to the *corpus callosum*, in which Lancisi established the seat of the soul —anticipating the late M. de la Peyronie, who illustrated the theory with a great many experiments.

After all the quadrupeds, birds have the most brains. Fish have large heads, but these are void of sense, like the heads of many men. Fish have no *corpus callosum*, and very little brain, while insects entirely lack brain. . . .

The imbecile may not lack brain, as commonly observed, but its consistency will be faulty, for instance, in being too soft. The same thing is true of the insane; the defects of their brains do not always escape our investigation; but if the causes of imbecility, insanity, etc., are not perceptible, how can we hope to discover the causes of the diversity of minds in general? They would escape the eyes of a lynx and an Argus. A mere nothing, a tiny fiber, something that the most delicate dissection cannot discover, would have made two idiots of Erasmus and Fontenelle, and Fontenelle himself makes this observation in one of his best dialogues. . . .

From animals to man, the transition is not violent, as good philosophers will admit. What was man before the invention of words and the knowledge of tongues? An animal of his species, who, with much less native instinct than the others, whose king he then considered himself to be, could not be distinguished from the ape and from the rest, except as the ape itself differs from the other animals; which means, by a face giving promise of more intelligence. Reduced to the bare "intuitive knowledge" of the Leibnitzians he saw only shapes and colors, without being able to distinguish between them; the same, old as young, child at all ages, he stammers out his feelings and needs, like a dog who asks for food when he is hungry or, tired of sleeping, wants to be let out.

Words, languages, laws, sciences, and the fine arts, have come, and by them our rough diamond of a mind has been polished. Man has been trained in the same way as animals; he has become an author, as they become beasts of burden. A geometrician has learned to perform the most difficult demonstrations and calculations, as a monkey has learned to take off or put on his little hat to mount his tame dog. All this has been done through signs, every species has learned what it could understand, and in this way men have acquired "symbolic knowledge," still so called by our German philosophers. . . .

All this knowledge, which blows up the balloon-like brains of our proud pedants, is therefore but a huge mass of words and figures, which form in the brain all the marks by which we distinguish and recall objects. All our ideas are awakened in the same way that a gardener who knows plants recalls, at the sight of them, all the stages of their growth. These words and the objects designated by them are so connected in the brain that it is comparatively rare to imagine a thing without the name or sign that is attached to it.

I always use the word "imagine," because I think that everything is imagined and that all the faculties of the soul can be correctly reduced to pure imagination, which gives form to them all. Thus judgment, reason and memory, are in no wise absolute parts of the soul, but real modifications of the kind of medullary screen upon which images of the objects painted in the eye are reflected as by a magic lantern.

But if such is the marvelous and incomprehensible result of the structure of the brain, if everything is perceived and explained by imagination, why should we divide the sensitive principle which thinks in man? Is not this clearly an inconsistency on the part of those who uphold the simplicity of the mind? For a thing that can be divided can no longer without absurdity be regarded as indivisible. This is where we come to through the abuse of language and those fine words "spirituality," "immateriality," etc., used haphazardly and not understood even by the most intelligent. . . .

We were not originally made to be learned; we have become so perhaps by a sort of abuse of our organic faculties, and at the expense of the State, which nourishes a host of loafers whom vanity has adorned with the name of "philosophers." Nature created us all solely to be happy —yes, all, from the crawling worm to the eagle that soars out of sight in the clouds. That is why she has given all animals some share of natural law, a share of greater or less delicacy according to the needs of each animal's organs when in good condition.

Now how shall we define natural law? It is a feeling which teaches us what we should not do, because we would not wish it to be done to us. Would I dare add to this common idea, that this feeling seems to me but a kind of fear or dread, as salutary to the race as to the individual? For perhaps we respect the purses and lives of others only to save our own possessions, our honor, and our own lives; like those "Ixions of Christianity" who love God and embrace so many fantastic virtues, merely because of their fear of hell.

You see that natural law is nothing but an intimate feeling which belongs also to the imagination like all other feelings, thought included. Consequently it evidently does not presuppose education, revelation or legislator, unless we confuse it with civil laws, in the ridiculous fashion of the theologians.

The arms of fanaticism may destroy those who maintain these truths, but they will never destroy the truths themselves.

Not that I call in question the existence of a supreme being; on the contrary it seems to me that the greatest degree of probability is in favor of this belief. But since the existence of this being does not prove that one form of worship is more necessary than any other, it is a theoretic truth with very little practical value. Therefore, since we may say, after such long experience, that religion does not imply exact honesty, we are authorized by the same reasons to think that atheism does not exclude it.

Furthermore, who knows whether the reason for man's existence is not simply the fact that he exists? Perhaps he was thrown by chance on some spot of the earth's surface, nobody knows how or why, but simply that he must live and die, like mushrooms that appear from one day to the next, or like the flowers which border ditches and cover walls. . . .

Let us conclude boldly then that man is a machine, and that in the whole universe there is but a single substance with various modifications. This is no hypothesis set up by dint of proposals and assumptions. It is not the work of prejudice, nor even of my reason alone; I would have disdained a guide which I believe so untrustworthy, had not my senses held the torch, so to speak, and induced me to follow reason by lighting the way. Experience has thus spoken to me in behalf of reason; and in this way I have combined the two.

But it must have been noticed that I have not allowed myself even the most forceful and immediately deduced reasoning, except as it followed a multitude of observations which no scholar will contest; and furthermore, I recognize only scientists as judges of the conclusions which I draw, and I hereby challenge every prejudiced man who is not an anatomist, or acquainted with the only philosophy which is to the purpose, that of the human body. Against such a strong and solid oak, what could the weak reeds of theology, metaphysics and scholasticism, avail; childish weapons, like our foils, which may well afford the pleasure of fencing, but can never wound an adversary. Need I say that I refer to the hollow and trivial notions, to the trite and pitiable arguments that will be urged, as long as the shadow of prejudice or superstition remains on earth, for the supposed incompatibility of two substances which meet and interact unceasingly? Such is my system, or rather the truth, unless I am very much mistaken. It is short and simple. Dispute it now who will.

D'Alembert

1717-1783

Jean Le Rond d'Alembert, illegitimate son of Mme de Tencin, was named for the church on the steps of which he was placed as a foundling. He became one of the mathematical geniuses of his age and as co-editor with Diderot of the *Encyclopedia* gave the enterprise the prestige of his membership in the Berlin Academy. He secured the cooperation of Voltaire and later, as perpetual secretary of the French Academy, was influential in bringing that distinguished institution into the camp of the *philosophes.*

The *Encyclopedia,* for which D'Alembert wrote the Preliminary Discourse, was France's greatest publishing venture of the century. From modest beginnings, it grew to thirty-five in-folio volumes, and was the parent of the Britannica and other modern encyclopedias. In expressing its purpose in his article "Encyclopedia," Diderot also stated his confidence in the theory of progress through enlightenment: "The aim of an encyclopedia is to assemble the knowledge scattered over the face of the earth, to expound its general system to the men with whom we live, and transmit it to the men who will come after us; in order that the labors of past centuries will not have been in vain for the centuries to come; that our children, better instructed than we, may at the same time become more virtuous and happy, and that we may not die without having deserved well of mankind."

D'Alembert's first concern in the Preliminary Discourse was the problem of knowledge (how we know), its unity and classification. He then presented an historical view of the progressive development of the human mind from ancient times.

Preliminary Discourse of the Encyclopedia (1751)

. . . The task that we are beginning and plan to finish has two objectives: as an encyclopedia, to set forth as far as possible the order and interconnections of the sciences of man; as a systematic dictionary of sciences, arts and trades, to include for each science or art, either liberal or technological, the general basic principles and the most essential details which form its body and substance. These two points of view, namely the encyclopedic and systematic, will therefore form the plan and divisions of the preliminary discourse. We will survey them, pursue them one by one, and account for the means by which an effort has been made to satisfy this double objective.

A little reflection upon the interdependence of discoveries makes it apparent that the sciences and arts are mutually helpful and that there is therefore a connecting link between them. But it is often difficult to reduce each particular science or art to a small number of rules or general ideas; it is no less difficult to embrace in a single system the infinitely diverse branches of human knowledge.

The first step to be taken in this search is to examine, if we are permitted the term, the genealogy and filiation of our realms of knowledge, the causes that must have given rise to them, and the traits that characterize them; in a word, to turn back to the very origins and creation of our ideas. Independently of the help we will obtain from this examination for the encylcopedic enumeration of the sciences and arts, it is not out of place at the head of a systematic dictionary of human knowledge.

The masterpieces in almost all genres left us by the ancients had been forgotten for twelve centuries. The principles of the sciences and arts were lost, because beauty and truth, which seem to appear to men on all sides, impress them little unless they are pointed out. Not that these unhappy times were more sterile than others in the production of men of genius; nature never changes. But what could these great men do, scattered as they always were over the face of the earth, occupied with different interests, and dependent in an uncultured society upon their own lights? The ideas that are acquired through reading and social intercourse form the basis of nearly all discoveries. This atmosphere is imbibed unwittingly and is the very breath of life; and the men we are speaking of had no such resource. They were like the first creators of the sciences and arts, whom their illustrious successors consigned to oblivion only because they came afterwards. The man who first invented wheels and pinions would have invented watches in another age. . . .

Yet most of the best minds of those dark ages were self-styled poets or philosophers. How little it cost them, to be sure, to usurp two titles which can be bestowed so cheaply and which were always assumed to owe little to borrowed ideas! They thought it useless to seek models for poetry in the works of the Greeks and Romans, whose language was no longer spoken, and they mistook for the true philosophy of the ancients a barbarous tradition which completely disfigured it. Poetry became for them a childish wordplay. The serious examination of nature and the great study of man were replaced by a multitude of frivolous problems concerning abstract and metaphysical beings; problems which required for their solution, whether true or false, a great deal of subtlety and consequently a great abuse of the mind. If we add to that disorder the state of slavery into which almost all Europe was plunged and the ravages of superstition born of ignorance and giving rise in turn to ignorance, we can see how complete were the obstacles in the way of the return to reason and good taste; for only freedom of action and thought are capable of producing great works, and freedom needs only enlightenment to guard against excess.

To emerge from barbarism man had to undergo one of

those revolutions from which the world takes on a new face: the Greek empire was destroyed, and its ruin spread over Europe the bit of knowledge that was still left on earth: the invention of printing and the protection of the Medici and Francis I gave new life to the mind, and light was reborn on all sides.

The study of languages and history which had to be abandoned during the centuries of ignorance was the first to receive close attention. The spirit of man, as it emerged from barbarism, passed through a sort of infancy. It was eager to accumulate ideas and yet was incapable at first of acquiring ideas of a certain order because of a kind of numbness, which had so long pervaded the spiritual faculties. The first of all these faculties to be cultivated was memory, because it was the most readily satisfied and because the knowledge acquired through memory could be the most easily stored. Instead of beginning with a study of nature, as primitive men must have done, the men of the Renaissance profited from a source unknown in early times, namely the works of the ancients, which the generosity of princes and the printing-press were beginning to popularize. They thought they had only to read to become learned, and it was much easier to read than observe. Thus they devoured without discrimination all that the ancients had left us in every genre; they translated and annotated, and were so grateful that they began to worship the ancients, long before they had begun to understand their true value.

Thus there appeared a great many men of profound erudition in the classical languages, to the point of disdaining their own. As a famous author has said, they knew everything about the ancients except their grace and discriminating taste, and were all the prouder of their vain show of learning, because the advantages which come with the least effort are ordinarily those that are most readily displayed. They were like those grandees who do not resemble their forebears through any real merit, but are inordinately proud of their ancestry. Moreover their vanity was not without pretext. The do-

J. D'ALEMBERT.

main of erudition and facts is inexhaustible. We believe, as it were, that we see our substance increasing day by day by painless acquisition. The domain of reason and invention, on the contrary, is rather limited, and often instead of learning something new, we succeed by dint of study in unlearning what we thought we knew. That is why, with much less merit, scholars are vainer than philosophers and perhaps poets; for the inventive mind, looking ever beyond, is always dissatisfied with its progress; and the greatest geniuses discover in their very self-esteem a secret but severe judge, which is silenced for a few moments by the approbation of others, but is never actually corrupted. We should not be surprised that these scholars gloried so much in their rude, often ridiculous, and sometimes barbarous learning.

It is true that our present age, which believes itself destined to change laws of all kinds and set them aright, does not esteem very highly those men who were once so famous. It is considered a kind of merit today to belittle them, a merit even that many people can relish. It seems that by despising these scholars, we try to punish them for their own exaggerated self-esteem or the unintelligent tributes of their contemporaries, and by casting these idols to the ground we hope to consign their very names to oblivion. But all excess is unjust. Let us rather take grateful advantage of the work of these laborious men. In order to teach us how to extract from the works of the ancients all that could possibly be useful, they had to extract much that was useless; gold cannot be drawn from a mine without a great deal of dross or less precious matter. Like us, they would have separated the good from the bad, if they had lived in later ages. Erudition was therefore a necessary guide to lead us to the literary arts. . . .

We would be unjust, as we enter into our detailed survey, if we did not recognize what we owe to Italy; from her we received the knowledge which since has fructified so bountifully in all Europe, and to her we owe the fine arts and good taste, of which she has furnished us with a multitude of inimitable models.

During the time that arts and letters were being honored, philosophy was very far from making the same progress, at least in any nation as a whole; it did not reappear until very much later. Not that it is basically easier to excel in letters than in philosophy; superiority in every genre is equally difficult to attain. But the reading of the ancients was to contribute more promptly to the advancement of letters and good taste than to progress in the natural sciences. Literary beauty can be sensed without prolonged review, and since men feel before they think, by the same token they judged what they felt before judging what they thought. . . . (Part II)

[*D'Alembert proceeded to illustrate the renaissance of philosophy with sketches of Francis Bacon, Descartes, Newton, Locke, Galileo, Huyghens, Pascal and Leibnitz, among others.*]

Helvétius

1715-1771

Son of a physician credited with saving the life of Louis XV, Claude Adrien Helvétius was appointed General Tax Collector at the age of twenty-three. In this most lucrative of all eighteenth-century occupations he amassed a large fortune and retired eleven years later to devote himself to letters and philanthropy. His literary merits were not great, but his ideas were original. In *On the Mind*, published in 1759 and condemned, along with the *Encyclopedia* and works of Voltaire and Diderot, he envisaged the behavioristic doctrine of the complete reconditioning of mankind through education and legislation. This work, which greatly influenced Jeremy Bentham's utilitarianism and theory of the greatest good of the greatest number, shocked Diderot by its complete neglect of hereditary factors, and Voltaire by its forthright materialism. It occasioned the Voltairean maxim: "I entirely disagree with what you say and will fight to the death for your right to say it."

Helvétius was forced to retract, but impenitently reinforced his doctrine in a sequel, *On Man*, published in 1772 immediately after his death. His beautiful and wealthy widow maintained a salon for liberals during the latter years of the century. She refused proposals of marriage by Turgot and Franklin, whereupon the latter wrote one of his most delightful minor literary pieces.

On the Mind

(1759)

On the Use Accruing to Morality

If moralizing hitherto has contributed little to the happiness of mankind, it is not owing to any want of perspicuity or beauty of style, or propriety and loftiness of sentiment in the moralists; but with all their superior talents it must be owned that they have not often enough considered the different vices of nations as necessarily resulting from the different forms of their governments; yet it is only by considering morality from this point of view that it can become of any real use to men. What have hitherto been the effects of all the splendid maxims of morality? If some individuals have been corrected by them of faults which perhaps they reproached themselves with, no changes in the manners of nations have been produced. What is this to be imputed to? It is because the vices of a people, if I may presume to say so, always lie at the bottom of its legislation. There one must search if the root from which its vices arise is to be destroyed. He who lacks either penetration or courage for such an undertaking is in this respect of little or no use to the universe. To try to wipe out vices inherent in the legislation of a people without making any change in that legislation is to attempt the impossible and reject the consequences that necessarily follow the accepted principles.

What can be hoped for from all the declamations against the falsity of women, if this vice is the necessary effect of a contradiction between the desires of nature and the feelings which, by the law of decency, women are forced to affect?

In Malabar and Madagascar all women are faithful, because they have gallants without number and never decide on a husband until after repeated trials. It is the same with the savages of New Orleans, those people among whom the relatives of the Great Sun, the princesses of the blood, may, if they find their husbands distasteful, repudiate them and marry others. In such countries no unfaithful wives are heard of, because it is not to their interest to be so.

I am far from inferring from these examples that the same customs should be introduced among us; I only say that women cannot reasonably be reproached with a breach of faith which decency and the laws, so to speak, imposed on them as a necessity; and that while the causes are allowed to subsist, the effects will continue. . . .

It follows from what I have said that no change in the ideas of a people can be hoped for until its laws have been changed; that the reform of morals is to be begun by the reform of laws; and declamations against a vice useful in the present form of government would be politically detrimental, even if they were not entirely fruitless. But so they will always be, for it is only the force of the laws that can ever act on the bulk of the nation. Besides, if I may make a passing observation, among moralists there are very few who know how to array our passions one against the other and use them to secure the adoption of their opinions; most of their admonitions are too virulent. Yet they should sense the fact that invectives can never prevail over emotions, for only a passion can get the better of a passion. . . .

By substituting the soft language of interest for the imperious clamor of invective, moralists may establish their maxims. I shall not enlarge further on this point, but return to my subject and say that all men tend only towards their happiness, that this is a tendency from which they cannot be diverted, and that the attempt would be fruitless, and dangerous if successful. Consequently they can be made virtuous only by making their personal interests coincide with the general interest. This being granted, it is evident that ethics is no more than a frivolous science, unless it is blended with public policy and legislation; whence I conclude that, if philosophers would be of use to the world, they should survey situations from the same point of view as the legislator. Though they are not invested with the same power, they should be animated with the same spirit. The moralist's duty is to indicate the laws, the execution of which the legislator insures by stamping them with the seal of his authority. (Essay II, ch. xv)

On the Means of Perfecting Morality

Every man who considers the picture of public miseries exhibited in history soon perceives that ignorance, which is still more barbarous than self-love, has caused most of

C. A. HELVETIUS

the calamities that have overflowed the earth. Struck with this truth, we are ready to cry out: Happy the nation in which the citizens are permitted to perpetrate only the crimes that spring from self-love! How greatly these crimes are increased by ignorance, and what blood has been spilled on its altars! However, man is made to be virtuous; and in fact, if force essentially resides in the greater number, and justice consists in the practice of actions useful to the greater number, it is evident that justice is in its own nature always armed with a power sufficient to suppress vice and place men under the necessity of being virtuous.

If audacious and powerful wickedness so often puts justice and virtue in chains and oppresses the nations, this is only brought about with the assistance of ignorance, which conceals from every nation its true interest, hinders the action and union of its strength, and by that means shields the guilty from the sword of justice.

To what contempt should be condemned anyone who would hold the people in the darkness of ignorance! This truth has not hitherto been insisted upon with sufficient force; no, all the altars of error must one day be overthrown. I know with what precaution we ought to advance a new opinion. I know that in destroying prejudices we ought to hold them in respect; and that before we attack an error generally received, we ought to send, like doves from the ark, some truths reconnoitering to see if the flood of prejudices has receded from the face of the earth, if error has begun to subside and if there can be perceived some isles where virtue and truth can gain a foothold and communicate themselves to mankind. . . . (II, xxiv)

On Probity, in Relation to the World in General

If there existed any such thing as probity in relation to all mankind, it would consist only in the habit of performing actions useful to all nations: but no action can have an immediate influence on the happiness or unhappiness of all men. The noblest of actions, by setting a good example, can produce in the moral world an effect no more perceptible than a stone thrown into the ocean can produce in the seas by raising their level.

There is then no practical probity in relation to the universe. With reference to probity of intention, which is nothing but a constant and habitual desire for the happiness of mankind and consequently only vague and inefficacious wishes for universal felicity, I maintain that it is nothing but a Platonic chimera. In fact if the mutual opposition of interests that subsists between different nations keeps them in a state of perpetual war; if a peace concluded between two nations is in truth merely a cessation of hostilities like that between two warships, which after a long fight take time out to repair their rigging and stop their leaks, only to renew the attack; if nations cannot extend their conquest and their commerce except at the expense of their rivals; in fine, if the felicity and grandeur of one nation is almost always connected with the misfortunes and weakness of another, it is evident that a spirit of patriotism, a passion so desirable, so virtuous, and so worthy of esteem in any citizen, is, as is proved by the example of the Greeks and Romans, absolutely exclusive of the love of all mankind.

It is necessary, in order to give existence to this kind of probity, that the nations by reciprocal laws and conventions should unite together as families composing one state; that the private interest of nations should submit to a more general interest; that the love of our country, becoming extinguished in the heart, should give place to the more extended flame of universal love: a supposition that will not be realized for a long time. From this I conclude that there can be no such thing as practical or even intentional probity with respect to all mankind; and on this point the mind is at variance with probity.

In fact, though the actions of an individual can contribute nothing to general happiness and though the influence of his virtue cannot extend perceptibly beyond the limits of an empire, it is not so with his ideas. If a man discovers a specific remedy or invents a windmill, these productions of the mind may render him a benefactor to all people.

Besides, in affairs of the mind the love of country is not, as in the case of probity, exclusive of the love of all mankind. A nation does not acquire knowledge at the expense of the neighboring states; on the contrary, the morc nations are enlightened, the more they reflect each other's ideas and the more the force and activity of the universal mind is augmented. From this I conclude that, though there is no probity relative to the universe, there are at least certain intellectual aspects that may be considered in this light. (II, xxv)

D'Holbach

1723-1789

Baron d'Holbach, a wealthy nobleman of German birth, married and settled in France, and through his prolific writings became the most forthright opponent of the eighteenth-century Church and State. His house in Paris and his château at Grandval were cultivated centers of freethought. His first publications were articles on metallurgy for Diderot's *Encyclopedia*, an enterprise which he generously supported throughout its stormy career. Patron and friend of the arts and sciences, he was especially friendly to Diderot, who often found a haven for work and rest in the baron's home.

D'Holbach was a materialist and atheist whose ideas were not particularly original but who succeeded in alarming the more moderate philosophers, including the theist, Voltaire. The excerpt on conscience given below is a characteristic and matter of fact examination of the conscience, which Voltaire considered a universal instinct and Rousseau hailed as the infallible voice of God.

Universal Morality

(1776)

On the Conscience

Our past experiences, the true or false opinions that we form or accept, the rational faculties that we more or less carefully cultivate, the habits that we contract, the education we receive, develop in us an inner feeling of pleasure or pain which we call conscience. This can be defined as the knowledge of the effect our actions produce upon our neighbors and in return upon ourselves.

A little reflection will convince us that, like the instinct or moral sense which we have just spoken of, conscience is an acquired characteristic, and that most moralists have very little foundation for regarding it as an inborn sense, or rather, as a quality inherent in our nature. If we want to agree in the field of ethics, we will be forced to admit that the heart of man is a *tabula rasa*, with a greater or lesser propensity to receive the impressions made upon it.

In the great majority of men, we discern only a faulty conscience, that is, a conscience which judges with little regard for truth or the nature of things, the result of false opinions that we formed or received from others, who succeed in applying the idea of good to actions that would, if closely examined, be considered very harmful. Many people are evil and even commit crimes in all security of conscience, because their consciences are vitiated by prejudice.

There is no vice that does not hide its deformities, when it is approved by the society in which we live; crime itself is glorified by the number and authority of the guilty. No one blushes at adultery or moral turpitude among a corrupt people. No one blushes at being abject as a courtier. The soldier is not ashamed of his plunder and crimes; he even boasts about them to his comrades, for he knows they are ready to do the same. It takes little investigation to find very unjust, mean, inhuman men who do not reproach themselves for their frequent unjust acts, which they often consider legitimate or within their rights; nor for their cruel acts, which they look upon as the results of praiseworthy courage or as duties. We see wealthy people whose consciences are silent about the acquisition of immense fortunes at the expenses of their fellow citizens. Travelers tell us of savages who feel obliged to put their parents to death when decrepitude has rendered them useless. We find zealots whose consciences, blinded by false ideas of virtue, incite them to exterminate remorselessly and without pity all who are not of their opinion. In short, there are nations so vitiated that conscience offers no reproach to men who tolerate plunder, homicide, dueling, adultery, seduction, etc., because these crimes or vices are approved or condoned by public opinion, or are not repressed by law; that being the case, all indulge in them without shame or remorse. These excesses are avoided only by a few who are more moderate, timid and prudent than the rest.

Conscience speaks only to reflective men who rationalize their acts and in whom a respectable education has given rise to an interest and desire to please and an habitual fear of incurring contempt or hatred. A man thus modified becomes capable of self-judgment; he condemns himself when he has committed some deed which he knows may prejudice the feelings he would constantly like to arouse in those whose esteem and love are necessary to his well-being. He experiences shame, remorse and repentance, whenever he does wrong; he examines himself and changes his ways through fear of experiencing again those unhappy feelings which often force him to detest himself, because he sees himself as others see him.

Hence it appears that conscience depends upon an imagination which paints in vivid and unmistakable colors the feelings that we arouse in other people; a man without imagination has little or no sense of these impressions or feelings; he fails to put himself in the place of others. It is very difficult to make a good man of a stupid person, whose imagination tells him nothing, or likewise of a senseless person whose imagination keeps him in a continual state of excitement.

All this proves to us, then, that conscience, far from being a quality inborn or inherent in human nature, can only be the fruit of experience, of imagination guided by reason, the habit of self-examination, the careful supervision of our acts, the foresight to measure their influence on others and their reaction upon ourselves.

Common Sense
(1772)

When we coolly examine the opinions of men, we are surprised to find that even in those opinions which they regard as the most essential, nothing is more uncommon than common sense; or in other words, nothing is more uncommon than a degree of judgment sufficient to discover the most simple truths, or reject the most striking absurdities, and to be shocked with palpable contradictions. We have an example of it in theology, a science revered in all times and countries, by the greatest number of men; an object regarded by them the most important, the most useful, and the most indispensable to the happiness of society. An examination, however slight, of the principles upon which this pretended science is founded, forces us to acknowledge that these principles, formerly judged incontestable, are only hazardous suppositions, imagined by ignorance, propagated by enthusiasm or knavery, adopted by timid credulity, preserved by custom which never reasons, and revered solely because not understood. "Some," says Montaigne, "make the world think that they believe what they do not; others, in greater number, make themselves think that they believe what they do not, not knowing what belief is." . . .

Oppressed by the double yoke of spiritual and temporal power, it has been impossible for the people to know and pursue their happiness. As religion, so politics and morality became sacred things, which the profane were not permitted to handle. Men have had no other morality than what their legislators and priests brought down from the unknown regions of heaven. The human mind, confused by its theological opinions, ceased to know its own powers, mistrusted experience, feared truth, and disdained reason, in order to follow authority. Man has been a mere machine in the hands of tyrants and priests, who alone have had the right of directing his actions. Always treated as a slave, he has contracted the vices of a slave.

Such are the true causes of the corruption of morals, to which religion opposes only ideal and ineffectual barriers. Ignorance and servitude are calculated to make men wicked and unhappy. Knowledge, reason, liberty, can alone reform them and make them happier. But every thing conspires to blind them and to confirm them in their errors. Priests cheat them, tyrants corrupt, the better to enslave them. Tyranny ever was and ever will be the true cause of man's depravity, and also of his habitual calamities. Almost always fascinated by religious fiction, poor mortals turn not their eyes to the natural and obvious causes of their misery, but attribute their vices to the imperfection of their natures, and their unhappiness to the anger of the gods. They offer up to heaven vows, sacrifices and presents, to obtain an end to their sufferings, which in reality are attributable only to the negligence, ignorance and perversity of their guides, to the folly of their customs, to the unreasonableness of their laws and, above all, to the general want of knowledge. Let men's minds be filled with true ideas, let their reason be cultivated, let justice govern them, and there will be no need of opposing to the passions such a feeble barrier as the fear of the gods. Men will be good when they are well instructed, well governed, and when they are punished or despised for the evil, and justly rewarded for the good, which they do to their fellow citizens.

In vain should we attempt to cure men of their vices, unless we begin by curing them of their prejudices. It is only by showing them the truth that they will perceive their true interests and the real motives that ought to incline them to do good. Instructors have long enough fixed men's eyes upon heaven; let them now turn them upon earth. An incomprehensible theology, ridiculous fables, impenetrable mysteries, puerile ceremonies, are too fatiguing to be any longer endured. Let the human mind apply itself to what is natural, to intelligible objects, sensible truths, and useful knowledge. Let vain chimeras be banished, and reasonable opinions will of their own accord enter into heads thought to be destined to perpetual error.

Does it not suffice to annihilate or shake religious prejudice to show that what is inconceivable to man cannot be made for him? Does it require anything but plain common sense to perceive that a being incompatible with the most evident notions, that a cause continually opposed to the effects which we attribute to it, that a being of whom we can say nothing without falling into contradiction, that a being who, far from explaining the enigmas of the universe, only makes them more inexplicable, that a being whom for so many ages men have so vainly addressed to obtain their happiness and the end of their sufferings: does it require, I say, anything but plain common sense to perceive that the idea of such a being is an idea without model, and that he himself is merely a phantom of the imagination? Is anything necessary but common sense to perceive, at least, that it is folly and madness for men to hate and torment one another about unintelligible opinions concerning a being of this kind? In short, does not everything prove that morality and virtue are totally incompatible with the notions of a God, whom his ministers and interpreters have described in every country as the most capricious, unjust, and cruel of tyrants, whose pretended will, however, must serve as law and rule to the inhabitants of the earth?

To discover the true principles of morality, men have no need of theology, of revelation, or of gods; they need only common sense. They have only to commune with themselves, to reflect upon their own nature, to consult their visible interests, to consider the objects of society and the individuals who compose it, and they will easily perceive that virtue is advantageous, and vice disadvantageous, to such beings as themselves. Let us persuade men to be just, beneficent, moderate, sociable, not because such conduct is demanded by the gods, but because it is a pleasure to men. Let us advise them to abstain from vice and crime, not because they will be punished in the other world, but because they will suffer for it in this. . . .

Diderot

1713-1784

Born in the ancient city of Langres, son of a highly respected master cutler, Diderot's ambition and promise as a student led his father to send him to one of the best colleges in Paris. The father hoped the son would distinguish himself in law or some other profession, but Diderot had too strong a craving for knowledge to settle down to a profession. His allowance was cut off and many difficult years followed, during which he mastered many languages including Greek, Italian and English, perfected his proficiency in mathematics and physics, and attended classes in the newly founded science of chemistry.

He first appears on the literary scene as a translator of English, especially of a work by Shaftesbury, English philosopher and moralist, and a dictionary of medicine. It was first as translator that he was associated with the publishers of the first great modern encyclopedia, of which he soon became editor-in-chief, with the help of D'Alembert for the mathematical parts. Early philosophical works, especially a *Letter on the Blind*, was found to be too bold by the authorities, and Diderot spent a few unhappy months in prison. The *Encyclopedia*, which under his direction was to become the greatest publishing venture of the century, kept him busy and gave him a livelihood for many long years. He managed, however, to write plays and essays on the drama, as well as a number of philosophical and scientific treatises. After the condemnation and suppression of the *Encyclopedia*, in 1759, he came to the conclusion that his ideas were too advanced for the age and withheld in manuscript his most notable and mature works, most of which saw the light only in the next century.

Diderot believed in thinking boldly and living conservatively. To save his library, which he was about to sell to provide his daughter with a dowry, Catherine II of Russia bought it, left it with him, and paid him to be its custodian. When his work on the *Encyclopedia* was finished in 1772, he set out for Russia at Catherine's invitation and in gratitude for her beneficence. On his return, his major work now accomplished, he lived in comparative tranquillity and died peacefully in 1784. His library and copies of his manuscripts then joined Voltaire's in St. Petersburg.

The Philosophy of Science

Diderot wrote no book under this title. His germinal ideas are scattered throughout his works and are nowhere systematically pursued. His early scientific works were of a practical nature. The Letter on the Blind *(1749) is the first serious study of the subject, a sound psychological investigation resulting from wide reading and actual consultations with persons afflicted with blindness. The* Letters on the Deaf and Dumb *(1751), beyond its purely scientific aspects, led him into serious consideration of gesture, language, and the art of communication, from which he derived theories of esthetics and literary criticism that clearly announce the poetry of Baudelaire and the French symbolists.*

The most important work published during his lifetime was his Thoughts on the Interpretation of Nature, *of 1754. Earlier works had hinted unmistakably at the theory of biological and cosmological evolution. In this work, he touches in germ upon the evolutionary ideas of transformism to be developed later by Lamarck and Darwin. The full development of his materialistic philosophy was achieved much later in a tripartite dialogue under the general title of* D'Alembert's Dream, *written in 1769 but not published until 1830. This brilliant amalgamation of the scientific and poetic imaginations is now regarded as a masterpiece, for the prophetic visions of his dream have now been realized. Physical, biological, psychological, esthetic and ethical considerations were all one for Diderot and all had a single cause at bottom—a physical cause—hence his concern with the material and physiological origins of the thinking, sensitive, moral and social human animal. To his correspondent, Sophie Volland, he wrote:*

"This work is of the utmost extravagance and at the same time of the most profound philosophy; it took some skill to put my ideas in the mouth of a man in a dream; but we must often present wisdom with an air of folly, to make it acceptable."

Diderot's philosophy of science has been described as humanistic naturalism, also, more scientifically, as dynamic organicism, a definite advance over the mechanistic materialism of La Mettrie, whose influence is apparent.

He thought of the areas of scientific knowledge as islands emerging from the sea of ignorance. With the advancement of science, the waters will recede and reveal the fact that the islands are all interconnected: there is no jump from the inorganic to the organic world, from the inanimate to the living and animate, from plant to animal to man. Why D'Alembert is different from a cow, he said, I do not quite understand, but some day science will explain.

Diderot's contribution to the philosophy of science was the result of an amalgamation of Bacon's empiricism, Locke's theory that all human knowledge is based on data received through the senses, and La Mettrie's persuasion that sense perceptions are definite physical modifications and leave indelible marks upon the brain. Stored perceptions can therefore be recalled voluntarily or sometimes arise involuntarily from the subconscious mind. From these insights many modern literary techniques and esthetic theories have been developed.

Thoughts on the Interpretation of Nature (1754)

Nature, it seems, has taken pleasure in reproducing the same mechanism in an endless variety of ways. She abandons one type of creation only after multiplying specimens with all possible variations. When we consider the animal kingdom and perceive that among quadrupeds there is not one whose functions and organs, especially the internal organs, are not entirely similar to those of every other quadruped, are we not inclined to believe that there has been only one first animal, the prototype of all other animals, which nature has formed by elongating, shortening, transforming, multiplying or obliterating certain organs? Picture to yourself the fingers of the hand joined together and the ungual material so abundant that it stretches and swells and envelops the whole; instead of a man's hand, you have a horse's foot. When we see the successive metamorphoses of the envelope of the prototype pass through imperceptible stages from one kingdom to another and populate the confines of the two kingdoms (if it is permissible to use the term confines where there is no actual dividing line)—and populate, then, the confines of the two kingdoms with beings that are indefinable, ambiguous, lacking in large measure the forms, qualities and functions that distinguish one kingdom from the other, who would not be inclined to believe that there has ever been but one being, the prototype of all other beings? But whether this philosophical conjecture be allowed to be true with Dr. Baumann [Maupertuis] or rejected as false with Buffon, it won't be denied that it must be embraced as an hypothesis essential to the progress of experimental science and rational philosophy, and to the discovery and explanation of the phenomena which result from organization. (XII)

I represent to myself the vast domain of the sciences as an immense body of land strewn with dark and with cleared areas. Our labors should aim at either pushing back the frontiers of the cleared areas or multiplying the centers of light. The second is a job for the creative genius; the first, for the wisdom which improves and refines. (XIV)

We have three principal methods at hand: the observation of nature, reflection, and experiment. Observation gathers the facts; reflection combines them; experiment verifies the result of the combination. The observation of nature must be assiduous, reflection profound, and experiment exact. These three methods united in one person are rarely seen. Hence creative geniuses are not common. (XV)

We have distinguished two kinds of philosophy, the experimental and the rational. The first is blindfolded and always feeling its way, seizes upon everything that falls into its hands, and at last stumbles upon precious things. The rational philosopher gathers these precious materials and tries to make a guiding light of them; but this assumed guide has, up to the present, been of less use than the groping of its rival, and necessarily so. Experiment puts no limit on its movements; it is ceaselessly in action; it spends in search of phenomena the time that reason employs in search of analogies. Experimental philosophy knows not what will result nor what will not result from its efforts; but keeps on working unremittingly. Rational philosophy, on the contrary weighs possibilities, makes a pronouncement, and stops there. It says rashly: "Light cannot be decomposed": experimental philosophy listens and is silent for long centuries; then suddenly it produces the prism and says: "Light is being decomposed." (XXIII)

Conversation Between D'Alembert and Diderot (1769)

D'ALEMBERT.—I confess that a Being who exists somewhere but in no fixed point of space; a Being who is not made of matter and yet who occupies a material universe; who subsists as a whole in each part of this universe; who differs essentially from matter and yet is united to matter; who follows it and moves it and is yet without motion; who acts upon it and yet is subject to all its vicissitudes; a Being of whom I can form no definite idea; a Being of such a contradictory nature is, I confess, difficult to accept. But other obscurities lie in wait for anyone who rejects this Being; for after all if that sensibility which you propose as a substitute is a general and essential attribute of matter, it necessarily follows that a stone feels.

DIDEROT.—Why not?

D'ALEMBERT.—That is hard to believe.

DIDEROT.—Hard indeed for anyone who cuts it, chisels it, crushes it, and doesn't hear it cry.

D'ALEMBERT.—I wish you would tell me what difference you see between man and a statue, between marble and flesh.

DIDEROT.—Not much. We make marble of flesh, and flesh of marble.

D'ALEMBERT.—But they are not the same thing.

DIDEROT.—Just as what you call animate force is not the same as inanimate force.

D'ALEMBERT.—I don't understand you.

DIDEROT.—I'll explain. The transfer of a body from one place to another is not movement, it's only the effect of movement. Movement is equally present in a moved body and a motionless body.

D'ALEMBERT.—That's a new way of looking at it.

DIDEROT.—But none the less true. Remove the obstacle that prevents a motionless body from moving in space and it will be moved. Suppress by sudden rarefication the air that surrounds that enormous oak trunk and the liquid that it contains, suddenly expanding, will shatter it into a thousand pieces. And I say the same thing about your own body.

D'ALEMBERT.—Agreed. But what connection is there between movement and sensibility? Could it be, perhaps, that you recognize an active sensibility and an inert sensibility, just as there is an active energy and a potential energy? An active force which is manifest in movement, a potential force which is represented by pressure? An active sensibility which is characterized by certain reactions that can be observed in animals and perhaps in plants? And an inert sensibility that can be ascertained by its passage to an active state?

DIDEROT.—Wonderful. You have guessed it.

D'ALEMBERT.—Thus a statue is only potentially sensitive; and a man, an animal, perhaps even a plant, is endowed with active sensitivity.

DIDEROT.—There is indeed that difference between the marble block and the flesh tissue; but you are well aware that that is not the only difference.

D'Alembert.—Of course. Whatever resemblance there may be between the exterior forms of a man and a statue, there is no relation at all between their interior organizations. The chisel of the most skilful sculptor can't make even an epidermis. But there is a very simple process by which an inanimate force can be changed into an animate force; that is an experiment that takes place repeatedly before our eyes a hundred times a day; whereas I don't see how a body with inert sensibility can be changed into one of active sensibility.

Diderot.—That's because you don't want to see it. It's a rather common phenomenon.

D'Alembert.—And this rather common phenomenon, what is it please?

Diderot.—I'll tell you if you want, to your own shame. It takes place every time you eat.

D'Alembert.—Every time I eat?

Diderot.—Yes, for what do you do when you eat? You remove the obstacles that stood in the way of the active sensibility of your food. You make it a part of yourself; you make flesh of it; you animalize it: you give it feeling: and what you do to food, I'll do if I want to marble.

D'Alembert.—How is that?

Diderot.—How? I'll make it edible.

D'Alembert.—Make marble edible? I think that won't be easy.

Diderot.—Then I'll have to show you the process. I take the statue you see there, I put it in a mortar, and with heavy blows of the pestle . . .

D'Alembert.—Gently, please; that is Falconet's masterpiece. Now if it were only a piece by Huez or some other person . . .

Diderot.—Falconet won't mind. The statue has been paid for, and Falconet cares little for his present reputation and none at all for the future.

D'Alembert.—All right. Pulverize away.

Diderot.—When the block of marble is reduced to fine powder, I mix this powder with humus or leaf-mould; I knead it all together; I water the mixture and let it putrefy for a year, two years, a century, time doesn't matter.

D. DIDEROT

When it is all transformed into a nearly homogeneous mass, into humus, do you know what I do?

D'ALEMBERT.—I'm sure you don't eat humus.

DIDEROT.—No, but there is a means of union or appropriation between humus and me, an intermediary, or *latus*, as the chemist would say.

D'ALEMBERT.—And that intermediary is a plant?

DIDEROT.—Very good. I sow peas in it, and beans and cabbages and other leguminous plants. The plants are nourished by the earth and I am nourished by the plants.

D'ALEMBERT.—True or false, I like your passage from marble to humus, from humus to the vegetable kingdom, and from there to the animal kingdom, to flesh.

DIDEROT.—I therefore make flesh, or soul, as my daughter says, an actively sensitive substance; and if I don't solve the problem that you proposed, at least I have come very close to it; for you will admit that there is a greater distance between a bit of marble and a feeling being than between a feeling being and a thinking being.

D'ALEMBERT.—I agree. But even at that, the feeling being is not yet a thinking being. . . .

DIDEROT.—Can you tell what constitutes the existence of a feeling being, from its own point of view?

D'ALEMBERT.—The awareness of having been itself, from the moment of first reflection to the present.

DIDEROT.—And on what is that awareness founded?

D'ALEMBERT.—On the memory of its acts.

DIDEROT.—And without that memory?

D'ALEMBERT.—Without that memory it would lose its identity, since if it feels its existence only at the moment of sense impressions it would have no life-history. Its life would be a broken series of sensations with nothing to bind them together.

DIDEROT.—Very good. And what is memory? What gives it birth?

D'ALEMBERT.—A certain organization which develops, grows weak, and is sometimes entirely lost.

DIDEROT.—Then if a feeling being who has this organization that produces memory binds together its sense perceptions and forms by this bond a history, its life history, and acquires self-awareness, it proceeds to deny, affirm, conclude, and think.

D'ALEMBERT.—So it seems to me; I have just one more objection.

DIDEROT.—You're wrong; you have many more than one.

D'ALEMBERT.—But one principal objection; it seems to me that we can think of only one thing at a time, and to be able to form, not those tremendous chains of thought which encompass thousands of ideas in their course, but a simple proposition, it could be said that there must be at least two things present, the object that the mind's eye rests upon, while the mind is concerned with the quality that it will either affirm or deny in that object.

DIDEROT.—I think so; and that has sometimes led me to liken the fibers of our brains to sensitive vibrant chords. The sensitive vibrant chord oscillates and resounds long after it has been plucked. And that oscillation, that sort of necessary resonance holds the object in view, while the mind is concerned with its true quality. But the vibrating chords have still another function, that of making other chords vibrate; thus a first idea calls up a second, these two a third, all three a fourth, and so on, with no fixed limit to the ideas awakened and linked in the mind of a philosopher who is meditating or musing in silence and darkness. This instrument makes astonishing leaps, and an awakened idea will sometimes set in vibration a harmonic across an incomprehensible interval. If the phenomenon can be observed between resonant, inert, and separate chords, how could it fail to take place between living and connected points, between continuous and sensitive fibers?

D'ALEMBERT.—If that's not true, it's at least ingenious. But it would be tempting to believe that you fall imperceptibly into the dilemma that you are trying to avoid.

DIDEROT.—What one?

D'ALEMBERT.—You don't like to make a distinction between the two substances.

DIDEROT.—I make no secret of that.

D'ALEMBERT.—And if you look at your argument closely, you are making of the philosopher's mind a being distinct from the instrument, a kind of musician who lends an ear to vibrating chords and decides whether they are harmonious or dissonant.

Diderot.—It's possible that I gave rise to that objection, which perhaps you wouldn't have made if you had considered the difference between the philosopher as instrument and the harpsichord as instrument. The philosopher is sensitive; he is at once both the musician and the instrument. As a feeling being, he has the momentary awareness of the sound that he renders; as an animal, he remembers it. This faculty of the organism, linking sounds together within itself, both produces and retains melody. Suppose the harpsichord has sensibility and memory and tell me if it won't repeat of its own accord the airs that you produced on its keys. We are instruments endowed with sensibility and memory. Our senses are so many keys struck by our natural surroundings and that often strike all by themselves; and here, in my opinion, is all that takes place in a harpsichord organized like you and me. There is an impression which is caused either within or without the instrument, a sensation born of that impression, a sensation which persists, for it is impossible to imagine that it is made and blotted out in an indivisible instant; another impression which follows and likewise is caused within or without the animal; a second sensation and voices which designate it by natural or conventional sounds.

D'Alembert.—I understand. Then if this sensitive, animate harpsichord were also endowed with the nutritive and reproductive faculties, it would live and engender, of itself or with its female, other little vibrating and resonant harpsichords.

Diderot.—No doubt. In your opinion, what else is a finch, or nightingale, a musician, or a man? And what other difference do you find between a canary and a wooden canary-whistle? Do you see this egg? With that are overturned all the schools of theology and all the churches of the earth. What is an egg? An insensitive mass before the germ is introduced; and after the germ is introduced, what is it? an insensitive mass, for the germ itself is only an inert, coarse fluid. How will that mass pass over into another organization, into sensibility and life? By means of heat. What will produce the heat? Motion. What will be the successive effects of this motion? Instead of replying, sit down and watch them from moment to moment. First there is a quivering point, a fiber which stretches out and takes on color; flesh which is being formed; a beak, wing tips, eyes, feet appear; a yellowish substance which unwinds and produces intestines; it is an animal. This animal moves, is agitated, cries; I hear its cries through the shell; it is covering itself with down; it sees. The weight of its head, in oscillation, brings its beak against the interior wall of its prison, which now breaks; it comes forth, walks, flies, is irritated, flees, approaches, complains, suffers, loves, desires, enjoys: it feels everything that you feel; all your actions, it performs. Do you claim, with Descartes, that it is a purely imitative machine? But little children will laugh at you, and philosophers will reply that if this is a machine, you are another. If you admit that between you and the animal the only difference is in organization, you will be sensible and reasonable and will do so in good faith, but it will be concluded against you that with inert matter disposed in a certain manner and impregnated with other inert matter, with heat and motion, there can be obtained sensibility, life, memory, self-consciousness, passions and thought. You have only one of two positions to embrace: either to imagine in the inert mass of the egg a hidden element which awaits development before manifesting its presence, or to suppose that this imperceptible element has worked its way through the shell at a determined moment of that development. But what is that element? Was it occupying space or not? How did it come or escape without moving? Where was it? What was it doing there, or elsewhere? Was it created at the moment of need? Was it already in existence? Was it awaiting a domicile? If homogeneous, it was material; if heterogeneous, neither its inertia before the development nor its energy within the developed animal is conceivable. Listen to what you are saying and you will be sorry for yourself; you will perceive that in order not to admit of a simple supposition that explains everything, namely sensibility as a general attribute of matter or a product of the organization of matter, you renounce common sense and cast yourself into an abyss of mysteries, contradictions and absurdities.

D'Alembert.—A supposition! It's nice of you to say so. But suppose it were a quality essentially incompatible with matter?

Diderot.—And how do you know that sensibility is essentially incompatible with matter, you who don't know the essence of anything, either matter or sensibility? Do you understand any better the nature of motion, its existence in a body and its passage from one body to another?

D'Alembert.—If I cannot conceive the nature of either sensibility or matter, I do see that sensibility is a simple quality, one, indivisible, and incompatible with a divisible object or agent.

Diderot.—Metaphysical-theological nonsense. What! don't you see that all the qualities, all the forms of the perceivable universe are essentially indivisible? There is no such thing as more or less impenetrability. A round body can be halved, but not roundness; a body can move more or less, but there is either motion or no motion; there is no more a half, a third, or a quarter of a head or an ear or a finger than there is a half, a third, or a quarter of a thought. If there is not a molecule in the universe that resembles another molecule, not a point in the molecule that resembles another point, admit that the atom itself is endowed with an indivisible quality and form; admit that division is incompatible with the essence of forms, since it destroys them. Be a physicist and admit the production of an effect when you see it produced, even though you are unable to explain the connection between cause and effect. Be a logician and do not substitute for a cause which exists and explains everything another cause which is inconceivable, of which the connection with the effect is no less inconceivable, which gives rise to an infinite multitude of difficulties and solves none of them.

D'Alembert.—But suppose I dispense with that cause?

Diderot.—There is only one substance in the universe, in man, in animal. The bird-organ is made of wood, man of flesh. The canary is flesh, the musician flesh diversely organized; but both have the same origin, the same formation, the same functions and the same ending. . . .

D'ALEMBERT.—Farewell, my friend. Good night and sleep well.

DIDEROT.—You're passing this conversation off as a joke, but you will dream about it on your pillow, and if it doesn't take on consistency, so much the worse for you, for otherwise you'll be forced to embrace very absurd hypotheses.

D'ALEMBERT. You're wrong there; a skeptic I go to bed, and a skeptic I arise.

DIDEROT.—Skeptic! Can a man be a skeptic?

D'ALEMBERT.—There you go again. You're not going to maintain that I'm not a skeptic? Who knows better than I?

DIDEROT.—Wait a moment.

D'ALEMBERT.—Hurry up then. I want to get to sleep.

DIDEROT.—I'll be brief. Do you believe there is a single question under discussion about which a man finds an exactly equal balance of strict logic for and against?

D'ALEMBERT.—No, that would be Buridan's ass.[1]

DIDEROT.—Then there is no such thing as a skeptic, since except for mathematical questions which do not admit of the least uncertainty, there are arguments for and against all the others. The scales are therefore never in balance, and must of necessity dip on the side which we believe the most probable.

D'ALEMBERT.—But in the morning probability appears on my right and in the afternoon on my left.

DIDEROT.—In other words you are dogmatic for in the morning and against in the afternoon.

D'ALEMBERT.—And in the evening, when I recall the fleeting nature of my decisions, I believe nothing, neither the morning's nor the afternoon's.

DIDEROT.—You mean you no longer recall the overbalance of the two opinions between which you have wavered; and that overbalance seems to you too slight a base for a

[1] The medieval philosopher Jean Buridan, confronted with a metaphysically insoluble problem, imagined an ass that died of hunger and thirst when unable to decide which to partake of first, a measure of oats or a bucket of water.

fixed idea; and you make up your mind not to bother with such problematical subjects, to leave the discussion to others, and dispute no longer.

D'ALEMBERT.—That could be.

DIDEROT.—But if someone takes you aside, questions you in a friendly way and asks you sincerely to which of the two sides you find the fewest objections, in all good conscience would you hesitate to reply and be like Buridan's ass?

D'ALEMBERT.—I don't think so.

DIDEROT.—Well, my friend, if you weigh the matter carefully you will find that in all things our true opinion is not the one about which we have never had doubts, but the one to which we most habitually revert.

D'ALEMBERT.—I think you are right.

DIDEROT.—I think so, too. Good night, now, and "remember that dust thou art and unto dust returneth."

D'ALEMBERT.—That's sad.

DIDEROT.—And yet necessary. Grant Man, I don't say immortality, but only a double span of life, and you'll see what will happen.

D'ALEMBERT.—What do you expect to happen? But what is that to me? Come what will, I want to sleep. Good night.

The Will

D'ALEMBERT.— . . . What is this free will, this will of a man in a dream?

BORDEU.[1]—What is it? The same as the will of a man wide awake: the latest impulse of desire or aversion, the latest result of all that a man has been from the time of his birth to the moment at hand: and I defy the most subtle mind to see the least difference between them.

D'ALEMBERT.—You think so?

BORDEU.—And you ask me that question! You, who, given over to profound speculation, have spent two thirds of

[1] Bordeu was a celebrated doctor and friend of Diderot.

your life dreaming with eyes wide open and acting without willing; yes, without willing, much less than in your dreams. In your dreams you were in command, you gave orders, you were obeyed; you were unhappy or content, you experienced contradiction, you met obstacles, you were incensed, you loved, you hated, you blamed, you came, and you went. In the course of your meditations, your eyes were hardly open in the morning when you were possessed by the preoccupations of the day before, you dressed, you sat at your desk, you meditated, you drew figures, you made calculations, you dined, you went back to your devisings, you even left your desk at times to verify them; you spoke to other people, you gave orders to your servants, you had supper, went to bed, and fell asleep, all without the least act of will. You were reduced to a single point; you acted, but did not will. Can we will, all by ourselves? Will is always born of some motive, interior or exterior, of some present impression, or reminiscence of the past, or passion, or future project. That being so I have just one word for you about free will, which is, that the latest of our acts is the necessary effect of a single cause—the self; a very complex cause, but single.

MLLE DE LESPINASSE.[1]—The necessary effect?

BORDEU.—Of course. Try to conceive of any other act resulting, supposing the agent to be the same.

MLLE DE LESPINASSE.—He is right. Since I acted thus, anyone who acted differently is no longer me; and to assert that at the moment I do or say anything, I can do or say something different is to assert that I am both myself and someone else. But doctor, vice and virtue? Virtue, that word so holy in all languages, so sacred among all peoples!

BORDEU.—It must be transformed into beneficence, and its opposite into malfeasance. We are born well- or ill-endowed by nature; we are irresistibly borne along by the general current which leads one man to glory, another to ignominy.

[1] Mlle de Lespinasse, famous for her salon, was D'Alembert's intimate friend.

MLLE DE LESPINASSE.—And self-esteem, shame and remorse?

BORDEU.—Childish notions, founded on the ignorance and vanity of a man who takes upon himself the merit or blame for a moment of time that had to be.

MLLE DE LESPINASSE.—And rewards and punishments?

BORDEU.—Ways of correcting the modifiable creature called wicked and encouraging the good.

MLLE DE LESPINASSE.—Isn't that doctrine a bit dangerous?

BORDEU.—Is it true or false?

MLLE DE LESPINASSE.—I think it is true.

BORDEU.—Which is to say that you think the lie has its advantages and truth, its inconveniences.

MLLE DE LESPINASSE.—I think so.

BORDEU.—So do I: But the advantages of a lie are momentary, and those of truth, eternal; the unfortunate results of truth, if present, pass quickly away, while those of a lie last as long as the lie. . . .

(from *D'Alembert's Dream*)

Memory

I am inclined to believe that all we have seen, known, perceived or heard—even the trees of a great forest, yes, even the disposition of the branches, the forms of the leaves and the variety of colors, the play of green and light, even the aspect of the grains of sand on the seashore, the unevenness of the waves, whether stirred by a light breeze or tossed by tempestuous winds; even the multitude of human voices, the cries of animals and physical noises, the melody and harmony of all tunes, all musical pieces, all concerts we have ever heard—all that exists within us and unknown to us.

I still review in my waking hours all the forests of Westphalia, Prussia, Saxony and Poland.

I review them when I dream as brilliantly colored as they would be in a painting by Vernet.

Sleep has brought back to me concerts executed all over again as if I were really there.

Comedies and tragedies presented thirty years ago come back to me, with the same actors, the same audience, the same men in the boxes, the same women, the same costumes, the same noise, either of hoots or applause. . . .

The sound of a voice, the presence of an object, a certain locality . . . and behold, an object recalled—more than that, a whole stretch of my past—and I am plunged again into pleasure, regret or affliction.

(*Elements of Physiology*)

Apologue of the Young Mexican (1777)

Diderot.—Weary from his labors a young Mexican was walking one day by the seashore. He saw a plank with one end dipped in the water and the other resting on the beach. He sat on the plank and there, looking over the vast expanse that stretched out before him, he said to himself: Nothing is truer than that my old grandmother is talking nonsense with her story of some people or other who, at some time or other, landed here from some country or other beyond our seas. It just doesn't make sense: can't I see that the sea ends at the horizon? And can I believe, against all evidence of the senses, an old fable the date of which is unknown, which everyone twists around to his liking, and which forms nothing but a web of absurd details over which they eat their hearts out and tear out their eyes?

While he was reasoning in this manner, the roll of the ocean rocked him gently on his plank and he fell asleep. And while he was sleeping, the wind came up, the waves floated the plank on which he was lying, and there was our young reasoner off to sea.

Madame de Broglie.—Alas! that is our human condition: we are all on our planks; the winds blow and the waves carry us away.

Diderot.—He was already far from the mainland when he awoke. And our young Mexican was surprised enough to find himself at sea, and even more so, after he had lost sight of the beach on which he had been walking just a moment before, and the sea appeared to merge on all sides with the horizon. He suspected then that he might have been mistaken; and that if the wind continued to blow in the same direction he might be carried to the shore among those people that his grandmother had so often talked to him about.

Madame.—But you say nothing of his anxiety.

Diderot.—He had none. He said to himself: What difference does that make, if only I land? I argued like a fool, I agree; but I was honest with myself; and that is all that can be expected of me. If it's not a virtue to be intelligent, it's at least not a crime to be a fool. Meanwhile the winds kept up, the man and the plank floated on, and the unknown shore began to appear: he touched land and stepped off.

Madame.—We will see each other there some day, Mr. Diderot.

Diderot.—I hope so, madam; and wherever that may be, I will always be very pleased to pay court to you. No sooner had he left his plank and stepped on the beach than he saw a venerable old man standing by his side. He asked where he was and to whom he had the honor of speaking. "I am the sovereign of this country," replied the old man. Instantly the young man knelt before him. "Get up," said the old man. "Did you deny my existence?" —"I did."—"And that of my empire?"—"I did."—"I forgive you, for I am he who sees into the depths of men's hearts and I have read at the bottom of yours that you acted in good faith; but the rest of your thoughts and deeds were not so innocent." Then the old man, who held him by the ear, reminded him of all the errors of his life; and on each count, the young man bowed his head, beat his breast, and asked forgiveness . . . Now, madam, put yourself for a moment in the place of the old man and tell me what you would have done. Would you have seized this young fool by the hair and taken pleasure in dragging him along the shore through all eternity?

MADAME.—Certainly, I would not.

DIDEROT.—If one of those six handsome children of yours, after escaping from the paternal roof and done all sorts of foolish things, came back truly repentant?

MADAME.—Why, I would run to meet him; I would take him in my arms and weep over him; but Monsieur de Broglie, his father, wouldn't take the matter so easily.

DIDEROT.—But Monsieur is no tiger.

MADAME.—Oh no. Far from it.

DIDEROT.—He might have to be teased into it a bit; but he would forgive.

MADAME.—Of course.

DIDEROT.—Especially if he happened to consider that, before fathering this child, he knew all that was going to happen to it, and that punishment for its faults would be of no use to himself, or to the child, or to his other children.

MADAME.—The old man and Monsieur are two different persons.

DIDEROT.—Do you mean to say that Monsieur is better than the old man?

MADAME.—Heaven forbid! I mean that if my sense of justice is not the same as Monsieur's, Monsieur's sense of justice may not be the same as the old man's.

DIDEROT.—Ah, Madam! you do not realize the consequences of that reply. Either the general definition of justice applies equally to you, M. de Broglie, and me, to the young Mexican and the old man; or I no longer know what justice is, nor how we can please or displease the old man. . . .

Political Observations

[*The manuscript of Diderot's* Observations *on the* Instructions *of Catherine the Great to her deputies, who were commissioned to recodify Russian law, went to Russia with his library in 1785. They have been published, imperfectly, only in the twentieth century. A critical text is being edited by Pierre C. Oustinoff and Edward J. Geary. The excerpts given below are translated from this text. From these observations, Diderot appears as the most forceful political writer of his age.*

Catherine had early been favorable to French liberal thought and, under the influence of Montesquieu and Beccaria, had sincerely contemplated reforms, which had been the subject of conversations with Diderot during his visit to St. Petersburg in 1773-4. By 1785, however, she was alarmed by the revolutionary course of events in France and considered Diderot's remarks unrealistic and completely out of place. She saw to it that they were kept under lock and key.

Although this text was unknown in France before the Revolution, Diderot had succeeded in making his influence felt through conversations and insinuations throughout the Encyclopedia *and other published works.*]

The only true sovereign is the nation. There can be no true legislator except the people. Rarely do people submit to laws that have been forced upon them. They will cherish them, obey them, defend them as their own work, if they are themselves the lawmakers. The laws are then no longer the arbitrary will of a single person; they represent the will of a number of men who have consulted one another on their happiness and security. They are useless if they do not apply equally to all men. They are useless if a single member of society can break them with impunity. The first article of a code should therefore inform us of the precautions that have been taken to assure the laws of their authority.

The first line of a well-drawn code should bind the sovereign. It should begin thus: "We, the People, and We, the Sovereign of this people, take solemn oath to uphold these laws, by which we are to be equally judged; and if it happens that We, the Sovereign, change or break them, as an enemy of our people it is just that they should be our enemy and be freed from their oath of allegiance, that they should pursue us, depose us, and even condemn us to death if the circumstances so require." And that is the first law of our code. May evil befall the sovereign who scorns the law, and the people who suffer it to be scorned. And since the authority of the sovereign alone endangers the law, this oath must be taken by the people and the sovereign for every law enacted; and on the original decree and all public copies, it must be certified that this oath has been taken. Any sovereign who refuses to take this oath is thereby declared to be a despot and a tyrant.

The second law is that representatives of the nation shall meet every five years to decide whether the sovereign has exactly conformed to a law that he has sworn to; to decide upon the penalty that he deserves if he has broken the law; to keep him in power or depose him; and to swear to uphold those laws of which the oath has been certified.

Nations, if you have authority over your sovereigns, draw up a code. If your sovereign has authority over you, leave a code alone. You will only be forging your own chains.

* * *

[Catherine had written: "My Lord, God, hear my prayer and grant me the intelligence to judge thy people according to thy holy law and in all truth. The Christian religion teaches us to do all the good we can to one another."]

It is a moot question whether we should submit political institutions to religious sanction. I do not like to include in acts of sovereignty people who extol a being superior to the sovereign and who interpret that being's will according to their own good pleasure. I do not like to transform a matter of rational concern into one of religious zeal. I do not like to give weight and consideration to those who speak in the name of the Almighty. Religion is a support that in the end almost always ruins the edifice.

The distance between the altar and the throne can never be too great. The experience of all ages and all countries has shown the danger to the throne of proximity to the altar.

* * *

[Catherine was long considered, and considered herself, a benevolent despot. "It is better to obey laws under a single master," she wrote, "than under several masters."]

I agree, but on the condition that the master be the first slave of the law. Laws should be principally directed against the master, the most powerful and dangerous of malefactors. Other malefactors can disturb the social order, but he alone can overthrow it. There is only one palace in an empire; there are a hundred million houses around that palace. For the one time that common sense, magnanimity, equity, fortitude, genius, fall upon the palace, there are a hundred million times when these qualities that make a king great miss their mark. We must expect then, according to an unalterable law of nature, to be governed by a fool, a reprobate or a madman. Nothing can be accomplished until this objection has been met.

Letters to Sophie Volland

Diderot's correspondence remains one of the most fascinating of his many accomplishments. His letters to Sophie Volland are particularly delightful and revealing. In the longer letter offered below, the life and conversation of one of France's most intellectual salons is realistically portrayed. The letter also gives us an insight into the way that Diderot's mind worked. His mastery in rendering lively conversation will enliven two of his masterpieces, Le Neveu de Rameau *and* Jacques le Fataliste. *The latter work especially exemplifies the literary techniques of suspension and digression, in imitation of the trends of general conversation which are here discussed.*

Diderot was a welcome guest at Grandval, the country estate of Baron D'Holbach, of which the baron's elderly mother-in-law (Mme D'Aine) was the gay and most considerate hostess. Among the distinguished guests assembled there were Mme Geoffrin, who presided over one of the celebrated salons in Paris, and Grimm and Abbé Galiani, both good friends of Diderot.[1] *Grimm's* Literary Correspondence, *a periodic report of the intellectual life of France (written in collaboration with Diderot), was addressed in general to the principal courts of Europe. It accounted for Catherine the Great's admiration of Diderot, revealed him as a great creative art critic in his report of the* Salons *(1759-1773) and gave Goethe and Schiller the opportunity to read a number of his important works in manuscript many years before they were known in France.*

Grandval, October 20, 1760.

Here, my dear, is how we pass our time. I might have made an amusing story of it, but how can we laugh and joke when our hearts are sad. I mean your mother's, your sister's, and yours. Your friend was born under such a lucky star! How I envy his character! Hope always remains in the bottom of his box, whereas when fate comes and opens the lid of mine, it's the first thing that flies off. Not that I don't perceive the strings that I could cling to; but they are so feeble and loose that I wouldn't dare trust them. I would almost as soon abandon myself to the torrent as grasp the leaf of a willow.

We have a lot of company here; M. Le Roy, as I wrote before, friend Grimm and Abbé Galiani, M. and Mme Rodier. I like M. Rodier's face. If he were only half as intelligent as it seems to promise! He is a mixture of tact and sensuality. In the morning when his long brown hair falls to his shoulders in loose curls, you would take

[1] "Father" Hoop was a disabused and forthright Scot, often a welcome guest of the baron. The other guests need no special identification.

him for Hymen, but as Hymen appears on the day after the wedding, pale and a bit weary. Mme Rodier was dressed in a deep red that did not become her, and Grimm said to her: "How now, dear sister? You are as beautiful as an Easter egg." D'Alainville and Mme Geoffrin, hardly bored at all, rare event. Mme de Charmoi, still with her beautiful eyes and entrancing mien, D'Aine, the monotonous son of the family, M. and Mme Schiester, Monsieur with his mandola and drum; and two or three others whom I don't know, for good measure.

I like my creature comforts everywhere, but especially in the country. I am lodged in a lady's apartment, the best in the house; in the midst of all these guests, I still have it, and like our hostess all the more for that.

The more numerous the company is, the freer we are. Left entirely to myself, I have never had so much time to read, to take walks, to be yours, to love you, and write to you.

Our dinner was very gay. M. Le Roy told of an unfortunate love affair of his. "Just one?"—"That is all." He slept on it his fifteen hours and got noticeably fatter. "But an unfortunate lover should be undone.—Or appear to be so, and I couldn't do it. That's what undid me." He rested because of the pain he had suffered, and when he had rested, he couldn't suffer any more because of the rest he had had. "Otherwise, you couldn't have stood it.—That's true; but from evening to morning I was all fresh to suffer again.—But if you sleep your fifteen hours when you are unfortunate in love, how long do you sleep when you are lucky?—Almost not at all.—Good fortune tires you little.—Not in the least, and besides, I pick up again quickly."

You will understand how all that sounds at table, at dessert, among twelve or fifteen people, with champagne, gayety, wit, and all the freedom of country living.

Mme Geoffrin behaved very well; I played piquet with her, D'Alainville, and the Baron. I always notice the noble yet simple taste of that woman's clothes. That day they were of plain material, sober in color, with ample sleeves, and the plainest and most delicate of linen, all as clean and neat as you could ask for. She asked after my wife and child. About the child, I replied that I was afraid her life would be stormy and unhappy, because she never could be still for a moment. "All the better," she said, for she will busy herself for the lazy ones," and she seized the occasion to sing the praises of Mme D'Aine, who was always on the jump taking care of the rest of us idlers.

But oh, my dear, where were you? What were you doing at Isle, when I wanted you here so much? Whenever I am having a good time, I wish you were sharing it. M. Schiester now takes his mandola, and now is playing something on it. Marvelous execution! How his fingers make his strings talk! It's unbelievable, and Mme D'Holbach and I didn't miss a word of it.—That's a fine fit of anger!—What a sweet lament!—He's becoming vexed; he's making up his mind.—You're right. Now they are reconciled again.—True.—How can anyone hold out against a man who offers such handsome excuses!—I'm sure we heard all that.

M. Schiester put down his mandola, and the keenness of our pleasure became the subject of the conversation. We let them talk to their hearts' content and preferred to enjoy in silence what was left of our emotion. The moment of excitement that follows great pleasure is a very enjoyable moment: for the heart beats faster both before and after pleasure.

Mme Geoffrin never sleeps away from home; at about six o'clock, she kissed us goodbye and got into her carriage with D'Alainville and off she went. At seven o'clock they sat down at the card tables, and Le Roy, Grimm, Abbé Galiani, and I chatted. Ah! this time I'll teach you to appreciate the Abbé, whom you have perhaps up to now thought of as just a pleasant sort of fellow. He's better than that.

Grimm and M. Le Roy were discussing the difference between creative genius and systematic method. Grimm detests the methodical mind; according to him, it's nothing but scholarly pedantry. Those who know only how to systematize might just as well save themselves the trouble; those who can learn only by system might just as well stay ignorant. "But method alone can evaluate.—And spoil everything.—Without it, no one would profit from anything.—Except by getting tired out, and that would be all the better. What's the need for so many people knowing anything more than their trade?" They said a lot of things that I won't repeat and would have said a lot more, if Abbé Galiani hadn't interrupted them as follows:

"My friends, I recall a fable. Now listen. It may be a bit long, but not boring.

One day in the depth of a forest, a singing contest took place between a nightingale and a cuckoo. Each of them boasted of his talent.—What bird, said the cuckoo, has as easy, as simple, as natural, and as measured a song as mine?

—What bird, said the nightingale, has a sweeter, more varied, more brilliant, more airy and touching song than mine?

The cuckoo: I say little, but that little carries weight, is orderly, and easy to remember.

The nightingale: I love to talk; but I am always original and never bore. I am the delight of the forest; the cuckoo brings sadness. He is so attached to his mother's teaching that he wouldn't dare risk a note he didn't learn from her. But I recognize no master. Rules are my playthings, and I am especially admired when I break them. Your fastidious method just can't compare with my happy outburst.

The cuckoo tried several times to interrupt the nightingale. But nightingales keep singing and don't listen: that's their failing. Our nightingale, carried along by his ideas, quickly followed them up without worrying about his rival's replies.

After several arguments back and forth, however, they agreed to abide by the judgment of another animal. But where find a third party intelligent and impartial enough to judge them? It's not easy to find a good judge. They went all around looking for one. They were crossing a meadow, when they saw a donkey, the gravest and most solemn of donkeys. Since the creation of the species, no donkey ever had such long ears.—Ah! said the cuckoo, when he saw them, we certainly are lucky; our quarrel is for ears to decide; here is our judge; God made him just for our purpose.

The donkey was browsing. He hardly dreamed that one day he would be a music critic. But Providence has fun in lots of different ways. Our two birds drop down in front of him, compliment him on his gravity and judgment, explain the subject of their dispute, and beg him very humbly to listen to them and decide. But the donkey, hardly turning his heavy head and not losing a mouthful of grass, makes a sign with his ears that he is hungry, and that his court is not in session that day. Browsing away, his appetite is soon satisfied. There were some trees growing along the edge of the meadow.—All right then, he said, go over there, and I'll come, too; you sing, I'll digest, I'll listen to you, and then I'll tell you what I think.

The birds swoop over and perch in the trees; the donkey follows them with the air and gait of a chief justice walking through the rooms of the courthouse. He arrives, stretches himself out on the ground, and says:—Begin; the hearing is open. He was all there was to the court.

The cuckoo says: Your Highness, not a word must be lost of my arguments; note well the nature of my song and deign especially to observe its skillful structure and method. Then puffing himself up and flapping his wings in unison, he sang: cuckoo, cuckoo, coo-coo-koo. cuckoo, coo-coo-koo. And when he had sung that in all possible combinations, he left off.

The nightingale, with no preamble, lets loose his voice, soars into the boldest of modulations, carries on with the most original and delicate of songs; trills or sustained notes that would take your breath away; now the notes could be heard tumbling and murmuring in the depths of his throat like the waters of a stream flowing deep down among resonant pebbles; now rising and swelling little by little until the whole air was filled with suspended song. It passed from one mood to another, sweet, airy, bright, or pathetic, and colorfully painted whatever spirit it was imitating; but it was not a song for the common herd.

Carried away by his enthusiasm, he would still be singing, if the donkey, who had already yawned a couple of times, hadn't stopped him and said: I suspect that all you have just sung is very beautiful, but it's over my head; it strikes me as odd, confused, all at loose ends. You are perhaps wiser than your rival, but he is more methodical, and I am all for method."

And the Abbé, addressing M. Le Roy and pointing to Grimm, said: "He is the nightingale and you, the cuckoo, and I, I am the donkey who awards you the victory. Good night."

The Abbé's stories are good, but he plays them up brilliantly. He breaks you down. You would have laughed your head off to see him stretch up his neck and mimic the soft voice of the nightingale; puff himself up and copy the raucous note of the cuckoo; prick up his ears and imitate the grave stupidity and dullness of the donkey; and all quite naturally, without apparent effort. He is all pantomime, from head to foot. M. Le Roy was minded to praise and laugh at the fable.

Speaking of the songs of birds, someone asked what made the ancients say that swans, with their nasal, raucous cries, sang melodiously when dying. I replied that the swan was the symbol of the man who talks on and on up to the very last moment, and I added that if I ever had to compose a poem of the last words of an orator, poet or statesman, I would call my poem "The Swansong."

The conversation then took a bit more serious turn. They spoke of the horror we all have of annihilation. "All?" exclaimed Father Hoop. "You'll excuse me, please. This life has been too rough on me to make me want to try it again. You could offer me immortality among the blessed in return for just one day in purgatory, and I wouldn't take you up: annihilation is best."

That set me dreaming, and it seemed to me that as long as I am in good health, I would agree with Father Hoop; but perhaps at the last moment, I would buy the happiness of living again for a thousand years, a thousand years of hell. Ah! my dear, we would be reunited, and I would love you still! I persuaded myself of what a daughter succeeded in persuading her dying father. He was an old usurer; a priest had sworn that he would be damned if he didn't make amends. He made up his mind to it, called his daughter, and said: "My child, you thought I was going to leave you rich, and so indeed you would have been; but here is a man who is going to make you destitute; he claims that I will burn forever in hell if I die without making restitution."—"Don't be ridiculous, father, with your ideas of restitution and damnation; I know you well enough to know that you won't be damned for ten years before you'll be quite used to it." He was convinced that that was true and died without restitution. A daughter will make up her mind to damn her father, a father to be damned in order to enrich his daughter; and an ardent lover or a man of honor will be afraid to do so. Isn't it a very nice idea to exist, and to meet again one's father, mother, loved one, friend, wife and children, all those whom we have cherished, even in hell?

And so now we are off, discoursing on life, death, the world and its assumed creator. Someone remarked that whether there is a God or not, it wouldn't be possible to introduce this mechanism either into nature or a problem without obscuring it. Another person, that if a supposition explained all phenomena, it wouldn't follow that the supposition was true; for who knows whether the general order of things has only one cause? What must we think, then, of a supposition which, far from resolving the only difficulty for which it was imagined, blossoms out into countless other difficulties?

My dear, I think our chatter by the fireplace always amuses you, so I carry on.

Among the difficulties that have been proposed since

the world began is that men suffer without deserving it, and there is still no answer to that. It's the incompatibility of physical and moral evil with the nature of the eternal being. This is how the difficulty is put: it's either powerlessness or ill-will on his part; powerlessness if he wanted to prevent evil and couldn't; ill-will, if he could have prevented evil and didn't want to.

A child would understand that. And that's what made people imagine the sin of a first parent, original sin, future rewards and punishment, incarnation, immortality, the two principles of the Manicheans, Ormazd and Ahriman among the Persians, emanations, the empires of light and darkness, the succession of lives, metempsychosis, philosophical optimism, and other absurdities accredited among the different peoples of the earth, where we always find a hollow vision in response to a clear, plain, and precise fact.

In these circumstances, what is the common sense solution? The one we have taken, my love: whatever the optimists tell us, we will reply that if the world couldn't exist without sentient beings, or sentient beings without suffering, the business should have been left alone. An eternity could well have passed without that blunder.

The world, a blunder! Ah, my dear, what a wonderful blunder, after all! According to some of the inhabitants of Malabar, it's one of the seventy-four comedies that amuse the eternal Being.

Leibnitz, founder of optimism, as great a poet as he was a profound philosopher, tells us somewhere that there was in a temple of Memphis a high pyramid of globes placed one on top of another; that a priest, asked by a traveler about this pyramid and globes, replied that they were all the possible worlds, and that the most perfect was at the top; that the traveler, anxious to see this most perfect of worlds, climbed up the pyramid, and the first thing that came into view as he looked at the top globe was Tarquin raping Lucretia. I don't know who brought up that story, which I knew and think I have already told you.

Conversation is a strange thing, especially when the company is a bit numerous. Just see how we have gone around and around; a sick man's dreams in a delirium are no more devious. However, just as there is nothing unconnected either in the head of a dreamer or a madman, so everything in conversation hangs together; but at times it would be hard to trace back the imperceptible links that have given rise to so many dissimilar ideas. A man throws in a word which he picks out from what has preceded and followed in his head; another does the same, and then pick it up who can. A single physical quality can lead an attentive mind to any number of diverse things. Take a color, yellow, for example: gold is yellow, silk is yellow, worries are yellow, bile is yellow, straw is yellow; and how many other trains of thought are tied to this one! Folly, dreams, the drift of conversation, consist in passing from one subject to another by the intermediary of a common quality.

The fool doesn't notice the shift. He holds a shiny yellow straw in his hand and says that he has caught a sunbeam. How many men are like this fool without suspecting it! And I, too, perhaps, at this very moment.

The word *rape* tied in Tarquin's crime with Lovelace's. Lovelace is the hero of the novel *Clarissa Harlowe*, and now we have jumped from Roman history to the English novel. There was great dispute about *Clarissa.* Those who held it in contempt held it in sovereign contempt; those who prized it, as excessive in their esteem as the former in their contempt, looked upon it as one of the triumphs of the human mind. I have it; I'm very sorry that you didn't put it in your trunk. I won't be happy about either you or me until I have led you to enjoy the truth of *Pamela*, *Tom Jones*, and *Clarissa*, and *Grandison.*[1]

So many wise and foolish things have been said and done here that I'd never be through if I didn't break the thread and proceed to two little adventures that I can't bear not to pass on to you, though I know very well that

[1] Works of Samuel Richardson and Henry Fielding, precursors of the realistic novel.

they are childish and of a color that hardly goes with your present complexion.

We are all lodged on the second floor, along the same corridor, some looking out on the entrance court and moats, others on the garden and countryside. Oh, my love, what a babbler I am! As Mme de Sévigné said, who was after all as much a babbler and glutton as I: "Will I ever be able to stop eating and shut up?"

In the evening we had all retired to our rooms. There had been a lot of talk about M. de Bagueville's fire, and so Mme D'Aine, once in bed, remembers that she had left a big log burning in the drawing-room fireplace; perhaps no one put up the fire screen and the log might roll out on the floor, as once happened. Fear seizes her; and as she never orders anything done that she can do herself, she gets up, puts slippers on her bare feet, and leaves her room in sleeping jacket and nightdress, with a little night lamp in her hand. She was going down the stairs as M. Le Roy, who is a night-hawk and was enjoying a book in the drawing-room, was coming up. They see each other, and Mme D'Aine runs, M. Le Roy runs after her, catches her, and now he has seized her around the waist and is kissing her; and she cries out: "Help! Help!" and the kisses of her ravisher keep her from speaking distinctly. However, something like this came out: "Help! my sons-in-law, help! if he gets me with child, so much the worse for you." The doors open, we enter the corridor and find only Mme D'Aine all disordered, looking for her nightcap and slippers in the dark; for her lamp had gone out and overturned, and our friend had shut himself in his room.

I left them in the corridor, where until two in the morning their outbursts of laughter equalled those of Homer's gods, who kept at it without end and sometimes with less reason; for you will agree that it is funnier to see a plump woman, white, chubby, and almost naked, in the arms of an insolent and lecherous young man, than an ugly, lame, clumsy fellow pouring drinks for his father and mother after a rather wretched family squabble. That's from the end of the first book of the *Iliad*.

The adventure became the joke of the day. Some claimed that Mme D'Aine called out too soon, others that she called only when she was sure there was nothing to fear and that she would have been as glad to remain silent for the sake of her pleasure as to call out for the sake of her honor; and a lot of other nonsense.

The other little story is impertinence to the highest degree. Picture fourteen or fifteen of us at table. Towards the end of the meal, "my son" was sitting at the left of Mme Charmoi. He is ordinarily familiar with her. He takes her hand, tries to look at her arm, pushes up her sleeve. They let him do it, either on purpose or through inattention. He sees great black hairs on a fairly white skin; he sets about plucking her arm; she tries to draw back her hand, but he holds it tight; to pull down her sleeve, but he pushes it back and plucks away. She exclaims: "Monsieur, will you stop that?" He replies: "No, madame, for what's all that good for?" And he keeps on plucking. He lets her grow angry, but plucks no less for that. Mme D'Aine, half choking with laughter and half with anger, holding her sides and trying to speak in a serious tone, said: "D'Aine, what are you thinking of?" and then she laughed. "Who ever plucked a lady at table?" And she laughed again. "Is that the way I've brought you up?" And all the table burst out laughing. As for me, the tears ran down my cheeks and I thought I would die of it.

However, a moment later, his mother signaled to her son, and he threw himself at the lady's feet and asked her pardon. She claimed he had hurt her, but that wasn't true; she was hurt by the mean joke and our inhuman laughter. . . .

(P.S.) I have just reread this letter. I was almost ready to burn it up, for fear it would tire you out reading it. If there is any chance of that, put it aside. You will come back to it, for it is obscure only because it was impossible for me to leave out anything that was said. And then these matters are not so familiar to you as they are to us here. I burn to see you again.

Paris, September 23, 1762.

The perpetual succession of useful and varied occupations makes a stay in the country so pleasant and residence in the city so dull for those who have had a taste of country life.

Why is it that the fuller life is, the less we are attached to it? If that is true, it's because a busy life is ordinarily an innocent life; because we think less often of death and fear it less; because without realizing it we become resigned to the common lot of the beings around us that are constantly dying and being reborn; because after we have attended for a number of years to the yearly recurring works of nature, we feel detached and weary of them; our strength departs from us, we grow weak and look forward to the end of life, just as after hard work, we look forward to the end of the day; because after living in a state of nature, we do not revolt against the orders that we see executed so necessarily and universally around us; because after going to sleep so many times on the surface of the earth, we are better disposed to sleep a bit under it; because, to return to one of the ideas above, there is not one of us who, after very wearying work, hasn't longed for his bed and looked forward with great pleasure to the bedtime hour; because, for certain persons, life is only a long and weary day, and death, a long sleep, and the coffin a bed of repose, and the earth a pillow on which it is good at last to lay our heads, never to raise them again. I assure you that death, from this point of view and after the many disappointments that I have suffered, is most desirable. I'm trying to become more and more accustomed to this viewpoint.

Voltaire

1694-1778

In 1750 when life in Paris again became impossible for Voltaire, he accepted the invitation of Frederick the Great and went to Berlin. He soon found that the philosopher-king, too, could exercise tyranny over men's minds, and Voltaire was only too glad to escape after a three year sojourn. Since the French court had not forgiven his departure, he was forced to seek refuge first in Alsace and finally, in 1755, in Geneva, where he leased a property which he called "Les Délices," and which now houses the Voltaire Institute and Museum. The Lisbon earthquake of 1755 and the Seven Years War (1756-1763) were the occasions of his undisputed masterpiece, *Candide*.

In 1758, Voltaire, now a wealthy man, purchased the château of Ferney in French territory just over the line from Geneva. Here, as resident landlord, he came to know the problems of the peasants and artisans of his domain and developed a genuine social conscience. At sixty-five, the major struggle lay still ahead of him. "In the liberation war of humanity," wrote Heine, "Voltaire's name will be forever memorable." In comparative safety from persecution—he was still being closely watched by the Bishop of Annecy, whom he outlived—he published a steady stream of treatises and pamphlets, demanding justice for Calas and Sirven, victims of religious fanaticism, attacking the foundations of Christianity in the name of which the Church exerted its persecuting power, and abolishing the last vestiges of serfdom. The *Philosophical Dictionary* (1764) with its many additions and the completion of a *Universal History, or Essay on the Manners and Spirit of Nations* were the major works of this period. As benefactor of Ferney he built more than a hundred houses, gave the town a church, a school and a hospital, improved the land, established a watch factory and a silk stocking mill, and planned an ideal village at Versoix where complete toleration was to reign, with Catholic and Protestant churches facing each other.

Social and Political Ideas

STATES. GOVERNMENT

[*This article was written in 1757, nine years after the publication of Montesquieu's* Spirit of Laws. *Voltaire here refutes a weakness in Montesquieu's book, namely, his generalizations concerning virtue as the guiding principle of the republic, and honor that of the monarchy. Although both authors reveal a theoretical fondness for the democratic form of government, not being revolutionaries, they saw little hope in France for anything more liberal than a constitutional monarchy with a fixed code of laws, a humane judiciary, security of person and property, and a balance of powers such as both had observed in England.*]

What is the best government? Up to the present time I have never known anybody who has not governed some state. I am not speaking of ministers, who really govern, some two or three years, some six months, and some six weeks; I am speaking of all other men who, at supper or in their studies, expound their systems of government, reform armies, the Church, the robe, and finances.

But we must agree that very wise men, worthy perhaps to govern, have written concerning the administration of states, in France, in Spain and in England. Their books have done a great deal of good: not that they have corrected ministers who were then in power, for a minister is not, and cannot be corrected; he has had his growth; he takes no more instructions, no more advice: he has no time to listen to them, for the current of affairs runs away with him; but these good books form young men destined to places of responsibility; they form princes, and the second generation is instructed.

The strength and weakness of all governments has been carefully examined in recent times. Tell me then, you who have traveled, who have read and observed, in what state and under what sort of government you would like to be born? I imagine that a landed lord in France would not be sorry to have been born in Germany: he would be sovereign instead of subject. A peer of France would be very glad to have the privileges of the English peerage: he would be legislator. The judge and the financier would be better off in France than elsewhere. But what country would be chosen by a wise and free man, a man with average means and without prejudices?

A rather learned member of the council of Pondicherry was returning to Europe by land with a brahmin better educated than most brahmins.

"How do you like the government of the Great Mogul?" said the councillor.

"Abominable," replied the brahmin; "how can you expect a state to be happily governed by Tartars? Our rajahs, our omras, our nababs, are very happy; but the citizens are not at all so; and millions of citizens are something, after all."

The councillor and the brahmin crossed the whole of upper Asia, reasoning as they went.

"I observe one thing," said the brahmin, "and that is, that there is not one republic in this whole section of the world."

"In former times, there was the republic of Tyre," said the councillor, "but it did not last long; there was still another towards Arabia Petrea, in a little corner named Palestine, if one can honor with the name of republic a horde of robbers and usurers, sometimes governed by judges, sometimes by a sort of king, sometimes by high priests; which fell into slavery several times, and was finally chased out of the country that it had usurped."

"I imagine," said the brahmin, "that one would find very few republics on the face of the earth. Men are rarely worthy of governing themselves. Such good luck should belong only to small peoples hidden on islands or among mountains, like rabbits which shun carnivorous animals; but in the long run, they are discovered and devoured."

When the two travelers had arrived in Asia Minor, the

councillor said to the brahmin: "Would you believe that there was a republic formed in a corner of Italy, which lasted more than five hundred years, and which possessed this Asia Minor, Asia, Africa, Greece, the Gauls, Spain, and all of Italy?"

"It must have become a monarchy very soon, then," said the brahmin.

"You have guessed it," said the other; "but the monarchy fell, and every day we write beautiful dissertations to find out the cause of its decay and fall."

"You put yourselves to a lot of trouble," said the Hindu; "that empire fell because it existed. Everything must fall; I hope that the same thing will happen to the empire of the Great Mogul."

"By the way," said the European, "do you believe that more honor is required in a despotic state, and more virtue in a republic?"

The Hindu, after an explanation of what was meant by honor, replied that honor was more necessary in a republic, and that more virtue was needed in a monarchy. "For," he said, "a man who wants to be elected by the people will not be elected if he is dishonored; but at court, he will easily be able to obtain a commission, according to the maxim of a great prince, that to succeed, a courtier should have neither honor nor temper. As for virtue, it takes a prodigious amount of it at court to dare to speak the truth. The virtuous man is much more at his ease in a republic; he has no one to flatter."

"Do you believe," said the European, "that laws and religions are made for climates, in the same way that furs are needed at Moscow and gauze stuffs at Delhi?"

"Certainly," said the brahmin; "all laws concerning physical things are calculated for the meridian which we inhabit; a German needs only one wife, a Persian needs three or four. The ceremonies of religion are of the same nature. How could you expect me, if I were a Christian, to say mass in my province, where there is neither bread nor wine? With regard to dogmas, it is another thing; climate has nothing to do with them. Did not your religion originate in Asia, from which it was banished, and does it not exist towards the Baltic Sea where it was unknown?"

"In what state, under what rule, would you prefer to live?" said the councillor.

"Anywhere except at home," said his companion, "and I have heard many Siamese, Tonkinese, Persians and Turks say the same thing."

"But once again, I ask," said the European; "what state would you choose?"

The brahmin replied: "That one in which laws alone are obeyed."

"That's an old answer," said the councillor.

"It's none the worse for that," said the brahmin.

"Where is that country?" said the councillor.

The brahmin said: "We have yet to find it."

Laws

Sheep live together in society very agreeably; we consider them very meek in character because we do not see the prodigious quantity of animals that they devour. We may believe that they eat them innocently, and without knowing it, just as when we eat a Sassenage cheese. The republic of sheep is the faithful image of the Golden Age.

A poultry-yard is plainly the most perfect monarchy. There is no king comparable to a cock. If he marches proudly in the midst of his people, it is not through vanity. If the enemy approaches, he does not order his subjects to go and be killed for him by virtue of his certain knowledge and plenary powers; he goes himself, lines up his hens behind him and fights to the death. If he is victorious, it is he who sings the *Te Deum*. In civil life, there is no one so gallant, so honest, so unselfish. He possesses all virtues. If he holds in his royal beak a grain of wheat or a worm, he gives it to the first of his subjects to present herself. Solomon in all his harem was not to be compared to a barnyard cock.

If it is true that bees are governed by a queen whose subjects all make love to her, that is a still more perfect government.

Ants are considered as forming an excellent democracy. It is superior to all other states because everybody in it is equal and every individual works for the common good.

The republic of beavers is better than that of the ants, at least if we may judge of them by their masonry.

Monkeys resemble mountebanks rather than civilized people; and they do not appear to be united under any fixed and fundamental laws, like the preceding species.

We resemble monkeys more than any other animal in the gift of imitation, in the levity of our ideas, and in inconstancy, which has never allowed us to have uniform and durable laws.

When nature formed our species and imparted to us a few instincts, self-love for our preservation, benevolence for the preservation of others, love which is common to all species, and the inexplicable gift of combining more ideas than all the animals put together; after having thus endowed us, she said to us: "Do the best you can."

There is no good code of laws in any country. The reason is evident. . . . Laws were established in nearly all states through the selfish interests of the legislator, to meet the need of the moment, through ignorance and superstition. They were made gradually, by chance, irregularly, just as cities were built. . . .

London became worthy of being inhabited only after it was reduced to ashes. From that time on, the streets were broadened and straightened: London was a city for having been burned. If you want to have good laws, burn your own, then, and make new ones. . . .

Your common law of Paris is interpreted differently in twenty-four commentaries: just so many proofs, then, that it is ill conceived. It contradicts one hundred and forty other common laws, all having legal force in the same nation, and all contradicting each other. . . .

The English nation has more uniformity; but having emerged from barbarism and servitude only at intervals and by fits and starts, and having conserved in her liberty several laws promulgated in former times by great tyrants disputing the throne, or by little tyrants invading prelacies, there was formed a fairly vigorous body, on which may still be seen many wounds covered with plasters.

The intellect of Europe has made greater progress in the last hundred years than the whole world had made since the days of Brahma, Fohi, Zoroaster, and Thaut of the Egyptians. Why is it that the spirit of legislation has made so little?

André Destouches in Siam

[*In this philosophical and allegorical satire on the government of France, Voltaire summarizes, paragraph by paragraph, what he considered to be the chief abuses of the Old Régime: the proliferation of monasteries, farming-out of tax collections, lack of a fixed code of laws, judicial use of torture of the first and second degree to secure confessions, severity of punishments, venality of public offices, payments of annates to the Pope, useless theological disputations, etc. Interested in music rather than politics, André Destouches mistakes the fundamental principle ("base fondamentale") of the Siamese government for the fundamental bass of Rameau's* Theory of Harmony, *thereby occasioning the prime minister's oath.*

Equivalences: Siam = France; Lao = England; barcalon = prime minister; talapoins = monks; question = judicial torture.]

André Destouches was a very pleasing composer in the great age of Louis XIV, before music had been perfected by Rameau and spoiled by those who prefer difficulties overcome to nature and art.

Before he exercised his talents he had been a musketeer; and before he was a musketeer he went to Siam, in 1688, with the Jesuit Tachard, who paid him very particular attention in order that there might be diversions on the boat; and Destouches spoke with admiration of Father Tachard all the rest of his life.

He made the acquaintance at Siam of the chief secretary of the barcalon; this private secretary was called Croutef, and he put in writing most of the questions he had asked Croutef, along with the replies of the Siamese. Here they are as they were found among his papers:

André Destouches: How many soldiers have you?

Croutef: Eighty thousand, and very poorly paid.

André Destouches: And how many talapoins?

Croutef: One hundred and twenty thousand, all do-nothings and very rich. It is true that in the last war we were badly beaten; but for compensation, our talapoins lived very well indeed, built fine houses, and kept very pretty mistresses.

André Destouches: Nothing could be wiser and better advised. And in what condition are your finances?

Croutef: In very bad condition. We have, however, ninety thousand men employed to make them prosper; and if they haven't succeeded it isn't their fault, for there isn't one of them who doesn't take honestly all he can get hold of and who doesn't fleece the farmers for the good of the state.

André Destouches: Bravo! And is your jurisprudence as perfect as all the rest of your administration?

Croutef: It is much superior; we have no laws, but we have five or six volumes about the laws. We are ordinarily guided by customs, for it is clear that a custom, having become established by chance, is always most wise. Moreover, since each custom has necessarily changed in each province, like clothes and headwear, the judges can choose at will the usage that was in fashion four centuries ago or the one that prevailed last year; that makes a variety of legislation which is the continual admiration of our neighbors; it means a sure fortune for the practitioners, a resource for all dishonest lawyers, and an infinite pleasure for the judges, who can, with clear consciences, decide cases without hearing them.

André Destouches: But for the criminal your laws are at least constant?

Croutef: From that, heaven preserve us! We can condemn to exile, to the galleys, to the gibbet, or dismiss the case from court, according to our fancy. We sometimes complain of the arbitrary power of Monsieur the Barcalon; but we want all our legal decisions to be arbitrary.

André Destouches: That is just. And you use the question?

Croutef: That is our greatest pleasure; we have found it an infallible secret to save a guilty man who has vigorous muscles, strong and supple hams, sinewy arms and a broad back; and we gaily break on the wheel all innocent people whom nature has endowed with feeble organs. Thus we go about it with marvelous sagacity and prudence. Just as there are half-proofs, that is, half-truths, it is clear that there are the half-innocent and the half-guilty. We begin then by putting them half to death, after which we go out to lunch; then we give them complete death, and that makes us very highly considered of men, and constitutes our reward for the price we pay for our charges.

André Destouches: Nothing could be wiser and more humane, that is agreed. Tell me what happens to the goods of the condemned.

Croutef: The children are deprived of them: for you know that it is most equitable to punish all the descendants for their father's crime.

André Destouches: Yes, I heard about that jurisprudence a long time ago.

Croutef: The nations of Lao, our neighbors, do not allow the question nor the arbitrary punishments nor the differing customs, nor the horrible deaths that constitute our practice; but we therefore consider them barbarians who have no idea of good government. All Asia agrees that we dance much better than they, and that consequently it is impossible for them to approach us in jurisprudence, commerce, finance, and above all in the arts of war.

André Destouches: Tell me, please, by what steps men become magistrates in Siam.

Croutef: By ready cash. You perceive that it would be impossible to judge well if the judge didn't have thirty or forty thousand pieces of silver ready at hand. In vain would he know by heart all the customs, in vain would he have pleaded successfully five hundred cases, in vain would he have an accurate mind and a heart filled with justice; no one can become a magistrate without money. That again distinguishes us from all the nations of Asia, and especially from the barbarians of Lao, who have the mania of rewarding all talents and selling no charges.

André Destouches, who was somewhat absent-minded, like all musicians, replied to the Siamese that most of the airs he had just heard sung seemed to him a little discordant, and he wanted to inform himself thoroughly concerning Siamese music; but Croutef, filled with his subject and passionately fond of his country, continued in these words:

"It makes little difference to me that our neighbors who live beyond our mountains have better music than we, and better paintings, provided that we continue to have wise and humane laws. That is the feature in which we excel. For example, there are a thousand instances in which, when a young woman has been delivered of a dead child, we repair the loss of the child by hanging the mother, through which instrumentality she is manifestly unable to have another unsuccessful delivery.

"If a man has skilfully stolen three or four hundred thousand pieces of gold, we respect him and we go to dine with him; but if a poor servant girl unskilfully appropriates three or four pieces of copper from her mistress's cash box, we do not fail to put her to death in the public square: first, for fear lest she mend her ways; secondly, in order that she may not give the state numerous children, among whom there might be found perhaps one or two who might steal three or four pieces of copper, or become great men: thirdly, because it is just to punish in proportion to the crime and it would be ridiculous to employ in the workhouse on useful jobs anyone guilty of so enormous a crime.

"But we are still more just, merciful and reasonable in the punishments we inflict on those who have the audacity to use their legs to go where they please. We treat so well our warriors who sell us their lives, we give them such prodigious pay, they play such a considerable part in our conquests, that they are surely the most criminal of all men when, after enlisting in a moment of drunkenness, they want to go back to their parents in a moment of reason. We have a dozen lead bullets fired into their heads at close range to make them stay in place, after which they become infinitely useful to their country.

"I shall not mention the countless number of excellent institutions which do not, to be sure, go so far as to shed the blood of men, but which make life so pleasant and agreeable that it is impossible for the guilty not to become honest men. If a farmer has not paid on the dot a tax which exceeds his ability to pay, we sell his kettle and his bed so that he may be able the better to cultivate his land when he is delivered from the embarrassment of his superfluous possessions."

André Destouches: Now that is quite harmonious. It makes a fine concert.

Croutef: To show our profound wisdom, know that our fundamental principle consists in recognizing as our sovereign, in many respects, a tonsured foreigner who lives at a distance of nine hundred thousand paces from us. When we give our finest lands to some of our talapoins, as it is very prudent to do, these Siamese talapoins pay the income for the first year to this tonsured Tartar, failing which it is clear that we would have no harvest.

But where are the times, those happy times, when this tonsured fellow had half of a nation cut the throats of the other half to decide whether Sommonocodom played at kites or pigeonhole; whether he disguised himself as an elephant or as a cow; whether he slept three hundred and ninety days on the right side or on the left? These great questions which are so essentially related to morality, used to excite the minds of all men: they shook the world; blood was shed for them; women were massacred over their husbands' bodies; little children were dashed against the rocks with a devotion, unction and compunction truly angelic. Woe unto us, degenerate children of pious ancestors, who perform no longer these holy sacrifices! But at least there are left to us, heaven be praised, a few good souls who would imitate them if they were allowed to do so.

André Destouches: Tell me, I beg of you, sir, whether in Siam you divide the major chord in two commas and two semi-commas, and whether the progression of the fundamental tone proceeds by one, three, and nine.

Croutef: By Sommonocodom! You are mocking me. You wander from the point; you asked me about the form of our government and now you are talking about music.

André Destouches: Music is related to all things; it was the basis of all the politics of the Greeks. But pardon me; since your ear is insensitive, let's return to the subject. You were saying then that to attain perfect concord . . .

Croutef: I was telling you that the tonsured Tartar used to claim the disposition of all the kingdoms of Asia, and that is very far from perfect concord; but a great benefit resulted therefrom: people were much more devoted to Sommonocodom and his elephant than in our day, when everyone takes it into his head, with a presumption that provokes pity, that he has common sense. However, it seems to work; people make merry, dance, play, dine, sup and make love: and that's enough to give the creeps to all men of good intentions.

André Destouches: And what more can you expect? All you lack is good music. When you have that, you will be able boldly to proclaim yourselves the happiest nation on earth.

Dialogues Between A, B, and C (1768)

Sixth Conversation: On the Three Forms of Government

[*In this series of dialogues, A is a member of the English Parliament, C is a wealthy French nobleman, and B is a republican-minded Voltaire.*]

B.—Let's get to the point. I confess I could get along well enough with a democratic government. I think that philosopher was wrong who said to a supporter of popular government: "Begin by trying it in your own house and you will repent quickly enough [Lycurgus, in Plutarch's *Banquet of the Seven Wise Men*]." Begging his pardon, a house and a city are two different things. My house is mine; my children are mine; my servants, when I pay them, are mine; but by what right would my fellow-citizens belong to me? All who have possessions in the same region have an equal right in the maintenance of order in that region. I like to see free men make the laws they choose to live by, just as they make their own dwellings. It is a pleasure for me when my mason, my carpenter, my blacksmith, who have helped me build my house, lift themselves above their trade and know more about public interests than the most insolent Turkish commissar. No farmer, no artisan, in a democracy, needs to fear vexation and contempt; no one is like the haberdasher who presented his bill to a duke and peer: "Have you not received something on account?"—"I beg your pardon, my lord, but I received a slap from your honorable agent."

It is very pleasant not to be liable to be hauled off to prison for not having paid to a man you don't know a tax, the value and purpose of which you don't know, and for life.

To be free, to live only among one's equals, is the true life, the natural life of man; any other is a shameful pretense, a poor comedy, in which one plays the role of master, the other that of slave; one the role of parasite and the other that of panderer. You will have to admit that men couldn't have fallen so far from their natural state except through cowardice and stupidity.

For this is clear: no one could have lost his freedom except through not having known how to protect it. There are two ways of losing it: when fools have been deceived by knaves, or when the weak have been subjugated by the strong. History tells us of a certain vanquished people whose conquerors deprived them of one eye; there are nations who have had both eyes put out, like old nags used to turn mill wheels. I want to keep my eyes; I like to imagine that in aristocratic states people have had one eye put out, and in monarchies, both eyes.

A.—You talk like a citizen of northern Holland, and are pardonable.

C.—But I like only aristocracies; the people are not fit to rule. I could never stand having my wigmaker a legislator; I'd rather never wear wigs. Only those who have had a very good education are in a position to lead those who never had any. The Venetian government is the best: that aristocracy is the oldest State in Europe. Next to that, I put the German government. Make me a noble Venetian or a count of the Empire, for I declare I can't live happily except in one or the other of these two capacities.

A.—You are a wealthy lord, Mr. C., and I heartily approve of your way of thinking. I note that you would be in favor of the government of the Turks if you were emperor of Constantinople. But although I am only a member of the British parliament, I look on my constitution as superior to all others; and as proof I will quote from an unchallengeable witness, a Frenchman who, in a poem dedicated to truths rather than to empty tales, speak thus of our government:

Three different powers at Westminster appear,
And all admire the ties which join them there.
Whom interest parts, the laws together bring,
The people's deputies, the peers, and king.
One whole they form, whose terror wide extends
To neighboring nations, and their rights defends.
[Voltaire, *Henriade*, I, 313-318.]

C.—A danger to itself! Then you have very great abuses in your system.

A.—Of course, just as was the case with the Romans and Athenians, and as it will always be among all men. The height of human perfection is to be powerful and happy along with enormous abuses; and that is what we have come to. It is dangerous to eat too much, but I like plenty of food on my table. . . .

Let's leave aside all this so-called ancient history; as for modern history, let each one try to learn from the faults of his own country and those of his neighbors. The lesson will be long; but also let's examine all the fine institutions for which modern nations are known. That will be a long lesson, too.

B.—And what will it teach us?

A.—That the closer positive laws come to natural law, the more supportable life will be.

A Letter to Jean Jacques Rousseau (1755)

[*Voltaire could hardly have been pleased with the theory of the corrupting influence of science and the arts, or the diatribe against private property and economic progress in Rousseau's* Discourse on the Origins of Inequality. *He wrote the following letter from his newly found retreat on the outskirts of Geneva, where he was already cultivat-*

ing his gardens. He first reduces to the absurd the primitive happiness of the savage state and then purposely mistreats the arguments against letters. Rousseau was still living on the fringes of Parisian society among men of letters and their patrons. The letter ends on a note of veiled, but cruel, sarcasm. When, contrary to Voltaire's intentions, the letter was published, Rousseau took the hint and left Paris for a "hermitage" furnished by a wealthy patroness in the woods of Montmorency not too far from the city.]

I have received, sir, your new book against the human race; I thank you for it. You will please men, to whom you frankly tell their faults, but you will not correct them. It is impossible to paint in bolder colors the horrors of human society, from which our ignorance and weakness lead us to expect so much consolation. Never has anyone employed so much wit in trying to make us witless; the reading of your book makes us want to creep on all fours. However, as it is now more than sixty years since I lost that habit, I feel unfortunately that it is impossible for me to take it up again, and I leave that natural attitude to those who are more worthy of it than you and I. Neither can I embark to go and live with the savages of Canada: first, because the ailments with which I am afflicted retain me by the side of the greatest doctor of Europe, and I could not find the same attentions among the Missouri Indians; secondly, because war has been carried into those countries, and the example of our civilized peoples has made the savages almost as wicked as we. I content myself with being a peaceful savage in the solitude that I have chosen near your native land, where you ought to be.

I agree with you that letters and sciences have sometimes caused a great deal of harm. The enemies of Tasso made his life a tissue of misfortunes; those of Galileo made him groan in prisons, at the age of seventy, for having recognized the movement of the earth; and what is more shameful, they forced him to retract. As soon as your friends had begun the *Encyclopedic Dictionary*, those who dared to be their rivals called them deists, atheists, and even Jansenists.

If I dared to count myself among those whose works have brought them only persecution for reward, I would show you people fiercely determined to undo me from the day that I produced the tragedy *Œdipus;* a library of ridiculous calumnies written against me; an ex-Jesuit priest, whom I saved from the gallows, repaying me with defamatory libels for the service that I had rendered him; a man, still more guilty, printing my own work, *The Age of Louis XIV*, with *notes* in which the grossest ignorance spews forth the most infamous impostures; another, who sells to a publisher some chapters of a so-called *Universal History* under my name; the publisher greedy enough to print this formless tissue of blunders, false dates, and mutilated facts and names; and finally men cowardly and wicked enough to ascribe to me the publication of this rhapsody. . . . But what shall I conclude from all these tribulations? That I ought not to complain; that Pope, Descartes, Bayle, Camoëns, and a hundred others, have suffered the same injustices and even greater ones; and that such is the fate of almost all those who have been too much enticed by the love of letters.

Confess truly, sir, that these are little individual misfortunes which society scarcely perceives. What matters it to the human race that a few drones steal honey from a few bees! Men of letters make a great stir over all these little quarrels, while the rest of the world knows nothing about them or laughs at them.

Of all the sorrows spread across human life, these are the least baleful. The thorns attached to literature and to a reputation however small are only flowers in comparison with other evils which in every age have inundated the earth. Confess that not Cicero, nor Varro, nor Lucretius, nor Virgil, nor Horace, had the slightest thing to do with the proscriptions. Marius was an ignorant man; the barbarous Sylla, the debauched Antony, the imbecile Lepidus, read very little in Plato and Sophocles; and as for that cowardly tyrant, Octavius Cepias, so scandalously surnamed Augustus, he was nothing but a detestable assassin when he was deprived of the society of men of letters.

Confess that Petrarch and Boccaccio did not originate the troubles of Italy! confess that the jesting of Marot did not produce the massacre of Saint-Bartholomew, and that the tragedy, the *Cid*, did not cause the disorder of the Fronde. The great crimes have almost always been committed by celebrated ignoramuses. What makes, and will always make of this world a vale of tears is the insatiable cupidity and indomitable pride of men, from Thomas Kouli-kan,[1] who did not know how to read, to a customs clerk, who does not know how to figure. Letters nourish the soul, rectify and console it; they are of service to you, sir, at the very moment that you write against them; you are like Achilles, who flies into a passion against glory, and like Father Malebranche, whose brilliant imagination wrote against the imagination.

If anyone should complain of letters, I am the one to do so, since in all times and in all places they have served to persecute me; but we should love them in spite of the abuse that is made of them, just as we should love society, the refined qualities of which are corrupted by so many men; just as we should love our native land, whatever injustices we must endure; just as we should love and serve the Supreme Being, in spite of the superstitions and fanaticism which so often dishonor his worship.

M. Chappuis informs me that your health is very bad; you should come and recover it here under your native skies, enjoy liberty, drink with me the milk of our cows, and browse our grasses.

I am very philosophically and with the greatest esteem, etc.

[1] A Persian usurper of the eighteenth century.

Liberty of the Press

In general, we have the natural right to use our pens like our tongues, at our own risk and peril. I know of many books which have been boring, but I know of none that has done any real harm. Theologians, or self-styled politicians, cry out:

"Religion is destroyed, the government is ruined, if you print certain truths or certain paradoxes. Never take it into your head to think until you have asked the permission of some monk or of some bureaucrat. It is contrary to good order for a man to think for himself. Homer, Plato, Cicero, Virgil, Pliny, Horace never published anything without the approbation of the Sorbonne doctors and the Holy Inquisition.

"See into what horrible decay the liberty of the press has brought England and Holland. It is true that they embrace the commerce of the entire world, and that England is victorious on land and on sea; but it is only false greatness and false opulence: they are marching with long strides to their ruin. An enlightened people cannot subsist."

One cannot reason more justly, my friends; but let's see, pray, what state has been ruined by a book. The most dangerous, the most pernicious of all books is Spinoza's. Not only as a Jew does he attack the New Testament, but as a scholar he ruins the Old; his system of atheism is a thousand times more consistent and better reasoned than the systems of Strato and Epicurus. It takes the most profound sagacity to reply to the arguments by which he attempts to prove that one substance cannot form another.

Like yourself, I detest his book, which I understand perhaps better than you, and to which you replied very weakly; but have you observed that this book has changed the face of the globe? Is there any preacher who has lost a florin of his pension through the sale of Spinoza's works? Is there any bishop whose income has diminished? On the contrary, their revenue has doubled since his time; all the harm boils down to a small number of peaceful readers who have examined the arguments of Spinoza in their studies and who have written, for or against them, works that are very little known.

You yourselves are inconsistent enough in having printed, *ad usum Delphini*, the atheism of Lucretius, and no confusion, no scandal has come from it; Spinoza was allowed to live in peace in Holland just as Lucretius was unmolested at Rome.

But if there appears among you some new book containing ideas which somewhat shock your own (supposing that you have ideas), or written by an author belonging to a party opposed to your faction, or, what is worse, to no party, then you cry, "Fire!" and there is nothing but noise, scandal, and universal hubbub in your little corner of the earth. Here is an abominable man who has written that if we had no hands, we could make neither stockings nor shoes; what a blasphemy! Pious women cry out, fur-robed doctors assemble, the alarm spreads from college to college and from house to house; entire bodies are set in movement; and for what? for five or six pages that are forgotten at the end of three months. If you don't like a book, refute it; if you are bored by it, don't read it.

"Ah!" you tell me, "the books of Luther and Calvin have destroyed the Roman religion in half of Europe." Why don't you say, too, that the books of the patriarch Photius[1] have destroyed that same religion in Asia, Africa, Greece, and Russia?

You are very seriously mistaken when you think that you have been ruined by books. The empire of Russia is two thousand leagues across, and there are not six men in it who understand the points of controversy between the Greek and the Latin Church. If Luther the monk, if John Calvin the canon, if Zwingli the curate, had been

[1] Photius was the chief instigator of the separation of the Greek Church from the Latin in 858. His voluminous works have been little read.

content with writing, Rome would yet subjugate all the states that she has lost; but those people and their adherents ran from city to city and from house to house, incited women to riot, and were upheld by princes. The fury which tormented Amata, and whipped her like a top, according to Virgil, was not more turbulent. Learn then that an enthusiastic, factious, ignorant, supple, vehement Capuchin friar, the tool of some ambitious man, by preaching, confessing, administering communion, and caballing can overturn a province much sooner than a hundred authors can enlighten it. It was not the Alcoran which brought success to Mohammed, it was Mohammed who brought success to the Alcoran.

No, Rome was not conquered by books: she was conquered for having revolted Europe with her rapacity, through the public sale of indulgences; for having insulted men, for having wished to govern them like domestic animals, for having abused her power to such an excess that it is astonishing that there is left to her a single village. Henry VIII, Elizabeth, the Duke of Saxony, the Landgrave of Hessia, the Princes of Orange, the Condés, the Colignys, accomplished everything, and books nothing at all. Trumpets never gained any battles and never brought down any walls except those of Jericho.

You fear books as certain small towns have feared violins. Let people read and let them dance; these two amusements will never do the world any harm.

Torture

Although there are few articles of jurisprudence in these honest alphabetical reflections,[1] a word must be said concerning torture, otherwise called the *question*. It is a strange manner of questioning men. It was not invented, however, out of idle curiosity; there is every likelihood that this part of our legislation owes its origin to a highway robber. Most of these gentlemen still are

[1] Most of the shorter articles of these *Selections* are taken from Voltaire's *Philosophical Dictionary*.

accustomed to squeeze thumbs, burn feet and question by other torments those who refuse to tell them where they have put their money.

When conquerors had succeeded these thieves, they found the invention very useful to their interests: they put it to use when they suspected that anyone opposed them with certain evil designs, such, for instance, as the desire to be free; that was a crime of high treason against God and man. They wanted to know the accomplices; and to accomplish this, they subjected to the suffering of a thousand deaths those whom they suspected, because according to the jurisprudence of these early heroes, whoever was suspected merely of entertaining against them any slightly disrespectful thought was worthy of death. The moment that anyone has thus merited death, it matters little that terrible torments are added for several days, and even for several weeks, a practice which smacks somewhat of the Divinity. Providence sometimes puts us to the torture by means of stone, gravel, gout, scurvy, leprosy, pox of both varieties, excruciating bowel pains, nervous convulsions, and other executioners of providential vengeance.

Now as the early despots were, by the admission of all their courtiers, images of the Divinity, they imitated it as much as they could. . . .

The grave magistrate who has bought for a little money the right to perform experiments on his neighbor tells his wife at dinner what took place during the morning. The first time, madam was revolted by it; the second time she got a taste for it, because after all women are curious; and now the first thing she says to him when he comes home in his gown is: "My dear, didn't you have anyone put to the question today?"

The French who are considered, I do not know why, a very humane people, are astonished that the English, who had the inhumanity to take all Canada from us, have given up the pleasure of putting the question.

When the Chevalier de la Barre, grandson of a lieutenant-general in the king's service, a young man of great intelligence and much promise, but possessing all the thoughtlessness of unbridled youth, was convicted of having sung impious songs and even of having passed in front of a procession of Capuchins without taking off his hat, the judges of Abbeville, men comparable to the Roman Senators, ordered not only that his tongue should be torn out, his hand cut off and his body burned by slow fire; but they applied torture to him to find out how many songs he had sung and how many processions he had seen pass with his hat on his head.

It was not in the thirteenth nor the fourteenth century that this adventure took place; it was in the eighteenth. Foreign nations judge France by its plays, novels and pretty poetry; by its opera girls, who are very gentle of manner; by its opera dancers who are graceful; by Mlle. Clairon, who recites her lines in a ravishing manner. They do not know that there is no nation more fundamentally cruel than the French.

The Russians were considered barbarians in 1700, and it is now only 1769; an Empress has just given to that vast state laws which would honor Minos, Numa and Solon, if they had been intelligent enough to invent them. The most remarkable is universal tolerance, the next is the abolition of torture. Justice and humanity guided her pen: she has reformed everything. Woe unto the nation which, though long civilized, is still led by ancient atrocious customs! "Why should we change our jurisprudence?" we say. "Europe uses our cooks, our tailors and our wig makers; therefore our laws are good."

Concerning the Horrible Danger of Reading[1]

We, Joussouf-Chéribi, by the grace of God mufti of the Holy Ottoman Empire, light of lights, elect among

[1] A satire in the form of a pastoral mandate. In Voltaire's vocabulary, a mufti was often an archbishop, and a dervish was a priest.

the elect, to all the faithful who these presents shall see, stupidity and benediction.

Inasmuch as Saïd-Effendi, former ambassador of the Sublime Porte to a little state named Frankrom, situated between Spain and Italy, has brought back among us the pernicious usage of the printing-press, having consulted concerning this novelty our venerable brothers the cadifs and imans of the imperial city of Stamboul, and especially the fakirs known by their zeal in combating intelligence, it has seemed good to Mohammed and to us to condemn, proscribe and anathematize the said infernal invention of the printing-press, for the reasons herewith set forth.

1° The faculty of communicating one's thoughts tends evidently to dissipate ignorance, which is the guardian and safeguard of civilized states.

2° It is to be feared lest among the books brought from the Occident, there be found some on agriculture and on the ways of perfectioning the mechanical arts, which books might in the long run, which God forbid, awaken the genius of our cultivators and manufacturers, excite their industry, increase their wealth, and inspire in them some day a certain exaltation, a certain love of the common weal, sentiments absolutely opposed to holy doctrine.

3° Things would come to such a pass that we would have histories free from that belief in the marvelous which keeps the nation in such a happy state of stupidity. One would be imprudent enough in these books to do justice to good and evil actions, and to recommend equity and love of country, which is visibly contrary to the rights of our position.

4° It might happen, in the course of time, that miserable philosophers, under the specious but condemnable pretext of enlightening men and making them better, might go so far as to teach us dangerous virtues which the people should never know anything about.

5° They might, while enlarging upon the respect

which they bear towards God, and stating in print in scandalous fashion that He fills the universe with His presence, diminish the number of pilgrims to Mecca, to the great detriment of the salvation of souls.

6° It would doubtless transpire that by dint of reading occidental authors who have treated of contagious diseases and the manner of their prevention we should be unhappy enough to protect ourselves from pestilence, which would be a heinous offense against the orders of Providence.

For these reasons and others, for the edification of the faithful and for the good of their souls, we forbid them ever to read any book, under penalty of eternal damnation. And lest they should be seized by the diabolical temptation to educate themselves, we forbid fathers and mothers to teach their children to read. And to prevent any contravention of our command, we forbid them to think, under the same penalties; and beseech all true believers to denounce to our officials whoever shall have pronounced four sentences in a sequence from which one might infer a clear and obvious meaning. We order that use be made, in all conversations, of terms that signify nothing, according to the ancient custom of the Sublime Porte.

And the prevention of the illegal entrance of any thought into the holy imperial city, we intrust especially to His Highness's chief doctor,[1] born in a swamp in the north of the Occident; which aforesaid doctor, having already killed four worthy persons of the Ottoman family, is more interested than anyone else in preventing the introduction of knowledge into the country: we give him power, by these presents, to seize upon every idea that might present itself in writing or by word of mouth at the gates of the city, and to bring before us the said idea bound hand and foot, in order that there may be inflicted

[1] Voltaire is here venting his spleen at the expense of a certain doctor of the Viennese court who opposed his ideas on inoculation.

by us upon it such chastisement as may be our pleasure.

Given in our palace of stupidity, the seventh day of the moon of Muharem, in the year 1143 of the Hegira.

Philosophical and Religious Ideas

"Metaphysics," Voltaire wrote to Frederick of Prussia, "is made up of two parts: the first, all that men of common sense know; the second, what they will never know." He was nevertheless intrigued by metaphysical problems throughout his long life. Most of his philosophical tales deal with the problem of evil. Nothing can be done about earthquakes, but there is an area in which reason and common sense can greatly alleviate the lot of mankind. His philosophy, eminently practical, can best be described as meliorism.

Religion, however, was his chief concern, and religious ideas predominate in all genres of his vast literary production. Born with an inquisitive and irreverent mind, his early work, the Epistle to Urania, *is a sharp criticism of the jealous and vengeful deity of the Old and New Testaments, for whom he would substitute a Supreme Being, creator of the universe, master architect of the heavens. He later became a serious student of the great religions of the world, from Confucius and Zoroaster to Unitarians and Quakers. A follower of Pierre Bayle like the other* philosophes, *he sought to establish a lay system of ethics entirely apart from religious sanctions.*

Unlike many of the philosophes, *however, he firmly defended his theistic beliefs. There runs throughout his work a vein of mysticism, which resembles the cosmic mysticism of Albert Einstein. From the* Adventures of Telemachus *of Fénelon, mystic and quietist, he learned to think of men as imperceptible objects crawling on the surface of the earth, as "atoms of mud" lost in the immensity of the universe. Tribal gods and a particular Providence could have no place in such a conception.*

On the practical side, Voltaire was soon aware that

every reform suggested for the good of humanity met the instant opposition of the Church. Only late in life did he decide that compromise was ineffectual and adopt the motto: Ecrasez l'infâme. *The infamous thing to be crushed was superstition, contrary to reason; fanaticism, which tried to suppress the progress of human thought by violent means, and which had put Calas to death on the wheel and atrociously tortured and burned the youthful Chevalier de la Barre for impiety and sacrilege; it was also by inference the Christian Church and the Christian religion. If the morality of the Old and New Testaments did not coincide with the morality of thinking men of the Age of Reason, so much the worse for that morality. Among reasoning human beings, morality was universally the same. Voltaire worked tirelessly during the last fifteen years of his life to upset the foundations of the Christian religion, attacking its history, its miracles, its prophecies, and its morality. His light mockery does not conceal the fact that he was in dead earnest. In his dictionary article "Religion" he was willing to accept Christianity only if he could prove that its founder was a deist who preached love and tolerance and forbearance among men, in direct opposition to the practice of the Church of his day.*

Liberty[1]

Either I am very much mistaken, or Locke, the definer, has very well defined liberty as *power*. I am again mistaken, or Collins, celebrated magistrate of London, is the only philosopher who has gone to the bottom of this matter, and Clarke replied to him only as a theologian. But of all that has been written in France on liberty, the little dialogue which follows seemed to me to be the clearest:

A. There is a battery of cannon firing in our ears; are you free to hear it or not to hear it?

B. To be sure, I cannot help hearing it.

[1] Free-will and determinism were discussed at this time under the terms liberty and necessity.

A. Do you want that cannon to take off your head and the heads of your wife and daughter who are walking with you?

B. What a strange proposition! As long as I am in my right senses I cannot wish such a thing; it is impossible for me to do so.

A. Good; you hear that cannon necessarily, and necessarily you do not wish to die, you and your family, from a shot of that cannon while you are out for a walk; you have neither the power not to hear nor the power to wish to remain here?

B. That is evident.

A. Consequently you have taken about thirty steps to get out of the way of the cannon, and you have had the power to walk with me these few steps?

B. That is again very evident.

A. And if you had been paralytic, you could not have avoided being exposed to that battery; you would not have had the power to be where you are: you would have heard and been hit by the cannon shot necessarily, and you would have necessarily died?

B. Nothing could be more true.

A. In what then consists your freedom, if it is not in the power that you as an individual have exercised in doing what your will exacted through absolute necessity?

B. You embarrass me; freedom is then nothing else but the power to do what I wish?

A. Reflect upon it and see if freedom can be otherwise understood.

B. In that case, my hunting dog is as free as I am; he has necessarily the will to run when he sees a hare, and the power to run if there is nothing the matter with his legs. I am then superior in no way to my dog: you reduce me to the animal state.

A. Those are the poor sophisms of the poor sophists who have instructed you. It makes you ill to be free like your dog. Do you not eat, do you not sleep, do you not propagate in essentially the same manner? Would you like the sense of smell otherwise than through the nose?

Why should you desire freedom of a different sort than your dog's?

B. But I have a soul which does a great deal of reasoning, and my dog reasons very little. He has also nothing but simple ideas, and I have a thousand metaphysical ideas.

A. Well, then, you are a thousand times more free than he: that is, you have a thousand times more power to think than he; but you are free only in the same way as he.

B. What! I am not free to will what I will?

A. Just what do you mean by that?

B. I mean what everyone means. Is it not said every day: "Wills are free?"

A. A proverb is not a reason: explain yourself more clearly.

B. I mean that I am free to will as I please.

A. Begging your pardon, there is no sense to that remark; do you not see that it is ridiculous to say: "I will will?" You will necessarily, in consequence of the ideas which present themselves to your mind. Do you wish to marry? Yes or no?

B. Suppose I told you that I did not wish one way or the other?

A. You would be replying like the man who said: "Some people believe that Cardinal Mazarin is dead, and others believe that he is alive, but I believe neither the one thing nor the other."

B. Well, then, I want to marry.

A. That is a real answer. Why do you want to marry?

B. Because I am in love with a beautiful young lady, gentle, well-educated, fairly rich, who sings very well, whose parents are very honorable people, and because I flatter myself that I am loved by her and would be welcomed by her family.

A. That's a reason. You see that you cannot will without reason. I tell you that you are free to get married: that is, that you have the power to sign the contract, to celebrate the wedding, and to lie with your wife.

B. What! I cannot will without a reason? Well, what becomes of that other proverb: *Sit pro ratione voluntas;* my will is my reason, I will because I will?

A. That is absurd, my good friend: there would be in you an effect without a cause.

B. Do you mean to tell me that when I play odd or even, I have a reason to choose even rather than odd?

A. Certainly.

B. And what is that reason, pray?

A. It is because the idea of even came into your mind instead of the contrary idea. It would be strange if there were cases where you will because there is a cause for willing, and if there were other cases where you might will without cause. When you will to marry, you evidently feel the dominant reason for it; you do not feel it when you play odd or even, and yet there must be one.

B. But once again, am I not free?

A. Your will is not free, but your actions are. You are free to do what you have the power to do.

B. But all the books that I have read on the liberty of indifference . . .

A. Are nonsense; there is no liberty of indifference; it is a word totally lacking in sense and invented by people who had little.

Morality

Loquacious preachers, extravagant controversialists, try to remember that your master never declared that the sacrament is the visible sign of an invisible thing; he never admitted four cardinal and three theological virtues; he never inquired whether his mother came into the world maculate or immaculate; he never said that little children who died without baptism would be damned. Stop making him say things that never entered his mind. He said, according to truth as old as creation: "Love God and your neighbor." Stick to that, wretched quibblers; preach morality and nothing else. But practice the morality that you preach: let the law courts no longer echo with your suits; no longer snatch, by the claw of an attorney, the crumb of bread from the mouths of widows and orphans; dispute no longer over some little benefice with the same fury that the papacy was disputed in the Great Schism of the West. Monks, no longer put, with all the power that in you lies, the universe under contribution; and then we may believe you.

I have just read these words in a declamation of fourteen volumes entitled *History of the Lower Empire:*

"The Christians had a moral code; but the pagans had none."

Ah! M. Le Beau, author of these fourteen volumes, where did you get that nonsense? But what of the morality of Socrates, Zaleucus, Charondas, Cicero, Epictetus and Marcus Aurelius?

There is only one morality, M. Le Beau, as there is only one geometry. But, I shall be told, the great majority of men know nothing about geometry. Yes; but with a little application to it everybody comes to an agreement. Farmers, laborers, and artists never took courses in morality; they have not read Cicero's *De Finibus* nor Aristotle's *Ethics;* but as soon as they reflect, they are unconsciously Cicero's disciples. The Indian dyer, the Tartar shepherd, and the English sailor know what is just and what is unjust. Confucius did not invent a system of morals, as one builds a physical system. He found it in the hearts of all men.

This morality was in the heart of the prætor Festus when the Jews urged him to put Paul to death for bringing strangers into their temple. "Learn," he told them, "that the Romans never condemn a man without giving him a hearing." (Acts of the Apostles, xxv, 16.)

If morality was deficient among the Jews or the Jews were deficient in morality, the Romans were not, and gloried in it.

Morality does not reside in superstition, nor in ceremonies, and has nothing in common with dogmas. It cannot be too often repeated that dogmas are all different and that morality is the same among all men who make use of their reason. Morality comes like light from God. Our superstitions are only darkness. Reader, reflect: spread abroad this truth; draw your own conclusions.

Soul

The article Soul and all articles which treat of metaphysics should begin with sincere submission to the indubitable dogmas of the Church. Revelation is doubtless more valuable than the whole of philosophy. Systems exercise the mind, but faith enlightens and guides it.

It is a vague and indeterminate term which expresses an unknown principle of known effects that we feel within us. This word *soul* corresponds to the *anima* of the Latins, to the *pneuma* of the Greeks, and to the term used by all nations to express what they understood no better than we.

In the proper and literal sense of the Latin and of the languages derived therefrom, it signifies *that which animates*. Thus people have spoken of the soul of men, of animals, and sometimes of plants, to signify their principle of vegetation and life. No one ever had, in uttering this word, anything but a very confused notion, as when it is said in Genesis: "God breathed into the nostrils of man the breath of life, and he became a living soul; and the soul of animals is in the blood; slay not the soul, etc."

Thus the soul was taken in general for the origin and cause of life and for life itself. That is why every known nation thought for a long time that everything perished with the body. . . .

We have no ground whatsoever to stand on to reach the slightest knowledge of what makes us live and what makes us think. How could we have any? we must first have seen life and thought enter a body. Does a father know how he produced his son? Does a mother know how she conceived him? Has anyone ever been able to guess how he acts, how he wakes, and how he sleeps? Does anyone know how his members obey his will?

has anyone discovered through what art ideas are traced in his brain and come forth at his command? Feeble automatons moved by the invisible hand which directs us on the stage of this world, which of us has been able to perceive the thread that guides us?

We dare to question whether the intelligent soul is *spirit* or *matter;* whether it is created before our own creation; whether it springs from nothingness at our birth; whether after animating us for a day on this earth, it lives after us in eternity. These questions appear sublime; what are they? questions of blind men asking other blind men: "What is light?"

When we wish to have a rude knowledge of a metal, we heat it in a crucible. But have we a crucible for the soul? One man says it is *spirit.* But what is *spirit?* To be sure no one knows anything about it; it is a word so empty of meaning that one is obliged to say what spirit is not, not being able to say what it is. Another says that the soul is *matter.* But what is matter? We know only certain of its appearances and properties; and none of these appearances, none of these properties appears to have the least connection with thought.

You say that it is something distinct from matter? But what proof have you? Is it because matter is divisible and figurable, and thought is not? But who told you that the first principles of matter are divisible and figurable? It seems very probable that they are not; entire sects of philosophers claim that the elements of matter have neither form nor extent. You exclaim triumphantly: "Thought is neither wood, nor stone, nor sand, nor metal; therefore thought does not pertain to matter." Weak and presumptuous reasoners! Gravitation is not wood, sand, metal, or stone; nor is motion, or vegetation, or life; yet life, vegetation, motion and gravitation are attributed to matter. To say that God cannot give thought to matter is to make the most insolently absurd assertion that anyone has dared utter in the privileged schools of insanity. We are not assured that God has done this; we are assured only that he has the power to do so. What matters all that has been said and all that will be said concerning the soul? what does it matter that people have called it entelechy, quintessence, flame, ether; that people have believed it universal, uncreated, transmigrant, etc.? Of what importance, in these questions inaccessible to reason, are these romances of our uncertain imaginations? What does it matter that the Church Fathers of the first four centuries of our era believed the soul corporeal? What does it matter that Tertullian, with an inconsistency quite customary with him, decided that it was at once corporeal, figured and simple? We have a thousand testimonies of ignorance and not one that affords us a ray of probability.

How then are we bold enough to affirm the nature of the soul? We know with certainty that we exist, that we feel, that we think. If we wish to go a step beyond that point, we fall into an abyss of darkness; and in this abyss we still have the foolish temerity to dispute whether this soul, concerning which we have not the slightest notion, is made before we are made or when we are made, and whether it is perishable or immortal.

[*Paying Voltaire a visit at Ferney in 1764, Boswell was rash enough to attempt the conversion of the patriarch, and after his departure, continued his arguments in a letter. Voltaire replied in English and with his usual charm, discussing the soul in a lighter vein:*]

You seem solicitous about that pretty thing call'd Soul. I do protest you, I know nothing of it; nor whether it is, nor what it is, nor what it shall be. Young scholars and priests know all that perfectly. For my part, I am but a very ignorant fellow.

Let it be what it will, I assure you my soul has a great regard for your own . . . etc.

Treatise on Toleration (1763)

On the Occasion of the Death of Jean Calas

[*Voltaire begins his* Treatise *with a brief account of the judicial "murder" of the sixty-eight-year-old Jean Calas of Toulouse on the preposterous charge that he hanged his own son to prevent him from departing from the family's Protestant faith. Religious fanaticism, fanned to white heat, finally intimidated the judges, who hoped that the old man, unable to bear the sufferings of torture, would confess his crime. Instead, as he lay dying on the wheel on which his body was stretched and his bones broken, he called God as a witness of his innocence and prayed that his judges be forgiven.*

Once convinced of the innocence of Calas, Voltaire set to work and after three years of constant effort succeeded in having the decision reversed and the judges rebuked. This was the most striking of a number of such cases. When Voltaire returned from Ferney to die in his native city, he was hailed by the populace of Paris as the "saviour of Calas."

The Treatise *ends with a plea for universal tolerance and the brotherhood of man.*]

Of Universal Tolerance

No great art or studied eloquence is needed to prove that Christians should tolerate one another. I go even further and declare that we must look upon all men as our brothers. But the Turk, my brother? the Chinese, the Jew, the Siamese? Yes, of course; are we not all the children of one father and creatures of the same God?

But these people despise us; they call us idolators! Then I'll tell them they are quite wrong. I think I could at least shock the proud obstinacy of an iman or talapoin, if I said to them something like this:

This little globe, nothing more than a point, rolls in space like so many other globes; we are lost in this immensity. Man, some five feet tall, is surely a very small part of the universe. One of these imperceptible beings says to some of his neighbors in Arabia or Africa: "Listen to me, for the God of all these worlds has enlightened me: there are nine hundred million little ants like us on the earth, but only my anthill is beloved of God; He will hold all others in horror through all eternity; only mine will be blessed, the others will be eternally wretched."

At that, they would cut me short and ask what fool made that stupid remark. I would be obliged to reply, "You yourselves." Then I would try to mollify them; but that would not be easy.

I would speak now to the Christians and dare say, for example, to a Dominican Inquisitor: "My brother, you know that every province in Italy has its dialect, and people in Venice and Bergamo speak differently from those in Florence. The Academy della Crusca has standardized the language; its dictionary is an inescapable authority, and Buonmattei's grammar is an absolute and infallible guide; but do you believe that the head of the Academy and in his absence, Buonmattei, would have been able in all good conscience to cut out the tongues of all those from Venice and Bergamo who persisted in using their own dialect?"

The Inquisitor replies: "There is a great difference; here it's a question of your salvation. It's for your own good the Director of the Inquisition orders that you be seized on the testimony of a single person, no matter how infamous or criminal he may be; that you have no lawyer to defend you; that the very name of your accuser be unknown to you; that the Inquisitor promise you grace and then condemn you; that you undergo five different degrees of torture and then be whipped or sent to the galleys, or ceremoniously burned at the stake. Father

Ivonet, Doctor Cuchalon, Zanchinus, Campegius, Roias, Felynus, Gomarus, Diabarus, Gemelinus are all agreed on the subject, and this pious practice can suffer no contradiction."

I would take the liberty of replying: "My brother, perhaps you are right: I am convinced that you wish me well, but couldn't I be saved without all that?"

To be sure, these horrible absurdities do not soil the face of the earth everyday, but they are frequent enough, and a whole volume could easily be written about them much longer than the Gospels which condemn them. Not only is it very cruel to persecute in this brief existence of ours those who differ from us in opinion, but I am afraid it is being bold indeed to pronounce their eternal damnation. It hardly seems fitting for us atoms of the moment, for that is all we are, to presume to know in advance the decrees of our own Creator. I am far from disputing the maxim: "Outside the Church, no salvation"; I respect it as I do all that the Church teaches us, but do we truly know all the ways of the Almighty and the full extent of His compassion? Are we not allowed to hope in Him as well as to fear Him? Is our faithfulness to the Church not enough? Must every individual usurp the rights of Divinity and decide the eternal fate of all men before God speaks?

When we wear mourning for the king of Sweden, or Denmark, or England, or Prussia, do we say to ourselves that we are mourning a man condemned to eternal hellfire? In Europe there are forty million souls outside the Roman Church; do we say to each one of them: "Sir, since it is agreed that you are damned without reprieve, I do not want to eat with you, or do business with you, or talk with you?"

What French ambassador, on being presented to the Grand Turk, will say in the bottom of his heart: "Your Highness will infallibly be burned through all eternity, because you have submitted to circumcision?" If he really believed that the Grand Turk was the mortal enemy of God and the object of His vengeance, could he so much as speak to him, and should he be sent to him in the first place? With what man could we hold commerce, what duty could we ever fulfill in civil life, if we were really convinced that we were dealing with the damned?

Oh, sectarians of a merciful God, if you had a cruel heart, if, while adoring Him whose only law consists in the words: "Love God and thy neighbor as thyself (Luke X, 27)," you had overloaded this pure and holy law with sophisms and incomprehensible disputations; if you had lighted the torch of discord either over a new word or a single letter of the alphabet; if you had made eternal punishment the penalty for the omission of a few words or ceremonies which other nations could not know about, I would say to you, as I wept in compassion for mankind: "Transport yourselves with me to the day when all men will be judged and when God will do unto each man according to his works."

"I see all the dead of all centuries, past and present, appear before His presence. Are you quite sure that our Creator and Father will say to the wise and virtuous Confucius, to Solon the law-giver, to Pythagoras, Zaleucus, Socrates, and Plato, to the divine Antoninus, good Trajan, and Titus, the flowering of mankind, to Epictetus and so many other model men: "Go, you monsters; go and suffer punishment, limitless in time and intensity, eternal as I am eternal. And you, my beloved, Jean Chatel, Ravaillac, Damiens, Cartouche, etc.,[1] who died according to the prescribed formulas, share forever at my right hand my empire and my felicity."

You draw back in horror from these words, and since they escaped me, I have no more to say. (ch. XXII)

Prayer to God

I no longer address myself to men, but to thee, God of all beings, all worlds, and all ages. If indeed it is allowable for feeble creatures, lost in immensity and im-

[1] Regicides and highway robbers.

perceptible to the rest of the universe, to dare ask anything of Thee who hast given all things, whose decrees are as immutable as they are eternal, deign to look with compassion upon the failings inherent in our nature, and grant that these failings lead us not into calamity.

Thou didst not give us hearts that we should hate each other or hands that we should cut each other's throats. Grant that we may help each other bear the burden of our painful and brief lives; that the slight difference in the clothing with which we cover our puny bodies, in our inadequate tongues, in all our ridiculous customs, in all our imperfect laws, in all our insensate opinions, in all our stations in life so disproportionate in our eyes but so equal in Thy sight, that all these little variations that differentiate the atoms called *man*, may not be the signals for hatred and persecution; that they who light tapers at mid-day to celebrate Thy name bear with them who are content with the light of Thy sun; that they who cover their robes with a white texture to say that Thou shouldst be loved detest not them who say the same thing beneath black woolen cloaks; that it be the same to adore Thee in a dialect derived from an ancient language as in a newer dialect; that they whose coats are colored with red or violet, who rule over a little parcel of this tiny mudpile of a world and who possess some rounded bits of a certain metal, may enjoy without pride what they call *grandeur* and *riches*, and that others may look upon them without envy; for Thou knowest that in these vanities there is no cause for envy or pride.

May all men remember that they are brothers; may they hold in horror tyranny that is exercised over souls, just as they hold in execration the brigandage that snatches away by force the fruits of labor and peaceful industry. If the scourge of war is inevitable, let us not hate each other, let us not tear each other apart in the lap of peace; but let us use the brief moment of our existence in blessing in a thousand different tongues, from Siam to California, Thy goodness which has bestowed this moment upon us. (ch. XXIII)

Miscellanies

Faith or Reason

[*Some of Voltaire's most forceful pages are hidden among the many volumes of* Miscellanies. *The following extract is taken from an imaginary letter from a student of divinity to his professor of theology. The student has met a very virtuous lord, whose opinions resemble strikingly those of M. de Voltaire, Count of Tournay, and whom he tries to convert to a more theological manner of thinking. The passage illustrates the profound sincerity of Voltaire's free-thought. The student writes:*]

"I did all that I could, and I did not succeed. I asked him what risk he ran in submitting his reason to faith.

" 'I run the risk,' he replied, 'of lying to God and to myself, of saying that I believe you when I do not believe you at all, and of offending the Being of beings who gave me my rational faculties. I am not in the position of an invincible ignorance, but rather of an invincible opinion. Do you think,' he added, 'that God will punish me for not having been of your opinion? And who told you that he will not punish you for resisting mine? I spoke to you according to my conscience; would you dare swear between God and me that you have always spoken according to yours? You told me that you believed that Jonah was three days and three nights in the belly of a fish, and I tell you that I don't believe it. Which of us two is nearer doubt? Which of us, in his secret heart, has spoken with the more sincerity? When I appear before God at my death, I will appear with confidence, but will you not be obliged to tremble in this fatal moment, you who, for the vain pleasure of subjugating me, have wished to make me believe things of which it is impossible that you yourself are convinced?' "

Providence

I was at the grating of the convent when Sister Fessue was saying to Sister Confite: "Providence takes visible care of me; you know how I love my sparrow: it would have died if I had not said nineteen *Ave Marias* to obtain its recovery. God brought my sparrow back to life; let's thank the Holy Virgin."

A metaphysician said to her: My sister, there is nothing so good as *Ave Marias*, especially when a girl recites them in Latin in a suburb of Paris; but I do not believe that God concerns himself much with your sparrow, however pretty it may be; consider, I beg of you, how much other business he has. He must continually direct the courses of sixteen planets and the ring of Saturn, in the center of which he has put the sun, which is as big as a million of our globes. He has billions and billions of other suns, planets, and comets to govern. His unchangeable laws and his eternal concurrence keep entire nature in motion: everything is bound to his throne by an infinite chain, of which no link can ever be out of place. If *Ave Marias* had made Sister Fessue's sparrow live an instant longer than it was to live, these *Ave Marias* would have violated all the laws established through all eternity by the Great Being; you would have deranged the universe; you would have necessitated a new world, a new God, and a new order of things.

Sister Fessue: What! You believe that God pays so little attention to Sister Fessue?

The metaphysician: I am sorry to say that like myself you are only an imperceptible link of the infinite chain; that your organs, your sparrow's, and my own are destined to subsist a determined number of minutes in this suburb of Paris.

Sister Fessue: If that is so, I was predestined to say a determined number of *Ave Marias*.

The metaphysician: Yes; but they did not force God to prolong the life of your sparrow beyond its term. It is inherent in the constitution of the world that in this convent, at a certain hour, you would pronounce like a parrot certain words in a certain language which you do not understand; that this bird, born like you through the irresistible action of general laws, having been sick, should get better again; that you should imagine that you had cured it with words, and that we should be holding this conversation together.

Sister Fessue: Sir, your discourse smacks of heresy. My confessor, Reverend Father de Menou, will infer from it that you do not believe in Providence.

The metaphysician: I believe a general Providence, my dear sister, from which has emanated through all eternity the law that governs everything, just as light springs forth from the sun; but I do not believe that a particular Providence changes the economy of the world for your sparrow or your cat.

Sister Fessue: But what if my confessor tells you, as he tells me, that God changes his intentions daily in favor of devout souls?

The metaphysician: He will be telling me the most stupid platitude that a confessor of girls can tell a thinking man.

Sister Fessue: My confessor a fool! Holy Virgin Mary!

The metaphysician: I did not say that; I say that only by means of a most stupid assertion could he justify the false principles which he has instilled into you, perhaps very cleverly, for your governance.

Sister Fessue: Indeed! I will think the matter over; it merits some reflection.

Superstition

The superstitious man is to the knave what the slave is to the tyrant. Moreover, the superstitious man is governed by the fanatic, and becomes one himself. Superstition, born of Paganism, adopted by Judaism, corrupted the Church from the earliest times. All the Fathers of the Church without exception believed in the power of magic. The Church always condemned magic, but always believed in it: she did not excommunicate sorcerers as madmen who were deceived but as men who really had commerce with the devils.

Today one half of Europe believes that the other half

has long been and still is superstitious. The Protestants regard relics, indulgences, mortifications, prayers for the dead, holy water, and almost all the rites of the Roman Church as superstitious madness. Superstition, according to them, consists in mistaking useless observances for necessary ones. Among the Roman Catholics there are some, more enlightened than their ancestors, who have renounced many of these customs formerly held sacred, and stand up for others which they have kept, saying: "These are indifferent, and what is merely indifferent cannot be an evil."

It is difficult to fix the bounds of superstition. A Frenchman traveling in Italy finds nearly everything superstitious, and is not far wrong. The Archbishop of Canterbury claims that the Archbishop of Paris is superstitious; the Presbyterians make the same objection to His Grace of Canterbury, and are in their turn treated as superstitious by the Quakers, who are the most superstitious of all in the eyes of the other Christians.

There is no agreement therefore in Christian countries as to what superstition is. The sect which seems the least attacked by this disease of the mind is the one which has the fewest rites. But if with few ceremonies it is strongly attached to an absurd belief, this absurd belief is alone equivalent to all the superstitious practices observed from Simon the Magician to the curate Goffredy.

It is evident then that the fundamentals of the religion of one sect are considered superstition by another sect.

The Moslems accuse all Christian countries of it, and are themselves accused. Who will judge this great controversy? Will it be reason? But each sect claims that they have reason on their side. It will then be force which will judge, while waiting for reason to penetrate into a large enough number of heads to disarm force. . . .

Up to what point does the state permit the destruction of superstition? This is a very thorny question; it is like asking at what point one should puncture a man with the dropsy, when he might die under the operation. That depends on the discretion of the doctor.

Can there exist a nation free from all superstitious prejudices? That is asking whether a nation of philosophers can exist. It is said that there is no superstition among the magistrates of China. It is likely that none will be left among the magistrates of a few European cities.

These magistrates will then prevent the superstition of the people from becoming dangerous. The example of these magistrates will not enlighten the rabble, but the bourgeois leaders will restrain them. There has perhaps not been a single riot, a single religious outrage, in which the bourgeoise of former times have not been implicated, because those bourgeois were rabble; but reason and time will have changed them. Their gentler ways will soften the manners of the vilest and most ferocious populace: of that we have striking examples in more than one country. In a word, the less superstition, the less fanaticism; and the less fanaticism, the less unhappiness.

Impiety

Who is the impious man? It is he who ascribes a white beard, feet, and hands to the Being of beings, to the Great Demiurge, to the eternal intelligence through which nature is governed. But he is only an excusable infidel, a poor infidel with whom we should not be angry.

Even if he paints the great incomprehensible Being borne on a cloud, which can bear nothing; if he is stupid enough to put God in a fog, in a rain, or on a mountain, and to surround him with little round, fat-cheeked, ruddy faces, between two wings; I laugh, and pardon him with all my heart.

The impious man who ascribes to the Being of Beings preposterous predictions and acts of injustice would make me angry if that great Being had not presented me with reason to repress my anger. This fanatical fool repeats to me, what others have said before, that it is not for us to judge of what is reasonable and just in the great Being, that his reason is not like our reason, that his justice is not like our justice. But how, my ranting fool, do you expect me to judge otherwise of justice and reason than by the notions I have of them myself? Do you expect me to walk otherwise than with my feet, or to speak otherwise than with my mouth?

The impious man who supposes the great Being to be jealous, proud, malicious and vindictive, is more dangerous. I should not like to sleep under the same roof with such a man.

But how will you treat the impious man who says to you: "See only through my eyes and do not think; I announce to thee a tyrannical God who has made me to be thy tyrant; I am his well-beloved; he will torment through all eternity millions of his creatures, whom he detests, in order to make me happy; I will be thy master in this world, and I will laugh at thy sufferings in the next world."

Do you not itch to drub this cruel blasphemer? And if you are born gentle, will you not run west with all your might when this barbarian utters his atrocious ravings in the east?

In regard to those impious men who fail to wash their elbows facing towards Aleppo and towards Erivan, or who do not kneel before a procession of Capuchin friars at Perpignan, they are doubtless guilty, but I do not think they ought to be impaled.

On Absurdities and Atrocities

Once your faith, sir, persuades you to believe what your intelligence declares to be absurd, beware lest you likewise sacrifice your reason in the conduct of your life.

In days gone by, there were people who said to us: "You believe in incomprehensible, contradictory and impossible things because we have commanded you to; now then, commit unjust acts because we likewise order you to do so." Nothing could be more convincing. Certainly any one who has the power to make you believe absurdities has the power to make you commit injustices. If you do not use the intelligence with which

God endowed your mind to resist believing impossibilities, you will not be able to use the sense of justice which God planted in your heart to resist a command to do evil. Once a single faculty of your soul has been tyrannized, all the other faculties will submit to the same fate. This has been the cause of all the religious crimes that have flooded the earth. (*Questions on the Miracles*, Letter XI)

The Questions of Zapata

(*Translated by Dr. Tamponet*[1] *of the Sorbonne*)

The licentiate Zapata, appointed Professor of Theology at the University of Salamanca, presented these questions to the assembly of doctors in 1629. They were suppressed. The Spanish copy is in the Brunswick library.

WISE MASTERS:

How am I to undertake to prove that the Jews, whom we burn by the hundreds, were for four thousand years God's chosen people?

How could God, who cannot without blasphemy be regarded as unjust, have abandoned the entire earth for the little Jewish tribe, and then abandon his little tribe for another, which was for two hundred years much smaller and much more despised?

Why did he perform a great number of incomprehensible miracles in favor of this paltry nation before the period called *historical?* Why has he performed no more for several centuries? And why do we never witness any, we who are God's chosen people?

If God is the God of Abraham, why do you burn the children of Abraham? and when you burn them, why do you recite their prayers in the process? How is it that you, who worship the book of their law, put them to death for observing their law? . . .

Is the book of *Genesis* science or allegory? Did God

[1] A doctor of divinity, enemy of the Encyclopedists. The attribution and the incident are, of course, purely fictitious.

truly take a rib from Adam to make a woman from it? and why is it previously said that he created male and female? How did God create light before the sun? How did he divide light from darkness, since darkness is nothing but the absence of light? How did he make day before the sun was created? How was the firmament formed in the midst of the waters, when there is no such thing as a firmament, and when this false notion of a firmament is only a fiction of the ancient Greeks? There are people who conjecture that *Genesis* was not written until the Jews had some knowledge of the erroneous philosophy of other peoples, and it would grieve me to hear it said that God knows no more about physics than he does about chronology and geography. . . .

Am I to confess or deny that the law of the Jews nowhere speaks of punishment or reward after death? How is it possible that neither Moses nor Joshua spoke of the immortality of the soul, a dogma known among the ancient Egyptians, the Chaldeans, the Persians and the Greeks; a dogma which was somewhat in fashion among the Jews only after the time of Alexander, and which the Sadducees always condemned because it is not in the Pentateuch? . . .

I beg of you to tell me by what trick Samson caught three hundred foxes, tied them together by their tails, and attached torches to their hind quarters to set fire to the harvests of the Philistines. Foxes are commonly found only in countries covered with woods. There was no forest in this district, and it seems rather difficult to catch three hundred foxes alive and to tie them together by their tails. It is said also that he killed a thousand Philistines with the jawbone of an ass, and that from one of the teeth of this jawbone there issued forth a spring. When it is a question of ass's jawbones, you owe me some enlightenment. . . .

I know not how I shall justify the conduct of Samuel, who cut into pieces King Agag, whom Saul had made prisoner and had put to ransom.

I do not know whether our King Philip would be approved if, having captured a Moorish king and made an agreement with him, he cut his royal prisoner into pieces.

We owe great respect to David, who was a man after God's own heart; but I fear I would not have sufficient knowledge to justify, by ordinary laws, David's conduct in leaguing himself with four hundred men of ill-repute and overwhelmed with debts, as the Scripture says; in marching to sack the house of Nabal, the king's servant, and, eight days later, marrying his widow; in going to offer his services to Achish, his king's enemy, and putting to fire and the sword the lands of the allies of Achish, sparing neither sex nor age; in taking new concubines as soon as he is on the throne; and not content even with his concubines, in ravishing Bathsheba from her husband, and accomplishing the death of the man he dishonors. I have some difficulty again in conceiving how God descends later in Judea from this adulterous and murderous woman, who is counted among the ancestors of the Eternal Being. I have already warned you about this article, which is extremely troublesome to pious souls. . . .

I have still greater need of your wise instructions concerning the New Testament; I am afraid I do not know what to say to reconcile the two genealogies of Jesus. For I shall be told that Matthew gives Jacob as the father of Joseph, and that Luke makes him the son of Heli, and that that is impossible unless we change *He* to *Ja*, and *li* to *cob*. I shall be asked how the one counts fifty-six generations and how the other counts only forty-two, and why these generations are all different, and again why, of the forty-two that are promised, there are found to be only forty-one; and finally, why this genealogical tree is Joseph's, who was not the father of Jesus. I fear lest I shall reply only nonsense, like all my predecessors have done. I hope that you will extricate me from this labyrinth. . . .

When I teach that the family went to Egypt according to Matthew, they will reply that that is not true, and that they stayed in Judea according to the other Evangelists; and if I then grant that they stayed in Judea, they will maintain that they were in Egypt. Is it not simpler to say that one can be in two places at once, as happened to St. Francis Xavier and several other saints? . . .

I beg of you, when you go to a wedding, to tell me how God, who also went to a wedding, went about it to change the water into wine for the benefit of people who were already drunk.

When you are eating figs for breakfast towards the end of July, I beseech you to tell me why God, being hungry, looked for figs at the beginning of the month of March, when it was not the season for figs.

After receiving your instructions on all such prodigies, I shall be obliged to say that God was condemned to be hanged for original sin. But if they reply to me that there never was anything about original sin, either in the Old Testament or in the New; that it is said merely that Adam was condemned to death the day that he should eat from the tree of knowledge, but that he did not die from it; and that Augustine, Bishop of Hippo, former Manichean, was the first to establish the system of original sin, I confess to you that, not having the people of Hippo as auditors, I might get myself laughed at while speaking much and saying nothing. For when certain wranglers came to point out to me that it was impossible that God should be put to death for an apple eaten four thousand years before his death, impossible that in redeeming the human race he should not redeem it, and should leave it still wholly in the clutches of the devil, except for a chosen few, I replied nothing but verbiage, and went off to hide myself for shame. . . .

They will ask me then whether Peter was at Rome; I shall reply, to be sure, that he was Pope for twenty-five years: and the big reason that I shall produce is that we have an epistle from this fellow who could neither read nor write, and that this letter is dated from Babylon; there is no answer to that, but I should like something stronger. . . .

Are you not as sorry as I am that the early Christians forged so many bad verses which they attributed to the Sibyls: that they forged letters from St. Paul to Seneca, letters from Jesus, letters from Mary, letters from Pilate; and that they thus established their sect through a hundred crimes of forgery that would be punished in all the law courts on earth? These frauds are today recognized by all scholars. We are reduced to calling them *pious*. But is it not sad that your truth should be founded only on lies? . . .

I know to be sure that the Church is infallible; but is it the Greek Church, or the Latin Church, or the Church of England, or that of Denmark and of Sweden, or that of the proud city of Neuchâtel, or that of the primitives called Quakers, or that of the Anabaptists, or that of the Moravians? The Turkish Church has its points, too, but they say that the Chinese Church is much more ancient. . . .

In short, would it not be better not to lose ourselves in these labyrinths and simply preach virtue? When God judges us, I doubt very much if he will ask whether grace is versatile or concomitant; whether marriage is the visible sign of an invisible thing; whether we believe that there are ten choirs of angels or nine; whether the pope is above the council or the council above the pope. Will it be a crime in his eyes to have addressed prayers to him in Spanish if one does not know Latin? Shall we be the objects of his eternal anger for having eaten twelve farthings worth of bad meat on a certain day? And shall we be rewarded eternally if we have eaten with you, wise master, a hundred piastres worth of turbot, sole and sturgeon? You do not believe so in the depth of your hearts; you think that God will judge us according to our works, and not according to the ideas of Thomas and of Bonaventure.

Shall I not render a service to men in announcing to them nothing but morality? This morality is so pure, so holy, so universal, so clear, so ancient that it seems to come direct from God, like the light of day which we consider his first creation. Did he not give men self-love to insure their preservation; sympathy, beneficence and virtue to control self-love; mutual needs for the formation of society; pleasure in the satisfaction of them; pain which cautions us to enjoy with moderation; passions which lead us on to great things, and wisdom to curb passions?

Did he not in short inspire all men united in society with the idea of a Supreme Being, in order that the adoration that we owe to this Being might be society's strongest tie? Savages who wander in the woods have no need of this knowledge; the duties of society, which they know nothing about, do not concern them; but as soon as men are assembled together, God manifests himself to their reason: they need justice, and they adore in him the principle of all justice. God, who does not want their vain adoration, receives it as necessary for them and not for him. And likewise he gives them the genius of arts, without which every society perishes, and he gives them the spirit of religion, the first and the most natural of sciences, the divine science whose principle is certain, even if uncertain consequences are daily drawn from it. Will you allow me to announce these truths to the Spanish nobles?

If you wish me to hide this truth; if you order me absolutely to announce the miracles of St. James in Galicia, and of Our Lady of Atocha, and of Mary of Agreda who exposed herself to small boys in her ecstasies, tell me how I must deal with the rebellious who dare to doubt: shall I have them given, along with edification, ordinary and extraordinary torture? When I meet Jewish maidens, shall I lie with them before having them burned? and when I put them to the fire, have I not the right to take a thigh or so for my supper with Catholic maidens?

I await the honor of your reply.

Dominico Zapata,
y verdadero, y honrado, y caritativo.

Zapata, receiving no reply, began to preach God in all simplicity. He announced to men the father of men, the rewarder, punisher and pardoner. He extricated truth from falsehoods, and separated religion from fanaticism; he taught and practised virtue. He was gentle, beneficent, modest; and was roasted at Valladolid, in the year of grace 1631. Pray God for the soul of Brother Zapata!

Declaration of the Rights of Man and of the Citizen (1789)

This most important political document of the age was the result of an intercommunication of ideas between France and America. Its articles were drawn up by a committee of five and presented to the National Assembly by Mirabeau in August 1789. It served as preamble to the Constitution of 1791 accepted by Louis XVI.

The committee consulted Thomas Jefferson, who was then American ambassador at the French court. The influence of the Bill of Rights of the Constitution of the State of Virginia is apparent. No less apparent is the fact that the document represents a concise summary of the reforms proposed by Montesquieu, Rousseau and Voltaire.

Declaration of the Rights of Man and of the Citizen (1789)

The representatives of the French people, constituted in National Assembly, considering that the ignorance, neglect, and contempt of the Rights of Man, are the sole causes of public misfortunes and the corruption of governments, have resolved to expose, in a solemn Declaration, the natural, inalienable, and sacred Rights of Man, in order that this Declaration, constantly present before all members of the social body, may ceaselessly remind them of their rights and duties; in order that the acts of the legislative power and those of the executive power, liable at any moment to be compared with the aims of all political institutions, may be the more respected; in order that the appeals of citizens, founded henceforth on simple and incontestable principles, may always tend to maintain the Constitution and the happiness of all men.

In consequence, the National Assembly recognizes and declares, in the presence and under the auspices of the Supreme Being, the following Rights of Man and of the Citizen:

1. Men are born, and remain, free and equal before the law. Social distinctions can be founded only on public utility.

2. The aim of all political associations is the conservation of the natural and imprescriptible rights of man. These rights are liberty, property, security, and resistance to oppression.

3. The principle of all sovereignty resides in the Nation. No body, no individual, can exercise authority which does not emanate expressly therefrom.

4. Liberty consists in being able to do whatever does not injure another. Thus the exercise of every man's natural rights is limited only by those which assure the other members of society of these same rights. These limits can be determined only by law.

5. The law has the right to prohibit only those actions which are harmful to society. All that is not prohibited by law cannot be hindered; and no one can be compelled to do what the law does not require.

6. The law is the expression of the general will. All citizens have the right to take part in person or through their representatives in its formulation. It must be the same for all, whether it protects or whether it punishes. All citizens being equal in the eyes of the law are equally eligible to all honors, offices, and public employments, according to their abilities and without other distinction than that of their virtues and talents.

7. No man can be accused, arrested, or detained except in cases determined by the law and according to the forms prescribed thereby. Those who solicit, promote, execute, or cause to be executed, arbitrary orders shall be punished; but a citizen summoned or seized by vir-

tue of the law must obey immediately: he becomes guilty if he resists.

8. The law must establish only those penalties which are strictly and evidently necessary; and no person can be punished except by virtue of a law that has been established and promulgated before the offense, and is legally applied.

9. Since every man is presumed to be innocent until he has been pronounced guilty, if it is judged indispensable to arrest him, all rigorous measures not necessary to secure his person ought to be severely repressed by law.

10. No man is to be molested on account of his opinions, even his religious opinions, provided that their manifestation does not disturb the public order established by law.

11. The free communication of thoughts and opinions is one of man's most precious rights. Every citizen may therefore speak, write, and publish freely; except that he shall be responsible for the abuse of that freedom in cases determined by law.

12. The guarantee of the Rights of Man and of the Citizen makes necessary a public force. This force is therefore instituted for the advantage of all, and not for the particular use of those to whom it is confided.

13. For the maintenance of public force and the expenses of administration, a common contribution is indispensable. It must be equally apportioned among all citizens according to their abilities.

14. All citizens have the right to determine, themselves or through their representatives, the necessity of public contributions; to consent to them freely; to watch over the use thereof; and to fix their amount, assessment, collection, and duration.

15. Society has the right to ask an accounting from all public agents of their administration.

16. Any society in which the guarantee of Rights is not assured, nor the separation of Powers determined, has no Constitution.

17. Since property is an inviolable and sacred right, no man may be deprived of it except when public necessity, lawfully constituted, evidently requires it; and on condition that a just indemnity be paid in advance.